THE JUST ONE JUSTICES:

The Role of Justice at the Heart of Catholic Higher Education

THE JUST ONE JUSTICES:

The Role of Justice at the Heart of Catholic Higher Education

The 1998 President's Institute on the Catholic Character of Loyola Marymount University

by

MARY K. MCCULLOUGH, PH.D., EDITOR

SCRANTON: THE UNIVERSITY OF SCRANTON PRESS

#43936960

© 2000 By The University of Scranton Press

Library of Congress Cataloging-in-Publication Data

(Not available at time of publication)

Distribution:

University of Toronto Press
2250 Military Road
Tonawanda NY 14150
800-565-9523

PRINTED IN THE UNITED STATES OF AMERICA

AS KINGFISHERS CATCH FIRE

As kingfishers catch fire, dragonflies draw flame;
As tumbled over rim in roundy wells
Stones ring; like each tucked string tells, each hung bell's
Bow swung finds tongue to fling out broad its name;
Each mortal thing does one thing and the same:
Deals out that being indoors each one dwells;
Selves—goes itself; *myself* it speaks and spells,
Crying *What I do is me: for that I came.*

I say more: the just man justices;
Keeps grace: that keeps all his goings graces;
Acts in God's eye what in God's eye he is—
Christ—for Christ plays in ten thousand places,
Lovely in limbs, and lovely in eyes not his
To the Father through the features of men's faces.

—Gerard Manley Hopkins

Dedication

Thank you Mother and Daddy for your
unconditional love.

Thank you Father Thomas P. O'Malley for your vision
and the Institute.

Publication of this volume was made possible with funding received from the Jesuit Community of Loyola Marymount University. The Jesuits wish to thank the directors of the University Hill Foundation for their continued support of Jesuit higher education: Howard B. Fitzpatrick, President; Edward F. Slattery, and Henry K. Workman.

TABLE OF CONTENTS

FOREWORD

THE UNIVERSITY THAT DOES JUSTICE

John A. Coleman, S.J.

I take my cue from the hustlers along Sunset or Hollywood Boulevards who hawk their road maps to the houses of the stars (to places, it turns out, where the genuine stars rarely deign any epiphanies). I take my cue most pointedly from the evaluations from earlier participants in former President's Institutes on the Catholic Character of the University who have consistently pleaded for a clearer road map, at the very beginning, of their week ahead. Even professors, it seems, can be apprehensive! But such a roadmap also well serves a book. I sketch this map, however, with a clear warning label (stealing from Jonathan Z. Smith's classic title) a map is not the territory! (Smith, 1978).

What are the authors in this book doing together? Their genre is unmistakable. It is called *conversation*. If the thematic topics of conversation for this symposium had been somewhat clearly set in advance by the title, "The Just One Justices," the rules for genuine conversation remain: that it goes where it goes and brings to the table, during the symposium and in the response of readers, without apology, whoever comes. There can be no pre-set outcome to a genuine conversation. There is no politically correct script. This is an exercise in conversation, not indoctrination or catechesis. But it is conversation—as Michael Engh, S.J., tells us in his contribution —about a very concrete school, with its own history, tradition, and distinctive *ethos*. It has a past of dealing with justice.

Genuine and engaged conversation is, of course, what any self-respecting university commits itself to practice. Universities are counter-cultural institutions which, embodying Jurgen Habermas's utopian model of ideal-speech (even if the professors have never heard of him!), seek to persuade (and never coerce or appeal to merely extrinsic authorities) by resort to the best argument (Habermas, 1987). Universities seek to expand horizons beyond a discipline, culture, or time frame. They seek not to exclude any voices. We also know how rare genuine conversation is, even in the hallowed halls of ivy.

University of Chicago theologian David Tracy, who has written so illuminatingly on conversation, reminds us that it takes discipline to listen intently, to be prepared to change our opinion on the basis of fresh horizons or evidence and to share what we genuinely believe and stay engaged in "conversation that matters," that makes a difference in who we are:

> The movement in conversation is questioning itself. Neither my present opinions on the question nor the text's original response to the question, but the question itself, must control every conversation. A conversation is a rare phenomenon, even for Socrates. It is not a confrontation. It is not a debate. It is not an exam. It is questioning itself. It is a willingness to follow the question wherever it may go. It is a dialogue.

> Conversation [has] some hard rules: Say only what you mean; say it as accurately as you can; listen to and respect what the other says, however different or other; be willing to correct or defend your opinions if challenged by the conversation partner; be willing to argue, if necessary; to confront if demanded . . . to change your mind if the evidence suggests it. (Tracy, 1987)

Conversation should serve as a prime metaphor for a Catholic university. The Catholic intellectual tradition (like any truly living tradition) is based on a lively conversation. As Alasdair MacIntyre puts it in his book, *After Virtue*, "tradition is an historically extended, socially embodied argument and an argument, precisely, in part, about the goods which constitute that tradition" (MacIntyre, 1981). Tom O'Malley and his respondents in their presentations present to us the principal goods they presume make up the Catholic intellectual tradition and imagination. That imagination constitutes a humanism rooted in matter and in the doctrine and reality of the incarnation of God in Jesus into history.

So, conversation can include argument. I suppose the ground rules for a productive conversation are simple: listen with respect; make sure that no internal censors block out the truth, experiential authority, and authenticity of any voice in the conversation; and, perhaps, follow the Ignatian rule for listening, with which St. Ignatius begins his *Spiritual Exercise* (a rule hard won from his own seering experiences in Salamanca of being misjudged by the Spanish Inquisition): "Every good Christian ought to be more eager to put a good interpretation on a neighbor's statement than to condemn it. Further, if one cannot interpret it favorably, one should ask the other how the other means it. If that meaning is wrong, one should correct the person with love. And if this is not enough, one should search out every appropriate means through which, by understanding the statement in a good way, it may be saved" (Ganss, 1992).

The topics the conversation turns on, in this book, are the two-fold phrases: (1) the faith that does justice; and (2) the university that does justice.

The Faith That Does Justice

In the recent Jesuit tradition, the faith that does justice is central to the mission of *any* Jesuit work or institution. Since General Congregation 32 of the Jesuits in 1974, it has been an overarching priority that Jesuits bring to any institution in which they work. At General Congregation 34 (1995), at which I was a delegate, it was clear that the Jesuits of the world did not want in any way to dilute this Jesuit commitment to the faith that does justice.

The document of the 34th General Congregation entitled "Our Mission and Justice" states that "the promotion of justice is an integral part of the Jesuit mission" (*Documents of the Thirty-Fourth General Congregation of the Society of Jesus* [*Documents*], 1995, Decree 3, p. 1). This document roots Jesuit commitment to justice in our wider Catholic faith:

> The vision of justice which guides us is intimately linked with our faith. It is deeply rooted in the scriptures, church tradition and our Ignatian heritage. It transcends notions of justice derived from ideology, philosophy or particular political movements, which can never be an adequate expression of the justice of God's kingdom. (*Documents*, 1995, Decree 3, p. 2)

This same document also asserts: "Every Jesuit ministry can and should promote justice in one or more of the following ways: (a) direct service and accompaniment of the poor; (b) developing awareness of the demands of justice and the social responsibility to achieve it; (c) participating in social mobilization for the creation of a more just social order" (*Documents*, 1995, Decree 3, p. 19).

But the conversation model I evoked also holds good for the understanding of the faith which does justice. As the document of the 34th General Congregation of the Jesuits entitled "Servants of Christ's Mission" almost lyrically puts it (evoking a dialogue and communication as central to any scheme or project of justice):

> Today we realize clearly:
> No service of faith without promotion of justice,
> entry into culture,
> openness to other religious experiences;

No promotion of justice without
communicating faith,
transforming cultures,
collaboration with other traditions;

No inculturation without
communicating faith with others,
dialogue with other traditions,
commitment to justice;

No dialogue without
sharing faith with others,
evaluating cultures,
concern for justice. (*Documents*, 1995, Decree 2, p. 19)

But—if it is not an oxymoron—Jesuit humility should admit that its slogan of the faith which does justice is merely a crystallization of the longer and richer Catholic tradition of justice in Catholic social teaching (which Peter Henriot slyly suggests is "our best-kept secret!") (Schulteis, DeBerri, & Henriot, 1992).

Catholic Social Teaching as a Conversation

Catholic social teaching also has a conversational character about it. It is addressed not just to Catholics but to men and women of goodwill everywhere. It has, to be sure, certain presuppositions which are communitarian rather than ruggedly individualistic, presuppositions about the dignity of the human person involving social as well as personal and civil rights; about a common good, which is defined in terms of justice in its rich variety and many forms: (1) distributive justice, dealing with the fair distribution of the public goods of society; (2) justice as participation, assuming that one must become an active agent in setting the agendas of society and not just passive recipient, even of necessary goods and welfare; (3) communitative justice, which looks to the more narrow justice of contracts but is subordinated to distributive justice and what is called (4) social justice, i.e., the social structures and institutional arrangements which guarantee and encourage human flourishing.

But the common good and the justice it presupposes is not some pre-ordained blue-print which Catholics then foist on others. It rests—as John Courtney Murray so insisted—on civic conversation with others about the goods we will pursue in common, the goods which make for human flourishing. In a classic essay, "Creeds at War Intelligibly," Murray talked about the need for a civil conversation across religious and secular creeds, to reach those social truths we can, by some genuine overlapping consensus, hold in common (Murray, 1964).

Nor can the high Catholic tradition of the common good hide the fact that justice is a relational concept within which ever lurks the volatile reality of power. As British sociologist, Steven Lukes, reminds us: power is an inherently contested concept (Lukes, 1974). Inasmuch as justice includes and presupposes for its enactment relations of power, it too is inherently contested. So argument about the contours of justice is to be expected. When the vision of justice gets translated into more concrete proposals for policy, the faith that does justice is never politically innocent. The justice which looks outward and takes society as one of its horizons must also look closely to the announcers of justice, the church and the university. And when they fail in justice, this must find redress.

Justice and an Ethic of Care

Ellen Marie Keane and her respondents ask us to expand the formula of justice to include a larger notion of care. Keane's main source is the work of Carol Gilligan, but the case for this expansion can also be made on more explicitly Catholic grounds (Gilligan, 1982). In the medieval city-states of Florence and Venice, there were vigorous debates just on this topic (we see an echo of this in Portia's famous speech in Shakespeare's *The Merchant of Venice*). Should we seek mercy and compassion to shield us from justice's often too stark dictates?

When Aquinas appealed to Aristotle in his ethical writings, he changed Aristotle's presupposition that justice is the first of the virtues in the *polis*. Aquinas did not simply pour baptism water on Aristotle. Aquinas made *caritas* (which means love, indeed the love of God poured out on us which the tradition also calls *agape*) the form of all virtues. *Caritas* is not what we call charity (i.e., a benevolent and free giving to those in need) but something much more radical which changes, even, the nature of justice and leads us to spell it with a capital J to include care (Pope, 1994). *Cura Personalis* (personal attentive care for students in the Jesuit tradition of education), another major attribute to Jesuit education, after all, does not get swept away by a conversation about justice. For justice includes respect for persons, for their inherent dignity and diversity. The Christian images of bearing one another's burdens and being part of one body call for something much more robust than just John Rawls's justice as fairness (Rawls, 1971). In Catholic social thought, justice also includes respect for cultures. The care for racial, ethnic, and gender diversity—in its faculty and student body—now found prominently in our universities, has deep roots in Catholic social thought (*Documents*, 1995, Decree 14).

The University That Does Justice

The university that does justice is also a very large theme. A university is neither a political party nor a social agency or social movement. Stephen Privett helps us articulate the vision of the university that does justice better. The university has its own appropriate ends and finalities. These lie primarily in the attempt to discover, shape, renew, or promote human knowledge, while respecting the integrity of disciplined knowing. The document on Jesuit Universities from General Congregation 34 issued a clear, even clarion, call for such disciplined scholarship and academic freedom—what it calls "the fundamental autonomy, integrity and honesty of a university, precisely as a university: a place of serene and open search for and discussion of the truth" (*Documents*, 1995, Decree 17, p. 6).

In that same document we also read these words: "While we want to avoid any distortion of the nature of a university or any reduction of its mission to only one legitimate goal, . . . a Jesuit university can and must discover in its own proper institutional forms and authentic purposes (which had been earlier described as dedication to research, teaching, publication and the various forms of service that correspond to its cultural mission) a specific and appropriate arena for the encounter with the faith which does justice." It continues that this "reflects the challenge to find concrete and effective ways in which large and complex institutions can be guided by and to that justice which God himself so insistently calls for and enables" (*Documents*, 1995, Decree 17, p. 8).

The martyrs of the Catholic University of El Salvador are, then, evoked in the Congregation's document on Jesuit universities, precisely because in and through their learning and research they testified to justice. Thus, Ignacio Martin-Baro, the Jesuit psychologist in El Salvador, was murdered, not for organizing peasants or working with guerrillas, but because he started the first genuine public opinion research organization in El Salvador and published the truth of how people there saw the government as oppressive and opposed its war against the insurgents (Martin-Baro, 1994).

Justice and Imagination

It will take imagination to explore in myriad forms (and not just through the dismal sciences of economics, politics, and sociology) the ways a university pursues, furthers, and embodies justice. Margaret O'Brien Steinfels calls us to this realm of imagination as does the Marymount presence at Loyola Marymount with its signature emphasis on culture and the arts. Steinfels had us read selections from literature, such as Dickens's *Hard Times,* and Ellen Marie Keane led us in a reading enactment of the play *Trifles*. Justice does involve learning to imagine differently and gaining empathy by passing over to the situation of the other.

Indeed, one of my own personal icons of the faith that does justice was my friend, Mev Puleo, a professional photographer. Her face adorns my office wall in a poster with the inscription: "Wake up and see you are the eyes of the world" (Puleo, 1994). As we have seen, the same 34th General Congregation of the Jesuits broadened the notion of justice to include dialogue with culture and interreligious dialogue as well. At its best, the Catholic tradition spelled with a big C cannot work unless it is also Catholic in the small c sense of inclusive. As James Joyce once put it, to be Catholic means "here comes everybody"!

So, if there is genuine conversation—even argument—about these two questions (the faith that does justice; the university that does justice), we will have significantly furthered the goal of considering the Catholic nature of the university. As Margaret O'Brien Steinfels insisted in her presentation, there is no one formula to address the catholicity of each and every university. But everywhere, sustaining a Catholic sensibility depends on fostering the ongoing conversation. We will in the process, I suspect, also help envision together some next steps for making our universities more concretely even more Catholic and, simultaneously, more a university (with its own important ideal of inclusiveness) than they have been.

References

Documents of the Thirty-Fourth General Congregation of the Society of Jesus (1995). St. Louis, MO: Institute of Jesuit Resources.

Dorr, D. (1992). *Option for the poor*. Maryknoll, NY: Orbis Press.

Ganss, G. E., S.J. (Trans.) (1992). *The spiritual exercises of Saint Ignatius: A translation and commentary*. St. Louis, MO: Institute of Jesuit Sources.

Gilligan, C. (1982). *In a different voice*. Cambridge, MA: Harvard University Press.

Habermas, J. (1984). In T. McCarthy (Trans.), *The theory of communicative action* (Vol. 1). Boston, MA: Beacon Press.

Habermas, J. (1987). In T. McCarthy (Trans.), *The theory of communicative action* (Vol. 2). Boston, MA: Beacon Press.

Lukes, S. (1974). *Power: A radical view*. New York, NY: Macmillan.

MacIntyre, A. (1981). *After virtue*. Notre Dame, IN: Nortre Dame Press.

Martin-Baro, I. (1994). In A. Aron & S. Corne (Eds.), *Writing for a liberation psychology*. Cambridge, MA: Harvard University Press.

Murray, J.C. (1964). *We hold these truths*. Garden City, NY: Doubleday Image.

Pope, S. (1994). *The evolution of altruism and the ordering of love*. Washington, DC: Georgetown University Press.

Puleo, M. (1994). *The struggle is one: Voices and visions of liberation*. Albany, NY: State University Press of New York.

Rawls, J. (1971). *A theory of justice*. Cambridge, MA: Harvard University Press.

Schulteis, M., DeBerri, E., & Henriot, P. (1992). *Our best kept secret*. Washington, DC: Center of Concern.

Smith, J. Z. (1978). *Map is not territory: Studies in the history of religions*. Leiden: E.J. Brill.
Tracy, D. (1987). *Plurality and ambiguity*. San Francisco, CA: Harper and Row Publishers.

AT THE HEART OF CATHOLIC CHRISTIANITY

Thomas P. O'Malley, S.J.

God so loved the world so as to give his only begotten son . . .
The Gospel of John.

Catholic Christians, east and west, believe that God is "Trinity." That is, God is one in three persons. While this is a central doctrine, it is a little difficult to access. When we say God is "Father," we are making an image. We are tempted to see an old man. When we say "Holy Spirit," we frequently see the image of a dove. But when we say "Son," we truly mean Son, for the very good reason that "the word became flesh." All that we really know of God is in the Son. The rest is silence. The rest is negative theology; the rest is sometimes helpful speculation.

God loved the world and sent his Son. To do what? To live, to show a style of life which is free, but bent on service. To show a way to be human which breaks through our isolation from one another, our inability to talk with one another; which certainly breaks the impenetrable silence of the mystery that all call God; which breaks through the sinful condition which leads us to do appalling things to one another; which breaks through the great *no*, death.

Jesus taught his followers to call God "Our Father." Simple, isn't it? The mysterious, the unknown, the dreadful, the unspeakable—Jesus had such a degree of intimacy with that mystery that all call God, that he was able to instruct us to call that mystery "Our Father." No doubt he came to that intimacy as he matured, by degrees; and at this point I am, of course, emphasizing what tradition has called "His humanity."

The gospels are filled with those nightly sessions in which Jesus went off to the hills to pray. As a consequence, we may guess, of this intimacy with God, Jesus came to this profound freedom which marks the gospel at so many points. And, he taught his followers to be free. Like all human beings, they were accustomed to making idols of habit, convention, religious practice, what people might think, blind prejudice. He especially wanted his followers to be free of those idols when it came to a question of helping others. This freedom of Jesus is related to his insight, to his friendship, to his intimacy with God in prayer.

1

Freedom

Epicurus would have his followers come to a freedom which is one of utter detachment. The spectacle of human life is as a battle seen from a refuge far off, on a hill. So Epicurus envisions God as wholly detached; and to become a philosopher is to be God-like—not falling in love, not embroiled in politics, not a creature of one's desires. But the freedom that Jesus (and Christianity after him) envisions, is one of freedom bent on service. Jesus is not a spectator, he is an actor. We see this in the gospel of Mark, in Jesus' energy, his passion to be up and doing. A wonderful passage is Mark 10:32 (*New American Bible*): "They were on the road going up to Jerusalem, and Jesus was leading the way; and the disciples were filled with awe while those who followed behind were afraid." It is impossible to imagine the Jesus, intimate with God his father in prayer, coming thus to freedom, and *not* being bent on service.

Freedom *from*, and *for what*? The world of Jesus was a human world; it was very much like our own. Cutting past all the enormous technological changes, it was a world in which people were being *lived by life*; caught up in habits of viewing the world, and other human beings, and indeed God, habits which were not calculated to bring them to freedom. Socrates would say: their lives were unexamined. Christians would say: their attachments to things, and to persons, were not known, not examined; such examination would bring them to the decisions to do away with those things that impede the liberty that serves. It is a long process, this coming to freedom. It means intimacy with God in prayer; it means a degree of inner self-consciousness; it means the painful and slow acquisition of virtues. It means the desire to avoid the temptation to be merely a spectator, but rather, to be one who serves. The world of Jesus, like our own, was a world where God was unknown and perhaps irrelevant; a world where nature was red in tooth and claw, a Hobbesian world, with the specter of death, and its *simulacra* everywhere. A world, therefore, where sin reigns. A world, as I say, much like our own. Niebuhr has said that "sin" or "original sin" is the only Christian doctrine which may be empirically observed.

Service

To serve: Whom? The Good Samaritan story echoes a theme in Jewish wisdom: we are to serve the one whom the Good Samaritan story calls "the neighbor," the case next door, the case that comes across your path. That is the need that requires service.

It strikes me that the Jesus of the gospel of St. Mark is a great model for teachers. He gets quite excited, indeed irritated, when his disciples find it so hard to understand. He is filled with the insight that he has won, filled with that familiarity with God in prayer, and it bothers him greatly when he sees people unable to grasp what it is that he is saying.

It is, in fact, difficult to grasp. It takes a whole afternoon of walking, which is to say a whole lifetime. You may remember those disciples on the road to Emmaus, one of the greatest of Easter stories (Luke 24:13–35), which is another good teaching model. Those disciples have many of the elements that would be in a Christian creed. That creed breaks off after they narrate Jesus' death. They are looking for Jesus for all the wrong reasons. They are looking for him in power, and demonstrable might. Jesus calls them foolish and slow of heart to believe. He claims that the Hebrew scriptures, as we would call them, have laid out all that the Messiah had to suffer. It is not so easy for us to grasp what Jesus means by this, unless you see the constant theme in those scriptures of *going down, so as to come up.* This is one of the mighty mysteries which is revealed to us by the "word of God," Jesus. We imagine what we might have done had we been there. We imagine what it might be like if he were to use his power, and to cure even more people, or to come down from the cross. Instead, he died, and then "God raised him up," as one theology of the resurrection puts it.

All that we know of God is in Jesus. The message is in the very person of Jesus. In his life, death, and resurrection; in his coming to glory, to his sonship in the fullness—all of this he comes to by suffering. Every Christian person has to embrace this necessity. And, great paradox: work to reduce that inevitable suffering in every "neighbor" that we meet. That is what a Christian person is called to do.

It follows, I believe, that the life, death, and resurrection of Jesus are all bound together. The resurrection is not simply a proof of the validity of his teaching. The resurrection is not a wholly disconnected miraculous event that puts the seal of approval on the way Jesus lived. Rather, the style of life that is in Jesus is what leads him to and through death, to life. It follows, for the believing person, that every healing, every brilliant medical break-through, every release from the captivity of addiction, every turning toward service arising out of familiarity with God with prayer—all of these—are little resurrections. For the believing eye, that is; faith and Christian life flow into every legitimate corner of human life.

It is important to notice that the disciples experienced this resurrection of Jesus, as they discover him, with the marks of his suffering still on him; where reluctance to believe, fear, and joy all are mixed together. We know with certainty very little about the risen body of Jesus—nothing of any great moment at any rate—except for the fact that it is in fact the person Jesus, the historically marked person of Jesus, who has broken through the great no of death. By his coming among us and by his resurrection, he has broken that silence of God. Christianity then goes on to say that he sends his spirit into times and places not his own, and where his foot never stepped, to draw by the Holy Spirit the power of God everyone who would make a leap of faith, into the "body of Jesus." That is not the only image of "Church," but it is one of the most famous.

Now, among the strands of the web of sin, everywhere observed in the world, is isolation of people, one from another. Isolation that leads to murder, already in the opening pages of Genesis. So, Jesus does not "save" people individually, though it is an individual act of faith; the natural process, drawn by the tether of the spirit, is to bring people into the body which is his Church. And this Church is a sign of the wholeness promised to us by God in Jesus exactly to the degree that it brings people together in communion.

Church

This Church, this community, this assembly, celebrates entrance into it by primal sacraments of initiation (baptism and confirmation); and while it celebrates three other critical sacraments of states of life, and a fourth of reconciliation, re-entrance into the community, the sacraments of initiation introduce the believer into *the sacrament* of all sacraments, the Eucharist.

Back to the disciples on the road to Emmaus. Notice that they walk on the road, they have all the elements of a creed except for death—and—resurrection; note that Jesus does not sit them down on a rock and tell them everything they need to know, but he walks with them on the road, explains the scriptures to them, introduces them into the profound mystery of "going down and coming up," and finally is known by them in the "breaking of the bread," that supper to which he was invited, though he himself is the inviter.

This is what Church does in the celebration of the Eucharist. She recalls the great things done by God in history (Old Testament and New Testament); she recalls, in every Eucharistic prayer, east and west, in a central passage, what God has done in Jesus (birth, life, death—and—resurrection); she recalls the expectancies of what he will yet do in the future, and now.

If the first part of the Eucharist is the reading of the scriptures, and the unfolding of them, the second part of the Eucharist is a great prayer of thanksgiving for all that God has done in the past, and in the world. There is a tantalizing hint in an early Eucharistic prayer that begins: "then he makes mention of the sun and the moon and the other stars. . . ." The author does not quote any further. But clearly the author intends to praise God not only for "saving history," but for the glories of the world itself. But the central kernel in all Eucharistic liturgies, east and west, begins "The night before he died. . . ."

There is an expectancy of a new future, certainly. "He will come again to judge the living and the dead." That expectancy is constantly there. But: because we have this future, the present must be taken seriously. The insistent demands of the *now* are presented to the believers, meeting in this assembly. Then every final prayer (post-communion) in the *Roman Missal*, the prime liturgical book of the Roman Catholic Church, the worshipers are reminded of the distance that exists between what they have celebrated—this act of perfect love—the death and resurrection of Jesus, and his presence in our midst—and where we are now, still partially caught in the web of sin. Luther would say: *Simul peccator et justus*; the language of the Missal will say: "To us, also, sinners. . . ."

It is a traveling church, a pilgrim church. It makes its way in various languages, and in various times, and with various architectures, and with various costumes. It sees itself to be continuous with the past. We have a description of a liturgy in what we would call modern day Turkey, someplace around A.D. 150, in which we can perfectly see the structure of today's liturgy. And beginning with the 4th century, we have a sudden flood of literature which introduces us to the sights, and the smells, and the sounds, and the shape of the liturgy of Augustine in North Africa, of Ambrose in Milan, of Cyril in Jerusalem.

This continuity with the past, this *tradition* is at once a gift, and something of a burden. The Church has always to be reformed. *Ecclesia semper reformanda*. Like people in general, she begins to make an idol of what was once a good practice. Like people in general, she begins to be somewhat deaf to the voice of God. She can become deaf to the insistent cries of the poor. She can be lost in the rite and its glory, and not hear the necessity of doing justice.

Intellect

Because she is always under the necessity of adapting to new times, and inculturating herself, she must necessarily be an intellectual church. That is, there has to be the power of intellect living within her, or she is bound to repeat the formulas of the past without understanding them, or without being able to frame the new announcements of the present. Church, of course, is not open only to intellectuals. It is not a Gnostic association. But she needs the services of intellect to be herself.

This is so because she must translate her scriptures, without which she is nothing. This is so because she always asserts that, because you accept God's saving action in Jesus (*God so loved the world . . .*) that it follows that certain actions are required of you. God does not love simply me, but he loves all human beings; the sign of this is the sending of his Son. It follows, therefore, that he wants all of those people to come to the fullness of human life. (I have made something of a leap here, as you may observe. It needs to be fleshed out. But we can do that in discussion.)

Finally, while the one central doctrine is to be found in Jesus, there are many reflections which theologians make, on how the mysteries cohere. How the sacraments of initiation relate to the Eucharist; how Eucharist relates to the style of life that is in Jesus; and, a most wonderful reflection, how the very self-giving that is at the heart of the life of Jesus, is to be found in the life of God, Trinity. There, as theologians reflect, we begin to see a mystery of otherness, of giving to the other, so that creation is not explained in terms of a purpose clause, but as a result clause. What does God want of creation? Nothing. Nothing. He can want nothing. But he is so good that . . . that goodness spills out into creation itself.

Very early on in the history of the Church (that laboratory where we see so much of how Church works well, and works badly), we see intellectual centers being formed. Paul himself is already an intellectual. Luke is a stylist. The author of Hebrews is a stylist and a theologian. A great catechetical school is founded at Alexandria. The apologists, in the second century, are constantly telling people of the reasonableness of Christianity. Towards the end of the second and the beginning of the third century, we have powerful intellects like Irenaus, Tertullian, and Origen—all of them explaining the scriptures, all of them relating the mysteries one to another, all of them insisting that there can be no profound, constant gap between faith and reason. (Tertullian, to be sure, fits into this with a little difficulty; but he is frequently saying that.)

All of them also insist that while intellect can see the reasonableness of it all, it cannot compel the assent, the leap of faith. If intellect cannot make that leap, faith can make the leap toward intellect.

Now we have a pilgrim people, a people on the march, through time, with certain constants—the celebration of sacraments, the recollection of the great things done by God in Jesus; with certain imperatives—the necessity of reflecting the wholeness of God (or holiness) in our lives, and doing justice in the world in which we live; accepting the fact that we are "all in the same boat together," and while the act of faith is an individual leap, it joins us to a body of believers; a pilgrim people who anticipate some future in which God will be all in all; but at the same time, because we have a future, taking the present seriously.

Intellect is a constant companion on that road. We see this in the catechetical school at Alexandria, and in Augustine (354–430), who all by himself formed an intellectual, theological center at his Basilica of Peace, where he preached for so long. Depending on the course of culture and of history, intellect is a constant companion and a necessary companion, of this believing people, this pilgrim people.

Connectedness

A recent papal document "Out of the Heart of the Church" (*Ex corde Ecclesiae*) says that the medieval university, and therefore the university in its seed as we presently know it, was born out of the heart of the Church (Abbott, 1966). It seems a paradox, but it is so. The Church has this sense of history, which gives her a strand of *connectedness* backward to her beginning, and beyond that, through the Hebrew scriptures, to the law and the prophets. There is an expectancy of the future, as has been said, but this sense of the future is not that proverbial "pie in the sky," but rather a mission to make things better in the here and now.

The body of Christ is of the very stuff of the earth. He is of the very stuff of human history. In one brilliant text from the New Testament (Hebrews 1:1), "When in times past God spoke to our forefathers, he spoke in many and varied ways through the prophets too. But in this the final age, he has spoken to us in his Son, whom he has appointed heir of all things; and through him he created the universe. He is the radiance of God's glory, the stamp of God's very being, and he sustains the universe by his word of power."

It is impossible, therefore, for a believing person to see any necessary alienation from the world itself, however violent and mindless it appears to be; and any alienation from other people, because we are called to be members of one body; any alienation from God, for God so loved the world. I might add, the work of our hands is something of great value, and alienation from that is most unlikely in this context of belief.

Because the Church believes with the famous words of (Genesis 1:31) ". . . and God saw that it was very good . . . ," all of the created world is good. Church has successfully resisted, in the laboratory of her experience, the temptation to regard matter as evil. It follows that Church has constantly used the things of the world in worship, music, dance, architecture, costuming, in her praise of God. She has also used the powers of the mind for her own self-understanding (as has been noted, again); but she has also gravitated toward the things of the mind, even when they did not immediately impinge on her interest of faith. You will see in the lower row of windows in Sacred Heart Chapel the desire of the iconographer to show this, by listing all the Catholics in the arts and sciences, the law, medicine, and other areas of intellect. The most famous calamity to befall her in this regard was in the case of Galileo, where there appeared to be a clash between faith and reason. The larger view, the perennial view, coming out of the experience of the Church itself, is that there can be no such contradiction. Intellect cannot make the leap, the saving leap of faith; but faith can certainly make the leap into all areas of human endeavor, taking them on their own grounds, and by their own rules; knowing that there is no shortcut, other than the long road of investigation, study, experiment.

Because the Church immerses itself in the world, finding everything in the world to be good, it necessarily inculturates itself. The way a sixteenth century Christian acted, prayed, sang, is different from the way in which a twentieth century Christian prayed. While we recognize ourselves in that liturgy described by Justin Martyr, in Asia Minor, around A.D. 150, we recognize that the manner in which the scriptures were read, the language, the music, the way in which people dressed, their relationship to the larger society—all of these were profoundly different from now. But the notion of inculturation is in tension with the counter-cultural nature of the gospel message, and Christian belief.

This means that Christianity cannot acquiesce to everything that the contemporary culture says. Not about the value of life, not about the value of sex, not about the meaningfulness of work, not about the infinite value of the individual, not about the possibility of coming to freedom; not about the value of habits which dispose people for the good, habits that we call virtues. The necessary bent toward reason which, I believe, has marked Christianity from its beginning means that it is constantly attempting to inculturate itself, and to find the language, and the other means of expression, to suggest to that culture that there is more, that there is a transcendent horizon that a given culture does not necessarily see.

Is it not amazing to think that it took the Christian churches some nineteen centuries to mount above the dominant culture to finally declare that slavery was an unspeakable evil? Is it not amazing that it took an equal amount of time, perhaps (though the question is very complicated) to come to the notion that color, sex, and condition in human society are not limits to being a Christian, nor limits to how Christians treat one another, or treat anyone who is human?

Saint Paul, especially in Galatians, came to the insight that God is not limited by space, time, ritual, dietary laws, or even to the chosen persons of Abraham, Isaac, and Jacob. This is also apparent in the drama of Luke— Acts where the good news is brought from Jerusalem to Rome, and thus symbolizing the radical universalism of Christianity. The Cornelius episode in Acts 10 is one of the dramatic ways in which Luke incessantly drives home this notion. This whole area is extraordinarily contemporary; and it is a good example of inculturation/counter-culturalism. There is a whole, immensely long period in which the Church was in many ways a prisoner of the culture in which she lived.

Paradox

Many paradoxes lie at the heart of Christianity. We assert that at the heart of the mystery that all call God, there is a kind of altereity, a community, a community of knowledge, of love, and of profound sharing. God is three, God is one. God has nothing to gain from creation; it is not to be described in terms of a purpose clause—God is so giving of self, diffusing of self, that the act of creation follows.

When we say that God became incarnate in Jesus, we go on to say that Jesus is God and man. The style of his life is so self-giving that it leads him by some mysterious process to the fullness of being a child of God, in his resurrection. It is in dying that we come to life.

Christianity says that we can be free, yet utterly depend on God to do the good. Christianity says that the individual is the one who must make the leap of faith, but the individual is also called to live in, and to be responsible for the community, especially the community of the Church. Christianity asserts that this belief in God, through Jesus, to which we are drawn by the power of the spirit is also one that holds the sanctity of individual conscience, expressing itself differently in religious views.

Christianity must necessarily root itself in the culture of its time, and at the same time profoundly criticize that culture. Christianity necessarily asserts the necessity of reason, and sometimes over against that reason, the primacy of faith. But it also asserts that they can never contradict one another. Christianity asserts the radical goodness of all the creation and, at the same time, teaches that human beings must learn to come to the ability to use these created things to the degree that they help, and avoid them to the degree that they hinder.

This radical goodness of Christianity leads one mystic, Saint Ignatius of Loyola (1491–1556), to see everything in creation, the universe itself and all its parts, and all creations of human genius, to be as it were gifts proceeding from God to the believing recipient. Since love is shown more by deeds than by words, and since love is a mutual sharing, Ignatius suggests that the believer then returns thanks to God, and "gives him glory," by acknowledging his presence in all of these things. *God so loved the world* . . . (John 3:16).

References

Abbott, W. M., S.J. (1966). *The Documents of Vatican II*. J. Gallagher (Trans. and Ed.). New York: Guild.

John Paul II (1990). *Ex Corde Ecclesiae* (Vatican trans.). Boston, MA: Pauline Books.

A WHOLE AFTERNOON OF WALKING

Timothy M. Matovina

Father O'Malley's major insight is that intellect and connectedness are important markers of Catholic Christianity. He contends that intellect underscores the ethical implications of faith, illuminates (at least partially) how the Christian mysteries cohere, and facilitates the vital task of adapting past formulas to new times. Connectedness, on the other hand, is a vision that links the past with the present, the various branches of learning with one another, and the human person with their fellow human beings and the entire created order. Since I agree wholeheartedly with Father O'Malley's position, in what follows I will respond to his paper by offering reflections on the teaching model of Jesus and the significance of intellect and connectedness as markers of Catholicity for a university such as Loyola Marymount.

Jesus the Teacher

Father O'Malley cited various gospel texts in his discussion of Jesus as a model teacher, among them the fascinating parable of the Good Samaritan (Luke 10:25–37, *New American Bible*). While frequently this parable is interpreted as a call to lend our neighbor a helping hand, it is also a most appropriate text for examining Jesus' teaching style. A lawyer asks him, "Teacher, what must I do to inherit everlasting life?" Upon Jesus' request, the man answers his own question by recalling the commandment to love God and neighbor. But the lawyer still is not satisfied and probes further: "Who is my neighbor?"

What he is really asking is, "Whom must I help?" He wants to know his responsibilities to the "have nots." Jesus does not criticize the lawyer, but in telling the story of the Good Samaritan he invites the lawyer to identify himself with one of the characters. The lawyer most certainly would not wish to identify with the priest or the Levite, who lack compassion. Nor would the lawyer identify himself with the Samaritan, to him a low and impure person. This leaves only one possibility: the man who fell among robbers and was left half-dead.

The effect of the parable was to reverse the lawyer's point of view completely. No longer powerful, he is placed in the situation of looking for help. From this perspective he learned that even a despised Samaritan is his neighbor.

This parable is not just about "doing what we can" for others. It is a challenge to see our world from a different point of view by imagining ourselves victimized and in the ditch rather than in control and walking on the road. It is a call to see ourselves and the world around us through a new set of eyes.

Father O'Malley's claim about the significance of intellect and connectedness reflects Jesus' encounter with the lawyer. This encounter begins with Jesus connecting the lawyer to the law and the covenant, continues with an imaginative exercise that reverses the lawyer's point of view, and ends with the recognition that the lawyer is to serve his neighbor. In other words, Jesus sparks the lawyer's intellect to perceive in a new way that his covenant relationship with God demands a connectedness with all of humanity.

A Community of Learning

What are the implications of Jesus' teaching style for Catholic universities and the quest to enhance the intellectual life and a sense of connectedness? I offer the following three observations from my perceptions as a faculty member in liberal arts, specifically theology and religious studies.

Distinguish history and memory

Often the detached analysis of historical treatises leaves readers with a sense of separation from the events related. Memory, on the other hand, implies a lived experience that connects us to the past and illuminates the ethical consequences that previous generations and events entail for contemporary life. In Jesus' encounter with the lawyer, he did not merely teach him Jewish history. Rather, he led the lawyer to remember and interpret the Sinai covenant in a way that invited a deeper understanding and commitment to that covenant.

One of the exercises I do with students in a course on the U.S. Latino religious experience is a genealogy assignment (an idea I learned from my colleague, Dr. Marie Anne Mayeski). After we spend some time examining the religious history of Latinos in the United States, the students interview their parents, grandparents, and other family members to trace their family lineage as far back as they can, noting the place and date of birth, religious affiliation, level of education, employment, and marital history of the successive generations they are able to identify. Then they write a short essay that connects events, movements, social changes, and other elements of the U.S. Latino experience to their family histories. Non-Latino participants in the class reflect in a similar manner on their own family background.

This assignment is most effective when students conduct extended conversations with their elders, at times hearing elements of their family saga for the first time. For many students who engage in these extended conversations, the memory of the past impels them to see their present and future in new ways. A few years ago one student discovered that his ancestors, who were from Mesilla, New Mexico, lived on the international boundary established by the 1848 Treaty of Guadalupe Hidalgo. For six years they remained residents of Mexico while the United States was a short distance from their home. The Gadsden Purchase of 1854 incorporated them into the United States, however, along with other residents of what is now the southern portions of New Mexico and Arizona. Family recollections about the arbitrariness of the international border helped this student and his classmates (as well as their instructor) envision the consequences of U.S. westward expansion in a more engaged and enlightened manner. His ancestral memory also taught us that borders like the one between Mexico and the United States are not immutable lines but human constructs that have substantial implications in our lives and in our responsibilities to citizens and immigrants alike.

Incite the imagination

Developing intellect is not limited to enhancing critical, analytical faculties. Jesus did not engage in philosophical arguments with the lawyer, but in an imaginative exercise that invited the lawyer to see his question about eternal life from an entirely different perspective.

His example has clear implications for a community of learning. The study of languages, history, anthropology, world religions, art, literature, and any number of subjects provides an opportunity to encounter a world radically different from our own. In my own experience as a student, a memorable moment of insight was the first time I realized that many words, phrases, and ideas cannot be adequately translated from one language to another. The idea that other people were walking around the planet thinking in patterns that were substantially distinct from my own enabled me to glimpse the complexity of the world and to reassess my place as one small actor within it. For me, translation assignments were not just a utilitarian exercise in language acquisition but a window into envisioning the wonderful diversity in the world's peoples and the challenge and opportunity that diversity presents for human relations and the pursuit of learning.

Foster active learning

In conversations with the lawyer and many others, Jesus used everyday stories and examples to call forth the wisdom of his hearers. Like the lawyer, students have an intellect that teachers are challenged to engage. As I look back on my own education, the most memorable learning experiences all occurred when a teacher engaged me in the learning process. An adage that I read on one teacher's office door has always stuck with me: "What we hear, we forget; what we see, we remember; what we do, we learn." Perhaps a golden rule for professors is, "Never give anyone an answer or an insight that they can discover for themselves." I mention this idea with humility because in my own teaching I so often fall short of the ideal. Nonetheless, Father O'Malley's call for recognizing the importance of the intellect in Catholic life suggests the vital significance of reminding ourselves frequently about respecting and engaging the intellect of our students.

Conclusion

There are, of course, various pitfalls which can potentially undermine attempts to enact the proposals outlined here and in Father O'Malley's paper. For example, connectedness or memory can be confused with nostalgia, a sanitized version of the past alongside which the present seems hopelessly degenerate, even irreformable. The intellect can be deluded or misguided, as critiques of the Enlightenment and modernity have demonstrated; the potential for short-sightedness and self-delusion with regard to imagination is also real. True conversation and dialogue and the humility of recognizing our own biases and limitations are constantly necessary if the marks of Catholic Christianity and a Catholic university are to endure authentically.

This is a lofty vision and neither Father O'Malley nor I have offered a comprehensive plan of action to realize it. As Father O'Malley states, in communities of learning like Loyola Marymount we must journey through "a whole afternoon of walking" as we struggle to live such a vision. Like the Catholic Christian tradition itself, our conversation about a Jesuit, Marymount, Catholic vision for the university enterprise requires ongoing adaptation in each generation. Certainly at Loyola Marymount we still struggle to grasp and act on our founding traditions and their development. Father O'Malley's address on the power of connectedness and the intellectual life, what I have called the life-giving forces of memory and imagination, offers some helpful markers for our ongoing task.

CONNECTEDNESS

Olga Celle de Bowman

"It is impossible, therefore, for a believing person to see any necessary alienation from the world itself . . . because we are called to be members of one body; any alienation from God, for God so loved the world" (O'Malley, 2000, p. 7). Although traditional forms of community are under attack, "community" is in a state of permanent reinvention and adaptation. German sociologist, Thomas Luckman, contends that in post-modern times, spiritual communities are abstract forms of identity characterized by the lack of "stable organization, canonized dogmas, recruitment systems, or disciplining apparatus" (Luckman, 1996, p. 2). Today, a deinstitutionalized and privatized form of spirituality is becoming the norm. This norm of privatization fosters alienation and creates barriers to connectedness—"members of one body."

Is there a contradiction between tradition and connectedness? The anti-authority and anti-tradition mood that characterizes postmodern times cannot be attributed only to a loss of spirituality and connection. The mood reflects the sinful state, or "original sin is the only Christian doctrine which may be empirically observed" (O'Malley, 2000, p. 2).

There is a loss of connectedness in the plight of those in search of institutionalized religion. Old solutions to new problems are accountable in part for the privatization of spirituality. Thus, there is not a contradiction between tradition and connectedness, but there is an urgent need for creative solutions to age-old questions. How do community members close the gap between this highly individualized form of spirituality and institutionalized religion?

A Return to the Basics

The experience of connectedness calls for a return to the basics. One essential component is the ability to see Christ in others—in our neighbor. The manifestation of this ability to see Christ means living out the practice of discouraging ourselves from doing to others what we would not like done to us. To reorient our lives to this basic tenet of connectedness is a difficult task. It is much easier to go to church every Sunday and to engage in rituals, than it is to commit to the principle of experiencing Christ in our

15

neighbor. Christian connectedness as a way of life is the most revolutionary strategy for social change.

Connectedness should be pragmatic. It refers to the actions and decisions we make every day to see Christ in our neighbor. The world would be a better place if we could raise moral indignation at the sight of injustice, or if we could allow ourselves to support justice even at the cost of our own comfort or security. Granted, we do not live in a perfect world. Individuals and organizations, both powerful and powerless, are constrained by their own social contexts. Like people, the Church begins to be somewhat deaf to the voice of God, and deaf to the insistent cries of the poor. The Church can be lost in the rite and its glory, and not hear the necessity of doing justice (O'Malley, 2000).

We are silent witnesses of injustice everyday in our comfortable place of work, in our neighborhood, and in our own family. "Now, among the strands of the web of sin, everywhere observed in the world, is isolation of people, one from another" (O'Malley, 2000, p. 4). The fight to right everyday injustices could jeopardize our private comfort. It could endanger the pleasure we gain from competition. And it could undermine our pride or our role of being a survivor in this difficult world. To placate our guilt, we find explanations for injustice and join the lynching crowd displaying our zealous veneration for the establishment. Secretly, we wish to become authority ourselves, hence our compliance and collaboration. The world would be a better place if we could do to others what we would like to have others do to us. This individual cost of connectedness is high for people without a transcendent sense of life.

In our everyday praxis, a spiritual community depends on the overt and covert support for victims of injustice, including those who fight injustice and endure the rigor of repression. For true connectedness how can we invest ourselves in the pursuit of justice two thousand miles away from home, while we witness injustice in our own home and remain silent?

What is the role of the Catholic university in the promotion of connectedness? What is the responsibility of Catholic university professors to live and practice justice? What lessons can the students learn from such lived example and/or such inconsistency? Every Christian's eternal dilemma is the choice between universal connectedness or selective connectedness. Christ showed us, with his death, a path of heroism and integrity that few can emulate. And yet, is there connectedness outside the praxis of everyday life? Do the students in Catholic universities experience and even seek connectedness? I believe not!

Sociology and Connectedness

Perhaps an answer to the question of spirituality and connectedness is therefore to orient our lifestyle toward a permanent connection between self and our neighbor, both immediate and global. We must teach by our example. Connectedness, as the essence of any form of spirituality, should be stressed in the culture and context of the Catholic university, as well as in the content of our teachings.

However, it is difficult to educate students in the broad normative guidelines of humanism. For many of them, it is uncomfortable to become aware of a responsibility that has no apparent personal advantage. The discipline of sociology supplies some answers and promises. There is an Argentinean folk ballad that warns:

When you sing verses of love, horses, trainers,
the sky and stars,
the Rich says: "what a beauty, this singer is such a charm!"
But if one goes the path of Fierro
throwing thoughts here and there
the Poor comes closer, pointing his ears toward you
and the Rich takes the back door
and goes away
the tail in between his legs. (Coplas del Payador Perseguido, Atahualpa Ypanqui)

Sociology promises to break the individual's self-centered view of life and society. As a discipline, sociology's promise is twofold. On the one hand, it is an effort to view society without prejudice. On the other, it remains a social science committed to social change. This humanist tradition focuses sociology's contribution on the elimination of human suffering, violence, and injustice—truly a taking care of self and neighbor endeavor.

After two centuries of its emergence, today sociology faces forbidding times. Never before have the young been so uninterested in a critical understanding of their own experience, not to mention the world in which they live and share with others. American sociologist David Ashley (1997) comments: "The postmodern masses are completely out of control; voyeurs without illusion mindlessly absorbed in the minutiae of the O. J. trial (or whatever happens to be the spectacle of the week), they are resistant to all pedagogies, to all socialist education" (p. 46). So too the Church continues a similar and longer struggle to understanding:

Is it not amazing to think that it took the Christian churches some nineteen centuries to mount above the dominant culture to finally declare that slavery was an unspeakable evil? Is it not amazing that it took an equal amount of time, perhaps (though the question is very complicated) to come to the notion that color, sex, and condition in human society are not limits to being a Christian, nor limits to how Christians treat one another, or treat anyone who is human? (O'Malley, 2000, p. 8)

The Internet, the media, and the youth subculture reach their hearts and minds earlier and more effectively than sociology. No other time in human history has had such an "absence of a public in which critical debate about important issues can take place" (Ashley, 1997, p. 47). In no other time has such a significant number of the public been so immune to social critique and reluctant to social commitment. These are not even good times for Psychology! It is instead the time of talk shows—personal problems and major social issues as entertainment, the tragic-comic scenario of hyper-reality or the simulacra of life.

The definitions of individualism and success have escaped the control of liberal social sciences or religion. The broad community orientation propagated by Christianity and liberal sociology has been lost in a celebration of hedonism that is not only anti-intellectual, but also anti-spiritual. The notion of purpose has long been disentangled from the ethos of hard work and civil responsibility that made the miracles of democracy and capitalism possible. The post–Soviet Union generation rejoices in its "hyperconformity." Materialism and consumerism have won the hearts and minds of our youth. If they are so focused, can they be persuaded to protect and embrace their neighbor?

The interplay of sociology and religion has not been harmonious or smooth. Take, for example, the concept of community. It refers to a social experience of harmony in sharing. However, sociological research consistently indicates that those images of harmony and happiness invoked by the word "community" conceal dynamics of oppression, e.g., workers within corporations (Morris, 1996). Since oppression is found in all institutions and organizations, it has been sociology's two-centuries-long task to disclose them all, one by one. This disclosure includes religious organizations. Sociology is the art of debunking myths, and in doing so contributes to the history of consciousness. However, the impact of sociology would have been insignificant, had human society not gone through huge and deep transformations. Sociology, feminism, and economics do not cause the crisis of community. They simply alert us to the corruption of power even within our most cherished institutions.

The crossroads of sociology and religion is the common concern for human suffering—the basic premise of connectedness. "Every Christian person has to embrace this necessity. And, great paradox: work to reduce that inevitable suffering in every 'neighbor' that we meet. That is what a Christian person is called to do" (O'Malley, 2000, p. 3). And yet, sociologists are human beings who find themselves adapting to the demands of their young audiences and, at times, abandoning their commitment to the struggle against injustice. The contribution of sociology will continue to be the effort to build social theories grounded on empirical research and aimed at improving the human condition. The contribution of professors in Catholic universities must be to make connections for the entire community to recognize suffering in the human condition, and to accept the responsibility to go the extra moral mile. "Christianity asserts the radical goodness of all the creation and, at the same time, teaches that human beings must learn to come to the ability to use these created things to the degree that they help, and avoid them to the degree that they hinder" (O'Malley, 2000, p. 9).

References

Ashley, D. (1997). *History without a subject: The postmodern condition*. Boulder, CO: Westview.

Luckman, T. (1996). The privatization of religion and morality. In P. Heelas, S. Lash, & P. Morris (Eds.), *Decentralization: Critical reflections on authority and identity*. Cambridge, MA: Blackwell.

Morris, P. (1996). Community beyond tradition. In P. Heelas, S. Lash, & P. Morris (Eds.), *Decentralization: Critical reflections on authority and identity*. Cambridge, MA: Blackwell.

O'Malley, T. P., S.J. (2000). At the heart of Catholic Christianity. In M. K. McCullough, (Ed.), *The just one justices: The role of justice at the heart of Catholic higher education* (pp. 1–9). Scranton, PA: University of Scranton Press.

JUST ONES PAST AND PRESENT

Michael E. Engh, S.J.

In the "Missions, Goals and Objectives" for Loyola Marymount University, we read a simple but profound statement: "Loyola Marymount understands and declares its purpose to be: the encouragement of learning, the education of the whole person, the service of faith and the promotion of justice" (1990). The first two clauses one would expect to find as the ideals of many if not most liberal arts colleges and universities in the United States. The "service of faith and the promotion of justice," however, are ideals that have evolved over the past thirty-five years in Catholic higher education. My purposes are: to place this growth in the broader context of first, the evolving social teaching in the Catholic Church, and second, within the framework of the history of the Religious of the Sacred Heart of Mary (the Marymount Sisters) and of the Society of Jesus (the Jesuits). With this background, I want to sketch the story of Loyola Marymount University within these dynamic traditions which exert enormous influence upon each of us and upon our campus culture.

This essay explores in particular the history of "education for justice" at Loyola Marymount University by the Marymount Sisters and the Jesuits. I am also including the contributions of the Sisters of St. Joseph of Orange, and other religious men and women, and lay men and women who historically have assisted in the mission of this University. These various *dramatis personae* form the cast for a play, but a play which finds us approximately at the end of the second act. I want to summarize the first two acts to date, and then suggest some of the action yet to come. We hear voices from off stage, from the direction of St. Louis and Rome, for example, and these are well worth cocking our ears in their direction.

Act One, Scene One: American Higher Education

Educational historian M. George Marsden (1994) provides us with a fascinating analysis of the growth and evolution of American higher education in his work, *The Soul of the American University*. He reminds us that American universities and colleges began as religiously inspired and administered institutions. The most important of these institutions were schools where Protestant Christianity trained not only its ministers, but also

21

lawyers, doctors, bankers, and other professionals. The vast majority of eighteenth and nineteenth century educators held the operative assumptions that to be American was to be Protestant; that Protestantism rested on the ideals of freedom, democracy, benevolence, justice, reform, inclusiveness, brotherhood, and service (Marsden, 1994). These educators further assumed that Roman Catholicism was the source of absolutism and of blind obedience, and thus the term, "Catholic university," was an oxymoron.

The founders and later administrators of the nation's colleges worked closely with public officials in extending the "free school" throughout the United States in the nineteenth century. Public schools were open to all citizens, but a Protestant ethos pervaded the classroom, from opening prayers and reading from the King James version of the Bible, to textbooks which denigrated Catholic countries, their governments and culture, as well as the Catholic Church. When Catholic immigrants began arriving in large numbers in the 1840s and 1850s, Catholic parents, parish priests, and bishops challenged the Protestant hegemony in education.

Charles Morris (1997) offers fascinating examples of the conflicts in the ensuing "school wars" and anti-Catholic riots in cities such as Philadelphia and New York. He also notes how Catholic leaders began constructing a separate world of institutions to protect the faith of the immigrant. Parochial schools, high schools, colleges, orphanages, hospitals, homes of the aged, and parish churches provided a safe haven from the threats to their religious sensibilities (Gleason, 1995). Bishops manifested a "custodial approach" toward parishioners (Dolan, 1985). In particular, the American Catholic hierarchy argued that "the Faith" could best be "preserved" if Catholics were educated separately from a highly suspect Protestant society. This extended to professional training as well, and this required Catholic schools of law, medicine, dentistry, education (for teacher training), and social work. Graduates of these institutions formed Catholic professional associations, such as the American Catholic Historical Association, where like-minded academics and practitioners could convene to discuss issues of mutual interest in an atmosphere that was more congenial—"safer" for the Faith—than that found in secular societies (Gleason, 1987).

Act One, Scene Two: Catholic Social Thought

Coinciding with these developments in the late nineteenth and early twentieth centuries, two popes began articulating a Catholic response to massive migrations of people, industrialization, and the rights of capital and labor. The first to set forth his views was Pope Leo XIII (r. 1878–1903), who issued an encyclical, *Rerum Novarum*, in 1893 which maintained that laboring people had the right to organize themselves in labor unions and to engage in collective bargaining. Subsequent popes expanded upon Leo's cautious first step, particularly Pius XI (r. 1922–1939), who issued *Quadragesimo Anno* in 1933. Other examples of this tradition include *Pacem in Terris* (1963), the letter which Pope John XXIII (r. 1958–1963) addressed to "all men of good will." The more recent examples of these writings on human rights are the letters of the present pontiff, John Paul II (r. 1978–), who has elaborated a sophisticated Catholic perspective on the dignity of the human person.

Few American bishops or clergy paid much heed to that early letter of Leo XIII. The massive influx of Catholic immigrants in eastern and midwestern cities taxed church resources and ingenuity. Historian David O'Brien observed that social action for the clergy means essentially ministering to the needs of the flock: provisions of religious services, assistance to people with personal problems, efforts to reach out and encompass within the Church the newcomers appearing daily in cities (O'Brien, 1971). For those who sought evidence of Catholic principles in matters of justice for workers, the papal teachings existed and could be cited. These letters actually inspired a small but significant number of laity and clergy whose numbers grew over the decades. We will see local examples of such concerned individuals in the story of our own institution.

Act Two, Scene One: Our Heritage at Loyola Marymount University

The predecessors of our University were known as Los Angeles College, which opened inauspiciously in 1911, and Marymount School, which first received students in 1923. The previously mentioned "custodial" approach to the laity marked the thinking both of the Jesuit and Marymount founders of their respective institutions. The bishop of the diocese in 1911, Thomas Conaty, was an Irishman who had been president of the Catholic University of America in Washington, D.C. He desired a Catholic college in Los Angeles which could offer professional training, such as in law, and he discovered that the administrators of the existing Catholic institution, St. Vincent's College, were not interested in his plans. They withdrew, and six Jesuits (two priests and four scholastics) opened a new school, Los Angeles College, in the fall of 1911. It began as a high school, and in 1914 initiated the first year of collegiate study until all four years were included in the curriculum by 1917.

The Jesuits obtained a state charter in 1918 and renamed the school Loyola College, in honor of their founder of the order, St. Ignatius Loyola. Two years later they opened the school of law which Conaty had so desired, and classes met in the evenings, 7:30 to 9:30 p.m., four nights per week. Undergraduates of the college were entitled to enroll in law school classes in those years, and students such as George Dunne, S.J., of the class of

1926, did just that. It is important to note two other features about the enrollment which distinguished the law school for its time and place. School records and yearbooks clearly document that women enrolled, received degrees, and even had their own sorority. While less easily verified, a strong oral tradition maintains that Loyola was the first law school in Los Angeles to admit Jewish students. Jews faced exclusion not only from law schools, but also from country clubs, and from the city's elite social institutions, such as the Jonathan Club and the California Club (Bradshaw, 1972; "The Jews," 1905).

A little over a mile to the south of the Jesuit school on Venice Boulevard at Normandie, the Marymount Sisters opened their school, "Marymount-in-the-West," in September, 1923. Conaty's successor, Bishop John J. Cantwell, had written the year previously and pleaded for Sisters to teach the daughters of the Catholic elite, whom he termed "poor little rich children." Cantwell feared that, "Unless something can be done the leaders in Catholic society in this city in years to come will be tainted with Protestantism, and our marriages among the well-to-do classes will be largely mixed" (Cantwell, 1922). Seven Sisters opened the school in a rented house on West 28th Street and on the first day they received six students, who ranged from first grade through the junior year of high school. Growth in enrollment and expansion of the curriculum led the Sisters to secure a new site and to build a permanent campus in 1931 in Westwood, on Sunset Boulevard on the north side of the then-new University of California, Los Angeles (UCLA) campus.

Loyola also grew, divided the administration into high school and college divisions, and expanded the curriculum to include new schools of Commerce and Engineering. In 1926, Father Joseph Sullivan, S.J., assumed the leadership of Loyola College, immediately planned a major fund drive, and created a Board of Regents which counted some of the most powerful men in the city and, significantly, included Protestants and Jews. One real estate developer, Fritz Burns, introduced Sullivan to another developer, Harry Culver, and persuaded Culver to give the Jesuits ninety-nine acres in the Del Rey hills (W. Hanna, personal communication, May 30, 1997). Sullivan switched the object of the fund drive from new buildings on Venice Boulevard to a new $20 million campus on the west side of the city. Sullivan broke ground on what we now know as the Westchester campus in May, 1928, in the presence of 10,000 spectators. Three buildings quickly appeared: St. Robert's Hall, Xavier Hall (a residence for faculty and students), and the locker room for athletics (previously incorporated into the Alumni gym). The great Depression intervened to forestall further construction and to defer the full realization of Sullivan's dreams.

In the area of work for justice, the Jesuits opened an extension division in 1935 and offered classes in Social Work at the Loyola High campus on

Venice Boulevard. They also responded to the wishes of their superior general, Wlodimir Ledochowski, S.J., to promote "social action" by combating the spread of Communism (McDonough, 1992). Because every Jesuit house was ordered to devise means to refute the teachings of Marx and Lenin, at Loyola, Father Joseph Vaughan, S.J., took to the radio and denounced Stalin and his followers. To form the moral character of students, the course of studies required eight semesters of "religion" and eight courses of philosophy. The goals of this education appear most clearly in a statement that appeared for many years in the school bulletin and described "the Loyola Man":

> Loyola aims to train a man for success and for possible greatness; but whatever a man's worldly achievement, Loyola's training insists that his design of living include the fulfillment of his obligations toward God and his own soul, prepares him to be, in the best sense, a Complete Man, a Citizen of Two Worlds. (*Loyola University Bulletin*, 1947, p. 33)

The Sisters at Marymount College shared similar goals for the women they taught and so strove to "give their pupils an education, moral, physical and intellectual, which will enable them to be, throughout their lives, models of every virtue and useful and accomplished members of society" (*Marymount Catalogue*, 1936). The curriculum emphasized the role that women played in society, an understanding and appreciation of the arts, and a realization of the fundamental spiritual values of life. The Sisters desired that each young woman achieve a "harmony of mind and soul and body," a goal not dissimilar to that sought by the Loyola Man. The statements of both schools strongly emphasized the necessity of religious training as part of the collegiate preparation for life after graduation. At both schools the custodial approach to Catholic education remained strong into the 1960s.

Both schools changed dramatically after World War II, in enrollment, to be certain, and in curriculum. Returning veterans took advantage of the GI Bill and boosted enrollment at Loyola to 1500 students by 1948; at Marymount, collegiate instruction began that year to accommodate demand from a burgeoning Catholic population. Both schools turned attention to problems of racial prejudice in Los Angeles through the establishment of campus chapters of the Catholic Interracial Council of Los Angeles. Catholic Interracial Councils were the largest Catholic organization responding to problems of race relations in the United States. In the Los Angeles branch, Reverend George Dunne, S.J., of Loyola's faculty, met with others to support efforts to combat racial prejudice, as in their successful challenge to the state's miscegenation law, struck down by the state Supreme Court in 1948 (Dunne, 1990).

The murder of an African-American family led Dunne to pen several articles and a play, *Trial by Fire*, which, among other work for social justice, led to his dismissal from Loyola's faculty and transfer out of the archdiocese of Los Angeles (Dunne, 1945, 1946, 1950). The persisting influence of the exiled Dunne and of others concerned about racial justice roused the ire of the new archbishop of Los Angeles, James Francis McIntyre, who resolutely maintained that Los Angeles had no race problem, save what was incited by outside agitators. McIntyre ordered the students to disband their campus chapters of the interracial council because he believed that they were being victimized by the Communist Party (E.F. Tighe, personal interview, October 17, 1992).

Shortly after Dunne's transfer, a new president assumed leadership at Loyola, the man most responsible for building a modern university out of a small local college. Reverend Charles Casassa, S.J., a thirty-nine-year-old priest with a degree in philosophy, possessed no previous presidential experience when he began his twenty-year tenure. The first president of the school with an earned doctorate, Casassa expanded the faculty, improved academics, conducted two major capital fund drives, improved faculty salaries, initiated the faculty sabbatical program, erected nine buildings on the Westchester campus, secured a new campus for the Law School on West Ninth Street, and enhanced University contacts with the broader community, particularly in the Jewish community.

Three events illustrate highlights of Casassa's record in the area of justice and warrant serious attention. The first concerns Loyola's football program, which dated back to Father Sullivan's tenure. The Loyola Lions in 1950 were a nationally ranked football team which entertained dreams of the school's first invitation to a post-season bowl. Alumni enthusiasm ran high until Casassa chose to forfeit a game in late September of 1950 against Texas Western University, now known as the University of Texas–El Paso. The Regents of the University of Texas then maintained a rule that no African American could play, either on the teams of their schools or of their opponents. Loyola University was fielding a squad that was all white except for one African American player, a starting defensive back by the name of Bill English. When Casassa learned of the Texas regulations, he negotiated with the Texas officials, who suggested that if Loyola relented, this rule would not be enforced at the Sun Bowl, to which Loyola would probably be invited to play. Casassa decided otherwise, and the coach, Jordan Olivar concurred; everyone on the squad played or no one played. Loyola forfeited the game, much to the ire of alumni fans—and to the praise of several fellow Jesuit schools across the nation *Los Angeles Loyolan*, 1950; D.G. Marshall, personal communication, October 4, 1950). (In the last game of the season, an undefeated Loyola fell to the University of Santa Clara, and no bowl bid ever came Loyola's way.)

The second area in which Casassa made a significant contribution to the University was in the establishment of the Human Relations Workshop, which began in 1953 and continued in various forms until the late 1980s (*Summary Report*, 1953). The purpose of this six-week summer institute was to train teachers, police, and public officials in improving community and racial relations within the Los Angeles area. The first director, Reverend Albert S. Foley, S.J., was a professor of sociology at Spring Hill College in Mobile, Alabama. Foley received his doctorate at the University of North Carolina and a post-doctoral fellowship at the Research Center for Group Dynamics at the University of Michigan. Casassa worked in partnership with the local branch of the American Jewish Committee to fund the institute and to assemble an Advisory Committee that included distinguished civic leaders such as John A. McCone, Attorney Martin Gang, and prominent figures such as Irving Stone and Bob Hope (A.S. Foley, S.J., personal communication, November, 1954).

Thirty participants enrolled that first summer, including four members of the Los Angeles Police Department, who received lectures from a large number of guest speakers, intensive training in intergroup dynamics and in the then-new practice of role-playing, and a series of field trips to public housing projects, jails, schools, and screenings of a series of films (*Summary Report*, 1953). One of the participants, an African-American in the L.A.P.D., later told Foley that he was a disenchanted and disillusioned police officer, but the workshop dramatically influenced his life. Tom Bradley decided to complete his law degree and to enter politics, and eventually was elected mayor of Los Angeles for five terms. When Bradley received an honorary degree from Loyola Marymount University in 1974, he publicly praised Foley and the workshop because it had "turned his life around" (Foley, n.d.).

Foley returned annually to conduct the successful and well-received workshop until 1957 when, once again, the archbishop of Los Angeles, McIntyre, detected the actions of Communists and fellow travelers at Loyola. McIntyre forbade Foley to return or to speak anywhere in the archdiocese of Los Angeles, and when Foley protested by letter, McIntyre contacted the superior general of the Jesuits, John Baptiste Janssens, to demand Foley's apology and obedience. Foley later recalled that the workshop had actually been organized, in part, because of McIntyre's actions and policies. Specifically, one of the principal aims of the Human Relations Workshop at Loyola was "to counteract the blatant anti-Semitism that Cardinal McIntyre was manifesting both in Archdiocesan policies and in the pages of the Archdiocesan weekly, the *Los Angeles Tidings*" (Foley, n.d.).

The third achievement for which Casassa warrants our consideration developed out of a further encounter with the archbishop of Los Angeles during the course of Vatican II. After the first session of the council had recessed in January of 1963, the University invited Reverend Hans Küng, a *peritus* at the council and professor of theology at the University of Tubingen, to speak on campus during a nationwide lecture tour. Casassa approached McIntyre for the requisite permission, which was refused, on the grounds that students were insufficiently prepared for the level of theological discourse expected from Küng. Casassa persisted until McIntyre relented to the extent that the faculty were permitted to hear Küng. Over 300 people attended Küng's presentation on April 3, 1963, in St. Robert's Auditorium, and at the open windows students thronged outside (Krebs, 1964; Weber, 1997).

Shortly after the Küng incident, Casassa approached McIntyre on another matter and requested permission for Loyola to admit women to undergraduate enrollment. McIntyre refused and cited the harm that would come to the Catholic women's colleges in Los Angeles. So matters rested at Loyola, while at Marymount College dramatic change was taking place. Continued growth in enrollment at their Westwood site prompted the Sisters to build a separate campus for the college. Learning that the California State University system would build a South Bay branch, the long-time president, Mother Gertrude Cain, R.S.H.M., decided to locate the new campus on the Palos Verdes peninsula (Kearney, 1965). Her successor, Mother Sacre Couer Smith, R.S.H.M., oversaw initial construction until her untimely death in 1964. Mother M. Raymunde McKay, R.S.H.M., from Marymount Manhattan College, assumed leadership and confronted dramatic difficulties. The administrators of the California State University system chose to build their new branch at Dominguez Hills (R. McKay, R.H.S.M., personal interview, August 13, 1996). This decision left Marymount College isolated both socially and academically, which gravely threatened future enrollment. Further, the accelerating national trend toward co-educational collegiate education also worried leaders of the all-women's college.

McKay took two major initiatives to confront these challenges, and she began by approaching Casassa about a partnership or affiliation of Marymount and Loyola. Hearing from Casassa of McIntyre's opposition to coeducation, McKay skillfully proposed to McIntyre that Loyola and Marymount initiate "co-instruction" at the Westchester campus. McIntyre readily agreed, much to the astonishment of Casassa (R. McKay, R.H.S.M., personal interview, August 13, 1996). Marymount College relocated to the Loyola campus and both schools began sharing one another's facilities and faculties in the fall of 1968. Marymount brought to the Jesuit campus a strong tradition in the arts, as well as creative academic programs in ethnic studies, international education, a reentry course of study for non-traditional students to complete their degrees, and a second community of women religious (R. Harrangue, personal communication, October 31, 1995).

McKay's second bold initiative was to enlist the larger community of the Sisters of St. Joseph of Orange as partners in supporting Marymount College. Possessing a collegiate program in the city of Orange for the training of their members, the Sisters of St. Joseph counted a respectable number of trained administrators and faculty members holding doctorates. When Marymount moved to Loyola, both women's religious communities arrived. Both groups also brought new benefactors to the Westchester campus, such as Thomas and Dorothy Leavey, and the Tenderich family, respectively. Women's enrollment at Marymount began to rise, and a broader array of courses and instructors were available to both male and female students.

After five years, the two schools agreed to merge, and in 1973 Donald P. Merrifield, S.J., Casassa's successor, was named first president of Loyola Marymount University, while McKay assumed the newly created post of provost. Numerous difficulties challenged the University in the next twenty years, not the least of which were issues concerning gender equity and the racial diversification of the student body and the faculty. Responding to changes in church and in society, Merrifield initiated programs to promote social justice both on and off campus. He fostered efforts to recruit greater numbers of minority students, as did his successors, James Loughran, S.J. (1984–1991) and Thomas P. O'Malley, S.J. (1991–1999). Merrifield also worked with Casassa in the area of ecumenism, such as continued contacts with the Jewish community of Los Angeles (Engh, 1989).

During Loughran's tenure, significant change originated through the blue-ribbon Commission on the Future of Loyola Marymount University, completed in 1989. For two years, 239 civic leaders reviewed operations of all aspects of the University, listened to its constituencies, and issued a thirty-four page assessment. Many recommendations affirmed University programs, but other statements challenged the school to go further, such as giving priority attention to attracting African-Americans (particularly males) and Latinos, and limiting enrollment increases in certain colleges in order "to attract more women and ethnic minorities to fields in which they are under-represented" (such as science and engineering). This blueprint for the direction of the University led to a revised Mission and Goals statement, which introduced this essay, as well as to a revision of the core curriculum with a mandatory American Cultures requirement to bring the benefits of racial and ethnic diversity into the curriculum (J. Jabbra, personal communication, February 11,1991).

During Loughran's administration, two other developments involved faculty and students in issues of justice. Campus Ministry coordinated delegations of faculty and staff to visit countries in the world experiencing significant injustice. Investigating conditions in El Salvador, Nicaragua, and Mexico brought University personnel face to face with the violence and grinding poverty of those nations (G. Wanser, S.J., personal communication, May 17, 1998). Students took the initiative in another area in 1988 when the Belles, one of the University's women's service organizations, inaugurated a requirement that all members devote at least twenty hours per semester in service to the off-campus community (J. Connolly, S.S.L., personal communication, May 17, 1998). Following the example of the Belles, the other four service groups instituted similar mandates so that at present members work in a wide variety of projects directly benefitting the poor (Dunne, 1990).

Thomas P. O'Malley, S.J., built on the foundations of his predecessors so that during his administration the enrollment of students of color reached unprecedented numbers, both for the University and among all Jesuit colleges and universities in the United States. Further, the Law School presently ranks second in the nation among all law schools for total enrollment of students of color. The Law School is also the first ABA-accredited law school in the state to establish an uncompensated public service requirement, and also maintains a summer program in Central America to study international environmental law (*Loyola Fact Sheet*, 1998). Funding from the James Irvine Foundation also financed the hiring of faculty members of color. These and other efforts earned the University the Theodore M. Hesburgh Award for 1998 from the Teachers' Insurance and Annuity Association–College Retirement Equities Fund (TIAA-CREF) for faculty development to enhance undergraduate teaching and learning. Further goals of O'Malley have been the establishment of endowed chairs of ethics in each of the colleges of the University, as well as an annual full scholarship for an undocumented person.

Act Two, Scene Two: Changes in the Roman Catholic Church Since 1965

Both the Society of Jesus and the Religious of the Sacred Heart of Mary received inspiration and mandates to change from meetings of the hierarchy of the Roman Catholic Church: the Second Vatican Council (1962–1965), and the Second Synod of Bishops (1971). These two international gatherings issued important documents which affected the renewal and direction of all religious orders. In several of their statements, the bishops of Vatican II enunciated their understanding of the nature of the Church and its mission in the modern world. They noted that members of the laity have particular and important roles to play and significant talents to offer to the church, free of clerical paternalism (Abbott & Gallagher, 1966). The Council began the process to end the custodial attitude toward the laity and to encourage their empowerment.

The Synod of Bishops in 1971 produced one of the turning-point documents in the history of the modern Catholic Church. Deeply concerned about the growing poverty in the world and the widening gap between the haves and the have-nots, they were also alarmed that the Church did not address itself directly to the structural and systemic inequities in national and international economies. The bishops wrote, "Action on behalf of justice and participation in the transformation of the world fully appear to us as a constitutive dimension of preaching the Gospel" (O'Brien & Shannon, 1992). Every religious order in the Catholic world met and discussed the implications of these new directives from Rome and the bishops, wrestled with their implications, and repeatedly returned to these texts for inspiration and guidance.

The Jesuits, response came in an assembly known as a "general congregation," with delegates from every Jesuit province (geographic division) and region in the world. A few words are necessary about the Jesuit jargon. The General Congregations in standard Jesuit shorthand are "GC 32" and "GC 34." The documents which were produced are known as "decrees," which is actually not the best terminology. "Decree" means "what has been decided." Actually, they are documents which set directions for the future and foster discussion. They can be juridical and they are binding, but they are primarily meant to be persuasive. They appeal to the Jesuits' sense of generosity and concern for the "magis," the greater good to be accomplished.

Meeting in Rome in 1974–75, Jesuits at GC 32 issued a series of statements, one of which, Decree Four, "The Service of Faith and the Promotion of Justice," committed the Jesuits to a "preferential option for the poor." They redirected the Order when they concluded that, "The mission of the Society of Jesus today is the service of faith, of which the promotion of justice is an absolute requirement . . . injustice not only personal but institutionalized: built into economic, social, and political structures that dominate the life of nations and the international community" (*Documents*, 1977). Similar commitments can also be found in the revised constitutions of the Religious of the Sacred Heart of Mary, approved in 1983. Section 8 reads, "Faithful to our heritage, attentive to the signs of the times and the call of the Church, we are committed to the service of evangelical justice, wherever we are and whatever our ministry" (*Constitutions*, 1983).

The implications of "the service of faith and the promotion of justice" have challenged educators around the world, but the principle has set deep roots in the psyche of the Marymount Sisters and the Jesuits. For Catholic higher education, the most striking example of the application of the summons to faith and justice took place at the University of Central America in El Salvador, in a school much like our own, when six Jesuits and two lay workers were murdered in 1989. Previously, the school's rector (president), Ignacio Ellacuria, explained the mission of the school:

> A Christian university must take into account the gospel preference for the poor. This does not mean that only the poor study at the university; it does not mean that the university should abdicate its mission of academic excellence—excellence needed in order to solve the complex social problems. It does mean that the university should be present intellectually where it is needed: to provide science for those who have no science; to provide skills for the unskilled; to be a voice for those who have no voice; to give intellectual support for those who do not possess the academic qualifications to promote and legitimate their rights. (Ellacuria, 1994)

Act Three

In January of 1995, Jesuit delegates gathered once again in Rome, this time for the Thirty-Fourth General Congregation, and in three months authored twenty-six decrees on a variety of topics (*Documents*, 1995). Three documents are included in the readings for the President's Institute: Decree Thirteen, "Cooperation with the Laity in Mission"; Decree Fourteen, "Jesuits and the Situation of Women in Church and Civil Society"; and Decree Seventeen, "The Intellectual Dimension of Jesuit Ministries." One delegate, Reverend John Padberg, S.J., explained to me last year that in drafting the statement on the Laity, the authors were stymied until they realized that they were approaching the matter in reverse. Instead of recommending that lay people be invited to work with Jesuits, perhaps it would be more helpful to recommend ways that Jesuits could assist the lay people who had already assumed the administration, staffing, and much of the operation of "Jesuit" institutions!

Permeating the entire statement is a spirit of cooperation and respect, not the paternalism of earlier decades. The first premise of the delegates is that the Catholic Church of the coming millennium will be called the "Church of the Laity," and this is to be welcomed as "a grace of our day and a hope of the future." Furthermore, the Society of Jesus offers "ourselves in service to the full realization of this mission of the laity" (*Documents*, 1995). [Note the shift in emphasis in these statements: NOT Jesuit leadership, but Jesuit service.] The delegates urge all Jesuits to cooperate with the laity, with other priests and religious, with people of all faiths and beliefs who seek a world of "truth, justice, freedom, peace, and love" (*Documents*, 1995).

Four major recommendations highlight Decree Thirteen which illustrate a shift from a custodial model of faith to one of empowerment. I draw attention to the third recommendation which states that Jesuits are to cooperate with laity in the works of the order, which includes lay people exercising "co-responsibility" and decision making—"where it is appropriate." A lay person can be the director of a Jesuit work, and the Society must take adequate steps to assure the "Jesuit identity" of the work (*Documents*, 1995). This section is probably the segment of the document with the greatest challenges for Jesuits, and it bears directly upon the options for the future of higher education. The document opens possibilities for what it terms "partnership of laity and Jesuits":

> Lay persons will rightly take on a greater role of responsibility and leadership within these works. Jesuits will be called upon to support them in their initiative by . . . promotion of Jesuit apostolic values. If our service will be more humble, it will also be more challenging and creative. (*Documents*, 1995)

Almost thirty years ago Jesuits and Religious of the Sacred Heart of Mary recruited and established civil boards of trustees to which they entrusted the ownership and operation of these schools (Fitzgerald, 1984). This movement swept the United States in the late 1960s and early 1970s for a variety of reasons, both ecclesial and financial. Thus, neither the Jesuits nor the Sisters "own" the University. Vatican authorities have had to struggle to understand these American developments in their own efforts to ensure that the Catholic colleges and universities in the United States remained truly "Catholic."

In 1990 Pope John Paul II drafted a document titled *Ex Corde Ecclesiae* to spell out the juridical relationship between the Roman Catholic Church and Catholic universities throughout the world. The application to the American situation proved complex because of our legal tradition of separation of church and state and our long cherished principle of academic freedom. With 235 universities and colleges in this country, American Catholics have the largest number of such institutions of any nation in the world. It took the bishops and Catholic higher education leaders six years to hammer out the solution in November of 1996, which harmonized Roman church law and American civil and educational practice (Stammer, 1996). Vatican officials rejected this compromise, and negotiation resumed.

This issue arose last year in the sale by St. Louis University of its hospital to the Tenet Corporation, a sale which the archbishop of St. Louis, Justin Rigali, challenged. Reverend Richard P. McBrien of the University of Notre Dame has summarized the issues at stake in this conflict. Suffice it to say that Archbishop Rigali and his supporters do not accept the fact that

Catholic laity can or ought to administer large corporate works formerly owned and operated by orders of religious men and women.

While discussing changes in the Catholic health care system, Cardinal Joseph Bernardin, the late archbishop of Chicago, asked, "What makes a hospital Catholic?" (Bernardin, 1996). What is important in that whole discussion is his astute observation that the Church "has not developed ecclesiological categories adequate to the new realities of expanded identity." Bernardin wondered, can the institutional Church comprehend these complex systemic organizations—in our case, in Catholic higher education—and cooperate with these changes?

Conclusion

This brings us to the present, territory in which any historian such as myself treads cautiously, while looking to the past Acts with their component Scenes. We have seen a shift in the approach to faith from a custodial model to one of empowerment. We have seen an ever broadening concern for issues of justice in our world and in our schools. We have also heard of the parallel development of new institutional ways to embody the Catholic nature of a school such as ours. Finally, we have heard of several important people from our past, people who faced questions and challenges which were daunting. How you write your lines or how you choose to interpret the ones you are given involves you in scripting the future of the University.

There is much to be worked out, much to be concretized. For today, though, I appreciate this opportunity to share with you the just ones past and present at Loyola Marymount University.

References

Abbott, S.J., & Gallagher, J. (1966). Pastoral constitution on the Church in the modern world. *The documents of Vatican II*. New York, NY: Guild Press.

Bernardin, J. (1996, May 4). What makes a hospital Catholic—A response. *America*, 9–11.

Bradshaw, J. (1972, August 6). The club game: Any number can't play. *Los Angeles Times Magazine*, 7–8.

Bulletin (1948). Los Angeles, CA: Loyola University.

Cantwell, J. J. (1922, May 27). Letter, to Reverend Mother Mary Joseph Butler, Religious of Sacred Heart. Available from the Archives of the Archdiocese of Los Angeles, California.

Constitutions of the Institute of the Religious of the Sacred Heart of Mary Immaculate Virgin. (1983). Rome: Religious of the Sacred Heart of Mary.

Documents of the 31st and 32nd General Congregations of the Society of Jesus (1977). St. Louis, MO: Institute of Jesuit Sources.

Documents of the Thirty-Fourth General Congregation of the Society of Jesus (1995). St. Louis, MO: Institute of Jesuit Sources.

Dolan, J. P. (1985). *The American Catholic experience: A history from colonial times to the present.* Garden City, NJ: Doubleday and Company.

Dunne, G.H., S.J. (1945, September 21). The sin of segregation. *Commonweal, 21,* 542–645.

Dunne, G.H., S.J. (1946 March 1). The short case. *Commonweal, 43,* 494–497.

Dunne, G.H., S.J. (1946 May 24). No accident. *Commonweal, 44,* 134–138.

Dunne, G.H., S.J. (1950, October 6). And who is my neighbor? *Commonweal, 52,* 623–625.

Dunne, G.H., S.J. (1990). *King's pawn.* Chicago, IL: Loyola University Press.

Ellacuria, I. S.J. (1994.) The task of a Christian university. In T. Whitfield, *Paying the price: Ignacio Ellacuria and the murdered Jesuits of El Salvador.* Philadelphia: Temple University Press.

Engh, M. E., S.J. (1989, January). Charity knows neither race nor creed. *Western States Jewish History, 21,* 154–165.

First annual catalogue of Los Angeles College (1911–1912). Los Angeles, CA: Los Angeles College.

Fitzgerald, P. A. S.J. (1984). *The governance of Jesuit Colleges in the United States, 1920–1970.* Notre Dame: University of Notre Dame Press.

Foley, A. S., S.J. (1954, November). The workshop way. *Interracial Review.*

Foley, A. S., S.J. (n.d.). Untitled manuscript. *Albert S. Foley, S.J., collection, archives of the New Orleans Province of the Society of Jesus.* New Orleans, Louisiana.

Gleason, P. (1995). *Contending with modernity: Catholic higher education in the twentieth century.* New York, NY: Oxford University Press.

John Paul II. (1990). *Ex Corde Ecclesiae.* (Vatican trans.). Boston, MA: Pauline Books.

Kearney, S. I, R.S.H.M. (1965). *Foundations of faith.* Tarrytown, NY: Privately printed.

Krebs, A.V. (1964, July 10). A Church of silence. *Commonweal, 80,* 472.

Los Angeles Loyolan (1950, October 3). p. 3.

Loyola Law School Fact Sheet (1998). Los Angeles, CA: Loyola Law School.

Loyola University of Los Angeles (1947). *Bulletin 1947–1948.* Los Angeles, CA: Loyola University.

Marsden, G. M. (1994). *The soul of the American university.* New York, NY: Oxford University Press.

Marymount Catalogue (1936). Los Angeles, CA: Marymount School.

McDonough, P. (1992). *Men astutely trained: A history of the Jesuits in the American century.* New York, NY: Free Press.

Morris, C. R. (1997). *American Catholic: The saints and sinners who built America's most powerful church.* New York, NY: Random House.

O'Brien, D. (1971). The American priest and social action. In J.T. Ellis (Ed.), *The Catholic priest in the United States: Historical investigations.* Collegeville, MN: St. John's University Press.

O'Brien, D.J., & Shannon, T.A. (1992). *Catholic social thought: The documentary heritage.* Justice in the world. Second General Assembly of the Synod of Bishops. Maryknoll, NY: Orbis.

Report of the commission on the future of Loyola Marymount University (1989). Los Angeles, CA.

Stammer, L. B. (1996, November 14). Catholic bishops OK new academic freedom rules. *Los Angeles Times,* pp. A1, A32.

Summary report: Human relations workshop, Loyola University (1953, Summer). In
    Department of University Archives and Special Collections, Charles Vonder Ahe
    Library, Loyola Marymount University, Los Angeles, CA.
The Jews and the Jonathan Club (1905, April 22). *The Graphic*, 22, 9.
The summer program in Latin America (1998, Fall/Winter). *Loyola Lawyer*, 18.
Weber, F. J. (1997). *His Eminence of Los Angeles: James Francis Cardinal McIntyre*.
    Mission Hills, CA: Saint Francis Historical Society.

GETTING INTO CHARACTER

Barbara E. Marino

Could Archbishop James Francis McIntyre, an avid opponent of coeducation at Loyola Marymount University, have imagined a day when a woman faculty member taught electrical engineering at this University? Could Reverend Charles Casassa, S.J., who refused to let Loyola Marymount participate in a segregated football championship, have imagined the rich diversity of the campus now? Can we imagine the changes and growth of Catholic universities which answer the call of the Jesuits' Thirty-Fourth General Congregation "to build a world of truth, justice, freedom, peace, and love" (*Documents*, 1995, p. 160). Michael Engh's paper, "Just Ones Past and Present at Loyola Marymount University" (Engh, 2000), asks us these questions and makes us look at the past, present, and future of Catholic universities.

Throughout his paper, Engh highlights several individuals who have greatly impacted the evolution of the University. Certainly, LMU did not evolve in a vacuum. What the LMU community is today has grown from the daily decisions of people both inside and outside the University. Therefore, it is important to examine the history of the Church and higher education along with their influence on the University and its development. These events, people, struggles, triumphs, successes, and failures tell a story. And so Engh begins his.

Engh sets the stage of the present-day University by presenting the very rich history of LMU beginning with its modest origins as Marymount School and Los Angeles College, small single-sex colleges founded in the early 1900s. Engh demonstrates a fascinating intertwining relationship between local/world events and the stages of LMU's evolution. One interesting example of this relationship is the fact that Catholic colleges were deemed essential to "protect" Catholics from an otherwise Protestant higher education. If higher education in this country had not had its start in the Protestant religion, Catholic colleges, and so Marymount School, Los Angeles College, and ultimately LMU, may not have seemed necessary.

Engh's story and its players captivate us as we meet those responsible for molding the University into what it is today. From Thomas Conaty, Bishop of Los Angeles in 1911, who was instrumental in the founding of Los Angeles College, to Mother M. Raymunde McKay, R.S.H.M., and

37

Reverend Charles Casassa, S.J., who were key actors in the merger of Marymount College and Loyola University and after in the formation of what is now known as Loyola Marymount University. Even Cardinal James Francis McIntyre, the often antagonist in the story fighting the changes LMU's administration wanted to make, such as the move to coeducation, helped shape the University. For without McIntyre, Loyola may have gone coeducational long before it did, potentially putting Marymount College out of business.

We as faculty are the present of LMU, and so this history belongs to us. Engh tells how Father Casassa stood up for racial equality by refusing to let the LMU Lions football team play against Texas unless the black athletes were allowed to play with the team (Engh, 2000). The pride I felt when I heard this story, and the disappointment I felt when I learned the provost's position created for McKay was simply a token, a powerless title (Engh, 2000), belong to me. I am connected to all that represents the past of the University. In accepting this I must also realize that I play a role in defining the present and future of LMU. How I choose to play my role will affect, perhaps only in some small way, the future of Catholic universities.

Armed with this realization I must now determine what this means to my position as a teacher, researcher, and member of the LMU community. Most obvious perhaps is my role as a member of the LMU community. Serving on committees which create, study, or enforce University policy is a very direct means of contributing to the direction of the University; however, other more subtle means exist. The simple act of discussing current events with fellow faculty over coffee in Huesman faculty commons may be the catalyst for such things as recognizing injustices and effecting change. Both direct and indirect, formal and informal, there are many opportunities to contribute to LMU's history in the making through an active involvement in the University community.

What is not as obvious is how my role as a teacher and researcher in electrical engineering plays a part in LMU's present and future. It is difficult to understand the connection between what happens in a course on the design of digital electronics and the University as a whole. Our classrooms, even in electrical engineering, give us an opportunity to present to our students what LMU is. The respect we show to our students and expect in return, the responsibility we teach our students to show in their work, and the academic excellence we encourage are just a few examples of subtle ways we daily affirm the Catholic character of the University. Through being just and consistent in classroom policies, without being bureaucratic or narrow minded, we teach the students about character just as our lectures teach them about science. Realizing that the classroom extends far outside the walls of lecture halls, I can reinforce these higher ideals if I am approachable and available after the class has ended.

Encouraging my students and interacting with them outside of the classroom, I form connections with my students that link us together and to the larger LMU family. These connections with students are made, whether we realize it or not, and they provide a valuable means for impressing upon our students what LMU is all about.

Further insight into the role of the faculty in defining the present and the future of Loyola Marymount University can be gained by studying the *Documents of the Thirty-Fourth General Congregation of the Society of Jesus* (1995). This collection of documents spells out the mission of the Jesuits and their position in a number of areas. Engh includes in his selected readings decrees in four such areas: Decree Thirteen, "Cooperation with the Laity in Mission"; Decree Fourteen, "Jesuits and the Situation of Women in Church and Civil Society"; Decree Sixteen, "The Intellectual Dimension of Jesuit Ministries"; and Decree Seventeen, "Jesuits and University Life." Of these four decrees, I feel particularly affected by the first two.

Decree Thirteen calls for a cooperation between the Jesuits and the laity in the Jesuit mission "to build a world of truth, justice, freedom, peace, and love" (*Documents*, 1995, p. 160). This cooperation seems particularly important and necessary in this day and age when the presence of religious is becoming less and less prominent. On the campus of LMU this translates to fewer Jesuits and more laity on the faculty and in the administration. In this document, the Jesuits recognize the unique contributions and gifts of the laity and invite the laity to help them to fulfill their mission. Reading their statement, I was struck by the support the Jesuits' proclamation offered to my efforts at LMU and by their emphasis on collaboration. By contributing fully as a faculty member in the decisions of the University and the ongoing campus dialogue, I walk along the path that historically only Jesuits tread.

Decree Fourteen echoes Pope John Paul II's call on us all "to make essential equality of women a lived reality" (*Documents*, 1995, p. 173). In a list of "practical" ways to work against gender discrimination, the Jesuits call for "the appropriate presence of women in Jesuit ministries and institutions" (*Documents*, 1995, p. 176). My presence at LMU is a direct, if not intentional, answer to this call. In a predominantly male field, I have the opportunity to serve as a role model for women. I can help further this call by encouraging my college to seek out qualified women candidates to add even more diversity to the faculty and administration.

In addition to trying to change the gender imbalance in the administration and faculty, I hope to change longstanding prejudices that have influenced the students of the sciences. As stated in Decree Fourteen, "The elimination of all forms of illegitimate discrimination between boys and girls in the educational process" (*Documents*, 1995, p. 176) is another "practical" way to work against gender discrimination. Groups I have worked with at LMU, including the Society of Women Engineers and Math Science Interchange, live out this decree by encouraging women to pursue study in the sciences, often overcoming years of discouragement. They recall the words in Galatians 3:28, *New American Bible*: "There is neither male nor female, for you are all one in Christ Jesus" (*Documents*, 1995, p. 178). Indeed, LMU has and will continue to benefit from struggling to live out this belief.

Loyola Marymount University and all of its students and faculty share a history of an evolving Catholic educational institution. We must live, as the Jesuits state, a shared mission both *for* others and *with* others (*Documents*, 1995, p. 160). In knowing this complex history, we are able to more fully participate in its further growth into a center of study, formation, and higher education, pursuing a path of justice, wisdom, and hope for all who enter her campus.

References

Documents of the Thirty-Fourth General Congregation of the Society of Jesus (1995). St. Louis, MO: Institute of Jesuit Sources.

Engh, M. E., S.J. (2000). Just ones past and present at Loyola Marymount University. In M.K. McCullough (Ed.), *The just one justices: The role of justice at the heart of Catholic higher education* (pp. 21–36). Scranton, PA: University of Scranton Press.

ST. AUGUSTINE AND THE COMMUNICATION OF ORGANIZATIONAL CULTURE

Steven C. Combs

Michael Engh's (2000) paper and presentation, "Just Ones Past and Present at Loyola Marymount University," offers an illuminating account of the history of higher education at Loyola Marymount University. My initial reaction to the paper was entirely positive. I was pleased to hear about some of the key people and events in the history of our University. I found the paper to be not only interesting but also extremely valuable, especially for new faculty who might not otherwise be aware of the rich traditions and history that underlie LMU.

What Father Engh is talking about, when related to my field of communication, is the background and contemporary culture of this University. While culture is typically thought of as the fundamental values and beliefs of a group of people, organizations also have cultures. Organizational culture is the underlying belief and value structure of an organization that is held by the employees (Clampitt, 1991). Organizational culture is created, maintained, and revised by communication practices. That is, culture is manifest in symbolic acts. It is enacted in the stories and other symbols used to express the essential nature of an institution. Strong cultures clearly communicate their business principles, value systems, heroes, heroines, and rites and rituals. According to Deal and Kennedy (1982), strong cultures help "provide practical meaning for people, both on and off the job" (p. 15). They also conclude that the most successful organizations have strong cultures.

While my initial reaction to Father Engh's paper was unambiguous, my feelings became a bit clouded. I wondered why I was hearing about many of our heroes, heroines, and achievements in great detail for the first time. I found myself asking if Father Engh's presentation could be videotaped and shown at workshops for new faculty. This led me to consider the general question of whether LMU and other Catholic universities do enough to enact and promote their organizational cultures. *LMU Vistas* and *LMU News*, published several times a year by the university relations group, and *Catholic Conversations* are examples of important and effective

41

promotional vehicles. Nonetheless, my central claim for this essay, and firm personal belief, is that Catholic institutions of higher education should do more to communicate their organizational cultures. Learning more about the heroines, heroes, myths, and rituals that reflect fundamental values will allow faculty, staff, and administrators to work more effectively within their roles. Communicating culture externally also allows for more positive and meaningful relationships with prospective students, local, national, and international communities, and various ancillary organizations.

There is a fascinating historical example that may serve as a parallel case for my point. St. Augustine, in advocating that the Church use the pagan art of rhetoric to promote its mission, provides a case study worth considering today. Augustine (354–430 C.E.), Bishop of Hippo, was schooled in the pagan arts, including rhetoric, the term used in antiquity to refer to the study of communication—especially persuasion. Augustine even taught rhetoric while he studied law. While Augustine held the title of Professor of Rhetoric, in Milan, he had the opportunity to hear St. Ambrose speak. This was a pivotal time, as Ambrose inspired Augustine to reflect on his spirituality (Kennedy, 1980).

Augustine eventually converted to Christianity, resigned his chair in rhetoric, and began his noted religious career (Corley, 1983). While Augustine appeared to be moving away from rhetoric and toward Christianity, he was actually preparing for a battle within the Catholic Church regarding whether to unite rhetoric with Christianity. His unique preparation—rhetorical and theological—allowed him to offer an invaluable contribution to both fields.

In the years leading up to and including Augustine's lifetime, the Church was poised for growth. The ecumenical (worldwide) council of the Church was held at Nicea in 325, establishing an elaborate organizational structure of dioceses. Official persecution of the Church ended in the middle of the fourth century. Finally, in 392 C.E., the Emperor Theodosius abolished paganism (Murphy, 1960). Thus, impediments to the spread of Christianity were being removed, and an organizational structure was taking shape.

A key remaining task was to more fully develop and define the intellectual base for the Church. Accordingly, a hotly debated and crucial issue became the extent to which Christianity should adopt the "contemporary culture" that Rome had taken over from Greece. James Murphy (1960) argues that, "From the Christian point of view, it was an age of selection, a time to examine the *sapienta saeculi* to extract from a thousand-year old heritage whatever would aid in the work of the Lord" (p. 406).

The debate regarding pagan culture and Christianity turned toward rhetoric because of the obvious need for a church to communicate its message. J. Russell Corley (1983) points out that, "Christianity depends upon the spoken word for preaching and evangelism" (p. 96). He also notes that, "Much of the materials in the gospels consist of spoken lessons delivered by Jesus" (p. 96). The obvious implication is that the Christian message, just like all other thoughts, relies upon communication and should be accounted for theoretically (Corley, 1983). Indeed, a theory of what constitutes successful Christian communication could be an important step in effective communication.

Although rhetoric was essential to the success of the Christian movement, the use of rhetoric posed two significant problems to Augustine. First, many theologians believed the Scriptures were inherently persuasive and there was no need for rhetorical adornment. These Church leaders believed so strongly in their new religion that they thought its truth was virtually inescapable and its eloquence was superior to that of any mortal. Quite simply, they believed the Bible needed nothing added by the communicator: it was persuasive *per se*. According to Corley (1983), many Christians "took the position that the possession of Christian truth automatically enabled the preacher to communicate that truth clearly. They felt they needed no help from any rhetorician to express their ideas in a persuasive manner" (p. 97). In fact, they distrusted oratorical techniques.

Second, many Church leaders perceived a conflict between Christian purity and pagan culture. The predominant rhetorical theories of the time were enunciated in Greece and then modified and carried on by the Romans. The rhetorical theories of Plato, Aristotle, Cicero, and Quintilian were viewed as pagan ideas. Murphy (1958) points out that, "Rhetoric at the end of the fourth century was associated with things pagan, Roman, non-Christian" (p. 26).

Many Christians rejected Roman culture as sinful, and Roman "literature was studded with man-like-gods parading what some Christian writers saw as a virtual gallery of sins" (Murphy, 1958, p. 51). Furthermore, rhetoric was associated with the Second Sophistic movement. Many "Christians felt that sophistic practices were deceitful, aimed at worldly success, and grounded in a philosophical acceptance of the relativity of truth" (Corley, 1983, p. 96). Finally, Rome had not long before committed many atrocities in its persecution of Christians.

The association with paganism was very serious. Murphy (1958) says, "There is a considerable body of evidence to indicate that some of the Church Fathers were violently opposed to anything smacking of pagan Roman culture" (pp. 26–27). Pierre Labriolle (1925) explains the dominant view of many Church scholars: "During the first centuries of the Empire there is hardly a Christian writer in whose case there does not intrude or show itself more or less sincerely, more or less diplomatically, a hostility in some regard to the different forms of pagan-learning" (p. 18).

Nonetheless, some of the most influential Christians were at least undecided about the role of rhetoric and indeed about many aspects of Roman culture. They found elements of pagan education, literature, and society that could possibly be adapted to a Christian lifestyle (Corley, 1983). As persecution faded from memory, there was a hot debate in the Church about the uses of pagan education. Saint Basil felt the conflict of embracing elements of pagan culture. He had mixed feelings, but nonetheless recommended gathering roses from among the thorns of pagan literature. Saint Ambrose was also aware of the potential cultural dilemma. He condemned sophistic abuses but admitted that rhetorical ornament may sometimes be useful. Indeed, this sometimes occurs in the Scriptures themselves (Murphy, 1974).

Augustine's response to the debate over the use of rhetoric was masterful and decisive. His response, articulated in *On Christian Doctrine*, is to claim that persuasion is necessary, synthesize key elements of pagan rhetoric, and disguise his reliance on questionable sources of insight by downplaying his debt to pagan theorists and highlighting the eloquence of Scripture.

While Augustine does not deny the perfection of Scripture, he does believe that audiences are flawed and may not always be moved to listen. Therefore, the first step in Augustine's creation of a Christian rhetoric is to argue that it is unfair that persuasion is used by heretics and skeptics but not by Christians:

> It is not right that the former can tell their lies eloquently while the latter speak in a manner which is tedious and inarticulate. For since by means of the art of rhetoric both truth and falsehood are urged, who would dare to say that truth should stand in the person of its defenders unarmed against lying, so that they who wish to urge falsehoods may know how to make their listeners benevolent, or attentive, or docile in their presentation, while the defenders of truth are ignorant of that art? Should they speak briefly, clearly, and plausibly while the defenders of truth speak so that they tire their listeners, make themselves difficult to understand and what they have to say dubious? (Robertson, 1983, p. 118)

Augustine's view stems from his notion that the duty of Christian eloquence "is to convert beliefs into works, to impel the faithful to the Christian life" (Kennedy, 1980, p. 157). Hence, the task is not necessarily to convert pagans to Christianity, but to convert apathetic Christians into active Christians. To accomplish this, according to Augustine, the clergy may not simply rely on the divine nature of the Scripture. Christians must be motivated to learn and avail themselves of the truths of their religion. The audience must not merely be instructed but also moved. Augustine says that if the Christian "desires also to delight or to move the person to whom he speaks he will not do it simply by speaking in any way at all; but the manner in which he speaks determines whether he does so" (Robertson, 1983, p. 136). Hence, one must study the means of expression as well as the Scriptures. It is desirable for the teacher to wish to speak not only wisely but also eloquently "since he can be of more worth if he can do both" (Robertson, 1983, p. 122).

In creating a Christian rhetoric, Augustine also makes good use of key ideas derived from pagan theorists. The framework for, and theory underlying, *Doctrine* comes from the works of Cicero, primarily *De Oratore*. M.L.W. Laistner (1967) says that, "His debt to Cicero is not superficial; for the parallelism in thought between the classical theory of oratory and Augustine's theory of Christian preaching can be traced right through the book" (pp. 70–71).

Augustine also makes use of Aristotle's position on the amorality of rhetoric by declaring the religious neutrality of rhetoric. Augustine, like Aristotle, contends that rhetoric is a neutral instrument, and whether it is good or evil depends on the person who uses it and the purposes to which it is put. Augustine asks, rhetorically, why Christians may not use rhetoric for good purposes: "Since then the faculty of eloquence is available for both sides, and is of great service in the enforcing of wrong or right, why do not good men study to engage it on the side of truth" (Robertson, 1983, pp. 118–119).

Finally, Augustine deviates from mainstream rhetorical theories of Aristotle, Cicero, and Quintilian by returning to a view of rhetoric popularized by Plato. While it was commonly accepted that rhetoric included the creation of ideas ultimately delivered in a speech, which the Romans referred to as "invention," Plato had previously argued against the Sophists of his time by saying that rhetoric was concerned solely with style and delivery of messages, but that the content of those messages must be derived from philosophy. Plato ultimately accepted the necessity for rhetoric in conveying "the truth" but insisted that only dialecticians were capable of knowing that truth which is fit for communication. By dropping the notion of "invention," Augustine avoids the argument that rhetoric is sophistic and removed from the truth. Instead, Augustine places the discovery of truth outside of rhetoric, saying that truth is already present in Scripture. Since the Old and New Testaments contain the totality of truth and wisdom, invention becomes the province of the Holy Spirit. Proof is a matter of locating the appropriate Scriptural references and explaining those ideas. Rhetoric is made palatable because it is no longer the discovery and presentation of ideas; it is concerned merely with the communication of truths derived from other disciplines.

Augustine's final move is to downplay his reliance on pagan theorists and highlight the rhetorical nature of Scripture. Laistner (1967) points out that, "Augustine writes throughout in his own language and very rarely makes a direct quotation from his pagan sources" (p. 70). This allows Augustine to extract pagan rhetorical theories without using pagan examples and images to which many Christians objected. Furthermore, Augustine uses the Bible for his examples, both praising the holy books and showing the rhetorical elements of the Scriptures. This is important, because Scripture became the example of eloquence and it was the basis of all knowledge. Kennedy (1980) argues that, "Christian rhetoric gives exclusive honor to the Old and New Testaments as the totality of wisdom and eloquence" (p. 158).

The genius of Augustine's work has not gone unnoticed. Kennedy (1980) argues that, "The great virtue of *De Doctrina Christiana* is that it made it possible for Christians to appreciate and teach eloquence without associating it with paganism" (p. 159). Murphy (1960) notes the importance of the book: "*De Doctrina Christiana* emerges, consequently, as a book written as a rebuttal to those who would deprive the Church of a useful tool in the work of winning souls. Significantly, the debate ends with its appearance" (p. 10).

Today, the art of rhetoric is called "communication," and Augustine, the man who bridged the classical and medieval worlds, would be astonished by our "post-modern society." Yet, the question remains as provocative today as it was for Augustine: How might principles of communication be used in the service of Catholic institutions? While this forum is not an appropriate place to exhaustively detail the many ways that Catholics might enhance the communication of their message, it is worth noting that Father Engh's paper, placed in a different context, may indicate that LMU and other Catholic institutions of higher education should think seriously about how they communicate their organizational cultures. Perhaps it is time to recover the spirit of Augustine and begin to formulate rhetorical theories and strategies appropriate to our missions. Murphy (1960) argues that, "The sin of the sophist is that he denies the necessity of subject matter and believes that *forma* alone is desirable. An opposite vice . . . [is] the belief that the man possessed of truth will *ipso facto* be able to communicate the truth to others. It is dependence upon *materia* alone" (p. 409).

References

Clampitt, P. G. (1991). *Communicating for managerial effectiveness*. Newbury Park, CA: Sage Publications, Inc.

Corley, J. R. (1983). Rhetoric in transition. In J. L. Golden, G. F. Berquist, & W. E. Coleman (Eds.), *The rhetoric of Western thought* (pp. 93–101). Dubuque, IA: Kendall/Hunt.

Deal, T. E., & Kennedy, A. A. (1982). *Corporate cultures: The rites and rituals of corporate life*. Menlo Park, CA: Addison-Wesley.

Engh, M.E., S.J. (2000). Just ones past and present at Loyola Marymount University. In M.K. McCullough (Ed.), *The just one justices: The role of justice at the heart of Catholic higher education* (pp. 21–36). Scranton, PA: University of Scranton Press.

Kennedy, G. A. (1980). *Classical rhetoric and its Christian and secular tradition from ancient to modern times*. University of North Carolina Press: Chapel Hill.

Labriolle, P. (1925). *History and literature from Tertullian to Boethius*. New York, NY: A. A. Knopf.

Laistner, M. L. W. (1967). *Christianity and pagan culture in the later Roman Empire*. Ithaca, NY: Cornell University Press.

Murphy, J. J. (1958). Saint Augustine and the Christianization of rhetoric. *Western Speech*, 2, 24–29.

Murphy, J. J. (1960). Saint Augustine and the debate about a Christian rhetoric. *The Quarterly Journal of Speech*, 46, 400–410.

Murphy, J. J. (1974). *Rhetoric in the middle ages: A history of rhetorical theory from St. Augustine to the Renaissance*. Los Angeles, CA: University of California Press.

Robertson, D. W., Jr. (1983). On Christian Doctrine. (St. Augustine, Trans.). Indianapolis, IN: Bobbs-Merrill.

THE UNIVERSITY AND THE STRUGGLE FOR JUSTICE

Stephen A. Privett, S.J.

The title of Loyola Marymount's Institute, "The Just One Justices," captures something central to the mission of a Catholic University. Gerard Manley Hopkins's use of "justice" as a verb reflects the classic Gospel standard for integrity: "By their fruits you will know them." There is a performative aspect to justice, which if neglected, leaves all manner of academic deliberations about the virtue of justice liable to charges of sterility. Just two weeks ago, I was privileged to be one of over 400 concelebrants at the funeral liturgy for the murdered Auxiliary Bishop of Guatemala City, Juan Gerardi. The homilist at the liturgy forcefully stated that Bishop Gerardi was killed because he struggled for an authentic peace not based on lies but rather founded on justice and truth. Just persons and action on behalf of justice are not abstractions. Real people "justice" at great personal cost to themselves. Some notable contemporary exemplars include Archbishop Romero, Dorothy Day, the four North American Church women of El Salvador, and the six Jesuits at the University of Central America in San Salvador. During the moving funeral liturgy for Bishop Gerardi, I found myself reflecting on why it is that Bishop Gerardi and other "just ones justice" even at the cost of their lives? Where did they come by the convictions and the courage to take their stands? What were the formative influences behind their decisions to live and die for something that flatly contradicted their own self-interest? I think these are pertinent questions for a Catholic University.

In his *Commonweal* article, Bob Egan, S.J., pointed out that questions about the Catholic identity of a university can only arise in a context such as ours which is characterized by religious and cultural pluralism (Egan, 1996). In the Middle Ages, for example, there were *only* Catholic universities. The challenge of maintaining a distinctively Catholic character in a particular university is a relatively recent issue and one that is both complex and urgent.

Campus conversations about a university's Catholic character generate a broad range of reactions from, "I can live with the mission statement," a less than ideal attitude from those entrusted with the future of an institution—to "things are fine the way they are," to unarticulated fears

49

about restrictions placed on academic freedom, to passionate convictions about responsibilities to and for society. The background for such conversations, as Egan points out, are "the dramatic changes during the last half-century, both in the basic characteristics and self-understanding of American Universities and in the basic characteristics and self-understanding of Roman Catholicism" (Egan, 1996, p. 11).

The impetus for those changes in self-understanding are rooted in the debates and deliberations at the Catholic Church's Second Vatican Council during the mid-1960s. The Post–Vatican II Catholic Church moved cautiously away from its polemical approach to other religions and its bleakly negative assessment of the post-enlightenment world and slowly opened itself to influences and perspectives it had previously resisted. The Church was beginning to understand itself as a learning as well as teaching institution or, perhaps more accurately, that good teaching is rooted in sound learning. It frankly admitted its desire to understand the world in which we live, its expectations, its longings, and its dramatic characteristics (Abbott, 1996). The Council challenged the universal church to make its own joys and hopes, griefs and anxieties of the people of this age, especially those who are poor or in any way afflicted (Abbott, 1996).

"The Council offered no more eloquent proof of its solidarity with the entire human family, . . . than by engaging in conversation about these various problems" (Abbott, 1996). The "various problems" that were the subject of these conversations were not narrowly parochial concerns or issues of Church discipline, but the pressing global issues of "hunger, poverty, illiteracy, oppression, war, international rivalries, and the whole purpose and meaning of human existence" (Abbott, 1996, p. 5).

The Jesuit order responded to the challenges of the Council and the contemporary world by convening in 1965, 1975, 1983, and 1995 what are called General Congregations—the order's highest legislative body—to elect the leadership and articulate the principles and values that would chart the Jesuit order's course into the next millennium according to the insights and the spirit of the Second Vatican Council. In 1974, the Thirty-Second General Congregation boldly declared that "the service of faith and the promotion of justice" was not "one ministry among others" for Jesuits but that it must be the "integrating factor" of whatever ministry Jesuits engaged in (*Documents*, 1977, Decree 2, p. 9). The most recent Congregation in 1995 soundly reaffirmed the order's commitment to the promotion of justice and pressed for an "ever fuller integration of the promotion of justice into our lives of faith, in the company of the poor and many others who live and work for the coming of God's kingdom" (*Documents*, 1995, Decree 3, p. 3). This brief essay on Catholic and Jesuit education distills some of the discussion and arguments which have engaged some 20,000 Jesuits from 114 different countries since 1965. It is important to realize that questions about Catholic and Jesuit character have been the catalyst for a dialogue and debate that stretches over three decades. The Catholic and Jesuit tradition is not, nor should it be, experienced as a kind of straightjacket that restricts thinking and acting within those institutions that would stand the Jesuit tradition. Tradition, we know, is not a bunch of people saying the same thing to each other over and over again but different people with different perspectives talking about the things they cherish (Egan, 1996). Tradition is constituted, in part, by an historically extended socially embodied argument precisely about what constitutes that tradition (Egan, 1996). Thus, dialogue, debate, and argument about the Catholic character of a University are quite traditional.

I propose three constituent qualities of the Jesuit educational tradition, each of which has its own internal dynamism that moves the enterprise toward the promotion of faith through justice:

(a) the religious vision that drives the entire enterprise,

(b) the humanistic ideals that support the curriculum,

(c) the normative mandate from the General Congregations for Jesuits to engage "in the crucial struggle of our time: the struggle for faith and that struggle for justice which it includes" (*Documents*, 1977, Decree 2, p. 2).

In the years that followed immediately after the Vatican Council, Jesuit scholars carefully and critically revisited the history of the order's foundational period. Their work reminded all of us that the Society of Jesus, unlike other Catholic religious orders up to that time, was not established by its founder, Ignatius of Loyola, for any specific work—staffing schools, caring for the sick, conducting retreats, or providing hospitality to pilgrims —rather its objective was to do "any service that may be for the greater glory of God and the common good" (Ganss, 1970, p. 3). Such a sweeping statement of purpose may not seem to offer much direction for us today. But this principle in the context of the early history of the Jesuits is quite illustrative. Within its first sixteen years, the order established an average of over one college a year and for reasons clearly stated in the Jesuit constitutions: "for improvement in learning and living . . . for the greater glory of God" (Ganss, 1970, p. 440). Colleges and universities were seen early on as effective means for serving the common good because of the presumed link between learning and a way of living that constituted the glory of God. The rationale that fired Ignatius Loyola's enthusiasm for colleges was clearly communicated in a letter to King Philip II of Spain in 1556: "All the well-being of Christianity and of the whole world depends on the proper education of youth" (O'Malley, 1993, p. 209).

Jesuit education has always situated itself within a context that linked learning with living "for the glory of God and the common good of humanity" as the constitutions have it. Jesuit universities are dedicated to the general purpose of any university: creating and communicating knowledge; but Jesuit universities further resolve to assess the impact of such knowledge on the lives of their students and the common good of humanity. One may build bridges or computers or stock portfolios, but it is unlikely one will contribute to the common good simultaneously without explicitly attending to do so.

The mission of a Jesuit university is, and always has been, the service of a God whose glory is men and women struggling to realize their full human potential through the pursuit of the truth. In Patristic theology the maxim was, "*Gloria Dei homo vivens*"—God's glory is the human person fully alive. Conversely, to steal another line from Hopkins, the extent to which people do not reach their full human potential is the extent to which God's glory is "seared . . . bleared, smeared . . . and wears man's smudge and shares man's smell . . ." (Hopkins, 1966). Erasing the smears and smudges from our world is central to our pursuit of the truth.

Within the Catholic intellectual tradition, the pursuit of truth is an implicit pursuit of that truth which at once extends our reach and exceeds our grasp. Theology names that ultimate truth, God, and the pursuit of truth is, at its core, the pursuit of God. To acknowledge the religious perspective that supports the Jesuit commitment to education does not vitiate the intrinsic integrity of an academic discipline to promote a narrowly religious goal. Being true to the internal integrity of a particular discipline and preserving the character and dynamic proper to formal education are essential if students are to contribute intelligently to their own development and that of society. There is no intention of religious fundamentalism or theological reductionism, rather an effort to situate the quest for knowledge in the larger context of the human pursuit of meaning and purpose which we believe is the divine spark that enkindles the human enterprise.

A number of campuses have established Catholic Studies Programs to promote the vital interaction of the Catholic tradition with the various sectors of learning represented across the university. Such programs offer students and faculty the opportunity to study the Catholic tradition and its manifold points of intersection with Western and other cultures, and with the leading issues of our time. This quarter I am involved in a course that uses episodes from the controversial television series "Nothing Sacred" to tease out the program's fundamental premises: the human is the divine, if only we can see it; when push comes to shove, mercy is justice; and there is a chosen people and they are everyone (Cain, 1998).

With regard to the second characteristic, humanism, an analysis of the earliest Jesuit rationale for the common curriculum adopted by all of its schools and colleges—what developed into the *Ratio Studiorum* revealed a strongly humanistic foundation (Ganss,1970, p. 351). In a thoughtful and provocative essay that relates traditional humanistic education to contemporary world conditions, Michael J. Buckley, S.J., has traced Jesuit educational theory and practice back to the educational reforms of the Italian Renaissance. Those reforms aimed at the humanization of students through contact with humanity's greatest accomplishments in literature, history, music, and science. The Renaissance emphasis on the liberal arts and science was reactive to a late medieval fixation with intellectual skills or disciplines that pushed learning to a level of abstraction and formality that rendered education irrelevant to living (Buckley, 1982). Renaissance reforms were directed toward specifying the content of education, because education was understood as the process whereby an individual claimed his or her full humanity through an association with and absorption of the finest expressions of the human spirit in literature, science, and the arts.

Today, we live with the spoiled fruits of the Renaissance focus on the content of knowledge—increasingly fragmented subdivisions of knowledge with little sense of the purpose that directs humanistic education: the full and integral development of the human person. True to the originating vision of humanistic education, Jesuit educational theory does not confuse the means of education with its end. We acknowledge that the hoped-for outcome of a Jesuit education is not simply an individual who has mastered this set of skills and/or that body of knowledge but a skilled and knowledgeable person who lives a fully human life. Recall that "human" is an adjective that names a distinctive way of being; thus "human being" does not simply denote an entity but also describes a way of being in the world that is characteristic of humans. The central concern of humanistic education is enabling or liberating—thus, "liberal" arts—persons to "be humanly" in the contemporary world.

Jesuit education directs itself toward creating and communicating that knowledge and those skills necessary to be humanly in this historical context. We are immunizing against what one educator calls, "mindlessness, the disease that afflicts those specialists whose training leaves them too narrow to know or care about the theory, or the history, or the impact—the human implications—of the work they do" (Belknap & Kuhns, 1977, p. 3). Civil engineers everywhere are taught how to construct bridges, dam rivers, and lay highways. Is it important for them to also learn how decisions are made about where and how such structures are built and whose interests they serve?

Jesuit educational theory does not so narrowly restrict teaching as to preclude a concern for nurturing those innate human qualities— compassion, integrity, and respect for others come immediately to mind— with such cavalier assertions as, "it's not my area of expertise" or "I was not hired to teach virtue." Questions of pedagogical method and classroom environment are quite germane to a humanistic education that hopes to nurture fully human persons who are skilled and competent practitioners of whatever profession. I recall a student who told me her best teacher was a philosophy professor. Why? Because, she continued, he stood just outside the door and greeted each student as she entered the classroom! A senior was completely taken aback when his finance professor instructed him to look at his senior internship experience with a big six accounting firm through the lenses of conscience and compassion, i.e., the presence or absence of these qualities in the conduct of business.

Decisions regarding the material one covers in a course are important and should be based on an understanding about the purpose of education and how this course "fits" with the overarching goals of the curriculum. In fact, such is the case, whether articulated or not. Every university has its own set of requirements and fixed set of courses, as does every undergraduate major. These various curricula embody value judgments— explicit or implicit—about the purpose of education, about which knowledge is valuable, and what skills and sensitivities are important in today's world. The central curricular issues should not revolve around "how much" English, Theology, Social Studies, Philosophy, or Natural Science but how and who do we want our graduates to be in this world. Once we answer those more difficult questions, we can begin to determine the content and sequence of courses that embody our educational goals and objectives.

The dark side of humanistic education is exposed in Pushkin's description of cultivated Russian nobility indulging their educated and refined appreciation for drama and ballet while their freezing coachmen waited for them in the bitter cold of St. Petersburg (Pushkin, 1978). The injured Paul Baumer wanders through a German military hospital ward filled with the mangled bodies of his wounded comrades and reflects on the contradictions inherent in his own humanistic education: "How senseless is everything that can be written, done, or thought, when such things are possible. It must be all lies and of no account when the culture of a thousand years could not prevent this stream of blood being poured out, these torture chambers in their hundreds of thousands" (Remarque, 1975, p. 227).

The axiom that all roads lead to Rome argues that there are many different routes to the same destination. That insight does not eliminate the need to decide where it is we want to go before mapping the journey and specifying the itinerary. Sensitivity and responsiveness to human suffering and a consequent passion for justice are essential elements of contemporary humanism and, as such, these concerns must have a place in the curriculum of a Catholic and Jesuit university. In this context, the social sciences have a central role to play in developing humane sensitivities and for providing tools by which the human condition can be thoughtfully addressed (Buckley, 1998). For example, a course in the sociology of aging places students in retirement homes where they confront, most for the first time, the practice of warehousing the elderly and the inherent failures of our health care system.

The third foundational principle for Jesuits is the mandate to engage in what the Congregations call "the crucial struggle of our time"—a struggle for the justice that authentic faith requires (*Documents*, 1977, Decree 2, p. 1). It is axiomatic that where we stand and whom we listen to determines what we hear. In trying to determine whether or not our education does, in fact, educate persons to live humanly in today's world an important piece of the evidence lies with the two-thirds of the world who are hungry, illiterate, homeless, or deprived of their most basic human rights and how present they are to us. One does not "be humanly" in the abstract but amidst the real pains and pleasures, hopes and sorrows of the all too human condition. The "justicing" of the just person is contextually specific and as concrete as the lives of Dorothy Day and Mother Theresa of Calcutta or the deaths of Oscar Romero and Stephen Biko.

Ours is not the 16th century Western European world of the first Jesuits. The answer to the question of how we link learning with living will not be found by an assiduous study of the past. Fidelity to the foundational principle of Jesuit ministry—doing what most effectively promotes the "glory of God and the common good"—demands rigorous analysis of our context before determining what may best serve the common good. One may not articulate the mission of a Jesuit University without engaging in what the Vatican Council called "reading the signs of the times"—or acquiring a disciplined sensitivity to the realities of the world in which we are preparing our students to live humanly.

This is how one General Congregation saw our world:

> There are millions of men and women in our world, specific people with names and faces, who are suffering from poverty and hunger, from the unjust distribution of wealth and resources and from the consequences of racial, social, and political discrimination. Not only the quality of life but human life itself is under constant threat. It is becoming more and more clear that despite the opportunities offered by an ever more serviceable technology, we are simply not willing to pay the price of a more just and more humane society. (*Documents*, 1977, Decree 4, p. 20)

Those suffering millions must be part of our conversation about the mission and goals of Jesuit education. Such a conversation is not the sum and substance of all education, but it is certainly central to Jesuit education. Jesuit education does what all education does: offers students knowledge, skills, and sensitivities, but it does so with the conviction that the complete development of a person's humanity demands the complete development of all humanity—especially those for whom "development" is at best a cruel hoax in the face of a daily struggle to merely survive. Those ghastly photographs from Rwanda or Bosnia bear heartbreaking witness to the world's desperate need for human development—theirs and ours. Development that comes at the expense of others dehumanizes us all. Each of us is really "a piece of the continent, a part of the main; if a clod were washed away by the sea, Europe is the less, as well as if a promontory were . . . any man's death diminishes me, because I am involved in mankind" (Donne, 1978, p. 17).

The millions of people in our world who struggle to stay alive are a challenge to our humanity and *a fortiori* to humanistic education. Michael Buckley asks the searing question that the world's voiceless pose for higher education:

> Even if your students do depart with such a sensitive development that they can appreciate the depth of human life reflected in the poetry of Goethe, Dante, and Eliot or in the sweeping histories of Thucydides and Gibbon or in the beautifully and carefully crafted argumentation of George Keenan, John Henry Newman, and George Steiner. Such students have been touched by some of the greatest achievements in the humanities and as they learned to appreciate and love them—they changed, they developed, they became more human. . . . Yes, all of that can be true. I grant all of this. But has your student become humane? (Buckley, 1991)

Education in these last years of the twentieth century—if it is to be humanistic, let alone Jesuit—must offer students a profound understanding of and sensitivity to the plight of those whom Franz Fanon named "the wretched of the earth." This understanding and sensitivity opens the minds and hearts of the truly educated and strengthens their resolve to engage somehow in the global struggle for human development. Such an education is neither expressive of a sectarian religious perspective nor reflective of a narrow ideology; it is simply the authentic embodiment of the Jesuit humanistic ideal. To be humanly at this point in history is to not ignore the two-thirds of the world who are poor, hungry, homeless, or illiterate. As the Salvadoran liberation theologian, Jon Sobrino, S.J., likes to point out, we—by virtue of being here in the United States and at a University—are the footnotes in the story of the contemporary world; the poor and the hungry are the text. We are the anomaly; they are the norm. Our learning must change their way of living if God is to be glorified and the common good secured.

How do we educate persons to live humanly in a world where 60,000 people die every day from hunger or hunger-related illnesses and nearly one in five people worldwide is chronically malnourished—too hungry to lead a productive life? What does one do in a world that spends in half a day for military purposes funds that would finance the entire malaria eradication program of the World Health Organization or where the amount spent on weapons every minute could feed 2,000 malnourished children for a year (Oxfam, 1998). Where an international debt structure leaves the poorest people in debtor nations in abject poverty by extracting interest payments from countries that have repaid the original capital many times over? It has been noted that if the world were reduced to a village of 100 people, only one person in that village would have a college education. Jesuit Universities are educating that person now; what should we be doing with them for the sake of the other ninety-nine?

The integration into academic courses of direct experiences with underserved populations is a powerful tool for educating students to the perspectives and issues of whole segments of the population who will never enter the halls of academe. Is it too farfetched to see the poor and marginalized—the other ninety-nine—as "adjunct faculty" from whom we have much to learn about a world very different from our own? Immersion experiences in developing countries or our own decaying inner cities are powerful means for "acting" faculty and staff into new ways of thinking about their disciplines and their responsibilities to and for the academy.

Those characteristics that distinguish an education that is Catholic and Jesuit—a religious perspective that understands the pursuit of the truth in whatever form as a graced expression of our hunger for the transcendent, a comprehensive humanism that develops sensitivity to human pain and social injustice, and a firm resolve to move against the unjust and the inhumane on a personal and global level—are best seen as threads that must be woven into the fabric of university life. These are not individual pieces of cloth but single threads which when woven together with the traditional strands of university life—teaching, scholarship, and service—make for a uniquely beautiful and brilliant tapestry. Simply tying together dangling threads or tacking on discrete patches over an existing pattern will disfigure the tapestry and ultimately unravel the whole piece. The challenge and the mission of Catholic education is to weave into the warp and woof of academic life the concerns and values of the Catholic tradition and thereby leaven society for good and offer a vibrantly distinctive pattern to American academic life.

References

Abbott, W.M., S.J. (1966). The Documents of Vatican II. *Pastoral constitution on the Church in the modern world (Gaudium et Spes)*. New York, NY: The America Press.

58 THE JUST ONE JUSTICES

Belknap, R. L., & Kuhns, R. (1977). *Tradition and innovation: General education and the reintegration of the university: A Columbia report.* New York, NY: Columbia University Press.

Buckley, M. J., S.J. (1982, June). The university and concern for justice: The search for a new humanism. *Thought, 57,* 219–233.

Buckley, M.J., S.J. (1991, May 6). Christian humanism and human misery: A challenge to the Jesuit university. Presidential lecture presented at Santa Clara University, Santa Clara, CA.

Buckley, M.J., S.J. (1998). The search for a new humanism: The university and the concern for justice. In *The Catholic University as promise and as project: Reflections in a Jesuit idiom.* Washington, DC: Georgetown University Press.

Cain, W., S.J. (1998, May). The Gospel according to "Nothing Sacred." Lecture presented at Santa Clara University, Santa Clara, CA.

Documents of the Thirty-First and Thirty-Second General Congregations (1977). St. Louis, MO: The Institute of Jesuit Sources.

Documents of the Thirty-Fourth General Congregation of the Society of Jesus (1995). St. Louis, MO: The Institute of Jesuit Sources.

Donne, J. (1978). *Devotions upon emergent occasions* (A. Raspa, Ed.). Montreal: McGill–Queens University Press.

Egan, B., S.J. (1996, April 5). Can universities be Catholic? *Commonweal,* 11–14.

Fanon, F. (1968). *The wretched of the earth.* New York, NY: Grove Press.

Ganss, G.E., S.J. (Ed.) (1970). *The constitutions of the Society of Jesus.* St. Louis, MO: The Institute of Jesuit Sources.

Hopkins, G. M., S.J. (1966). "God's grandeur." In J. Pick (Ed.), *A Hopkins reader.* New York, NY: Image Books Edition.

O'Malley, J. (1993). *The first Jesuits.* Cambridge, MA: Harvard University Press.

Oxfam America (1998). Why hunger? Netscape: Online Posting.

Pushkin, A. S. (1978). *Eugene Onegin.* New York, NY: Viking Press.

Remarque, E. M. (1975). *All quiet on the western front.* New York, NY: Fawcett Crest.

SOCIAL JUSTICE, URBAN POVERTY IN THE UNITED STATES, AND LOYOLA MARYMOUNT UNIVERSITY'S RESPONSE

Lance H. Blakesley

Although the participants in the 1998 President's Institute on the Catholic Character of Loyola Marymount University frequently talked about justice and social justice as we explored the topic "The Just One Justices," we gave little attention to how these concepts might be defined. During one session, several of the participants appeared to suggest that justice is the same as fundamental fairness. Certainly this is often thought of as one element of social justice; however, social and political theorists generally contend that the concept includes a good deal more. Of the several formal papers presented at the Institute, the paper written by Stephen Privett, S.J., entitled "The University and the Struggle for Justice," focused most upon issues concerning social justice that are frequently examined by social and political theorists, but the terms "justice" and "social justice" were not clearly defined in this paper (Privett, 2000).

What I intend to do in this reaction paper to Stephen Privett's presentation is to clarify how leading social and political theorists tend to conceptualize the terms "social justice" and "equality" and then explore ways that Catholic universities might more effectively promote social justice in the United States.

The words "social justice" and "equality" have been used in a wide variety of ways. Definitions are usually based on one's political ideology, as well as moral and ethical positions. Certainly there is no neutral, scientific approach for developing a universally acceptable conceptualization. It is possible, however, to identify three enduring conceptualizations which social and political theorists, political practitioners, and the public have used. Classical conservatism, classical liberalism, and socialism/progressive liberalism are three systems of thought which have distinctly different perspectives on both social justice and equality.

Classical Conservatism's Approach to Social Justice and Equality

Classical conservatism is a system of thought that arose in aristocratic and feudal societies. It is currently almost nonexistent in the United States. Unlike the contemporary core political culture of the United States—which emphasizes values such as progress, change, individual initiative, mobility, equal opportunity, and political equality—classical conservatism is committed to stability, order, harmony, social inequality, and governance by a natural aristocracy.

Plato is the most renowned proponent of classical conservatism. In his book, *The Republic*, Plato describes an ideal society where order and harmony exist because individuals perform functions appropriate to their innate capacities. Social justice is achieved, Plato contends, when the natural abilities of individuals are identified, where people can be assigned appropriate roles, and where people can be convinced to be happy in the performance of their assigned functions. Because of their superior intellect and philosophical training, only a very small class of people is capable of understanding true knowledge and equipped to govern in a just society. In feudal Europe, both the nobility and the Christian clergy held essentially a conservative world view, stressing harmony, obedience, order, narrowly restricted personal initiative, and the static places of various classes of people in the just society. Few Americans today appear to be proponents of classical conservative conceptualizations of social justice and social inequality.

Classical Liberalism's Approach to Social Justice and Equality

Classical liberalism is the bedrock of contemporary American political culture, and the classical liberal perspective on social justice and equality appears to be the one most familiar to and widely held by Americans today. Classical liberals believe that the just society is one in which people enjoy political equality (i.e., due process of the laws, equal protection of the laws, and each citizen's vote counts equally) and equal opportunity to pursue their self-interest in the marketplace. Social and material inequalities, while not celebrated, are thought of as natural by-products of a free-market economy, and collective efforts to lessen these inequalities are seen as potentially dangerous to the efficient operations of the free market. Classical liberalism is a system of thought derived from the reflections on early market societies by theorists such as Adam Smith, David Ricardo, and John Locke.

Social justice, according to this world view, is about process (where people are free to pursue their self-interest in an ideal free market and to acquire property). The existence of significant inequalities in income, wealth, housing, health care, and other social conditions tells the classical liberal nothing about how just or unjust is a society. A just distribution of scarce resources is any distribution that results from a just process, entailing political equality and voluntary participation and free competition in the society's economy. Classical liberal values of self-reliance, economic competition, equal opportunity to pursue one's self-interest, and the right to accumulate wealth are used to justify severe inequalities in social and material conditions. Today, classical liberalism is essentially what we call political conservatism in the United States: the conservatism of William F. Buckley, Milton Friedman, and the Republican leadership in Congress.

Socialism's and Progressive Liberalism's Approaches to Social Justice and Equality

While classical conservatism celebrates inequality, and while classical liberalism promotes both equal opportunity and political equality, but allows for significant social and material inequalities—socialism holds that social justice is based on the presence of equal opportunity, political equality, and equality in material conditions in a society.

By virtue of their common humanity, all people, according to the socialist world view, should enjoy political equality and equal opportunity to achieve their potential. The foundation of the socialist view of social justice, however, is the principle of equal material conditions in society: the distribution of scarce resources of a community in a manner that meets the basic needs of all its members. Most socialists don't call for an exact mathematical (or absolute) type of material equality, but they do insist on a level of sharing of those goods and services among all members of society that are necessary for a life of decency and self-respect.

Socialists generally believe that only when there exists equality of material conditions does it become possible for people to effectively exercise their legal and political rights and to develop fully as human beings. Only when lower-order physiological and security needs are met, are people free to develop their talents and interests and thereby meet their higher-order self-esteem and self-actualization needs. Socialists believe that notions of equal opportunity and political equality are only false promises in a society of extreme inequalities in material conditions. The tremendous obstacle, of course, that socialists confront when they attempt to realize their goal of social justice is that, in order to expand the opportunities for self-fulfillment of the many, the freedom of the privileged few to acquire and hold wealth is somewhat diminished.

Most people who think of themselves as liberals in the late twentieth century in the United States, while continuing to support the institutions of private property and the capitalist marketplace, have felt uncomfortable with the severe material inequalities that are either allowed to exist or are created in a capitalist economic system. Like socialists, these liberals tend to support various public policies that attempt to provide some measure of greater equality in material conditions in the United States. These progressive liberals, while retaining a belief in the capitalist marketplace, also believe that, in order to establish a just society, government needs to intervene in the economy to lessen sharp material inequalities.

Thus, it is evident that there is no single definition of social justice. The socialist and progressive liberal conceptualizations, however, which hold that social justice includes equal opportunity, political equality, and greater equality in material conditions than presently exists in most of the world, appears to be in keeping with the modern Catholic Church's concern for poverty in the world and the Jesuit commitment to a "preferential option for the poor."

Social Justice and Poverty in the United States

Unlike both classical conservatism and classical liberalism, which contend that individual factors alone largely determine one's fate in the world, both socialism and progressive liberalism maintain that how a person fares in the world is largely a consequence of three sets of factors: individual, family, and structural characteristics of the society. Individual factors, including one's level of motivation, intelligence, education, self-reliance, health, and willingness to postpone present gratifications for future gains, are seen as being important. Also, children whose parents are well-educated, highly motivated, economically secure, and have a multitude of social connections are more likely to fare well as adults. Economic, social, and political structural factors, which often are beyond an individual's control, are important as well. Global economic change, the neighborhood where one lives, the school that one attends, and institutional racism are all examples of structural factors that greatly determine a person's opportunities for self-fulfillment in the United States. Socialists, progressive liberals, and many social scientists (like myself) who are concerned about the problem of poverty in the United States tend to focus their attention on structural factors that have caused poverty in the United States and on structural changes that might be introduced to tackle the problem of poverty.

In the last ten years, no social scientist has more profoundly influenced serious discussions of the structural causal factors that have given rise to and allowed for the persistence of concentrated, inner-city poverty in the United States than William Julius Wilson. In his 1987 book, *The Truly Disadvantaged: The Inner City, The Underclass and Public Policy*, Wilson argues that low-income, urban African-Americans have become caught in a web of institutional and industrial change. The decline of manufacturing, the suburbanization of employment, and the rise of a low-wage service sector, according to Wilson, have reduced the number of jobs in the United States that pay wages adequate to support a family. These economic changes have been accompanied by an increase in spatial concentration of poverty in inner-city neighborhoods due to the movement away from the inner-city areas of a growing black middle class. As well-educated, middle-income blacks have moved largely to new middle-class black neighborhoods, the class structure of the urban black community has bifurcated into a black middle-class living in their own neighborhoods, and a more concentrated and destitute urban black underclass lacking the institutions, resources, and values necessary for success in the highly competitive postindustrial economy (Wilson, 1987). Both racial segregation in the housing market and the above-mentioned economic and demographic changes have confined lower-income blacks to a small number of geographically isolated and racially homogeneous neighborhoods in the nation's central cities. In his 1996 book, *When Work Disappears: The World of the New Urban Poor*, William Julius Wilson outlines a comprehensive public policy framework designed to attack the structural factors that have made for concentrated inner-city poverty. Wilson recommends both race-neutral, class-specific national policies—designed to improve the quality of public schools, to provide adequate health care, to create high-wage employment, to reduce crime, and to strengthen the family—along with race-based national policies to reduce racial segregation in housing through more effectively curtailing exclusionary zoning practices and more aggressive enforcement of Federal Fair Housing laws (Wilson, 1996).

There appears to be a high degree of congruence with William Julius Wilson's theoretical thrust and the perspective on poverty of both Jesuits and members of the Religious of the Sacred Heart of Mary. Michael Engh, S.J., has reported that at the conclusion of a general congregation meeting of Jesuits in Rome in 1974–75, with delegates from every Jesuit province and region in the world in attendance, a statement was issued, entitled "The Service of Faith and the Promotion of Justice," which proclaimed that, "The mission of the Society of Jesus today is the service of faith, of which the promotion of justice is an absolute requirement." The Jesuit community was directed to address "injustice not only personal but institutionalized: built into economic, social, and political structures that dominate the life of nations and the international community." Engh reports that, "Similar commitments can be found in the revised constitution of the Religious of the Sacred Heart of Mary, approved in 1983" (Engh, 2000).

Loyola Marymount University's Response

During the twenty-five years I have been a faculty member at Loyola Marymount University, I have witnessed some of the many ways that members of the University community have promoted social justice and provided assistance to the poor. The Campus Ministry, Educational Participation in Communities (EPIC) and other service organizations, groups sponsored by the several academic colleges and departments, and individual faculty, staff, and students have been involved in numerous worthwhile efforts. Several examples that seem to be particularly noteworthy include assistance provided by faculty and students in the School of Business to help residents in local public housing projects form tenant-management organizations, students who have worked closely with youngsters in Los Angeles juvenile correctional institutions, and faculty members and students in the School of Education who have tutored students and have provided assistance in curriculum-development and administrative-reform endeavors in low-income, inner-city schools. Certainly LMU's efforts to recruit low-income, minority students, along with LMU academic and financial-aid supportive services, have helped many disadvantaged individuals develop the capacities to more readily move into the mainstream economy in the United States. Rather than attempt to provide an exhaustive inventory of everything the University has done and is presently doing to promote social justice and to tackle the problems of poverty, it might be more useful if I were to suggest how we could improve some of our current efforts and also recommend new initiatives.

Presently a substantial number of students at LMU are participating in immersion activities intended to provide direct assistance to the poor and to familiarize our students with the multiple problems confronting the poor. These immersion experiences are also assumed to increase student empathy for the poor. Unfortunately—because these immersion activities are frequently brief, unstructured, lack adequate faculty supervision, and are not systematically examined in an academic setting—too often the student's preexisting negative stereotypes are reinforced rather than the student becoming more empathetic and more motivated to provide assistance to the poor. During the 1980s, the dominant explanation voiced by national opinion leaders for why there was poverty in the United States was that the poor suffered from individual moral and character defects. Only through increased self-reliance, self-restraint, self-discipline, and individual effort, and not through depending on governmental social welfare programs, could the poor, according to the proponents of this theory of individual responsibility, become self-sufficient and productive in the mainstream American economy.

After brief encounters with the social disorganization and dysfunctional individual behaviors that are associated with the culture of poverty, students participating in immersion activities that are not supplemented with scholarly reading materials and reflective, analytical discussions are likely to intuitively sense that their direct observations provide solid evidence supporting the causal theory of individual responsibility.

In order to make immersion experiences a more effective learning experience, I believe we should take steps to make sure that they are incorporated into formal courses that focus on the problem of poverty in the United States. One approach, which appears to deserve serious consideration, would be to require all students to complete at least one course that systematically focuses on the causal factors of poverty; the nature of the problems encountered by the poor; and alternative individual, family, and public policy remedial strategies. The goals of this required course would be to produce greater student empathy for the poor and help students to understand that the fate of all people is largely determined by a combination of individual, family, and structural factors and that a multi-pronged set of remedial strategies, including collective efforts such as governmental social welfare programs, is needed to effectively tackle the problem of poverty in the United States.

Being an urban university, located in the city of Los Angeles, which has a relatively large low-income African-American population, and an urban underclass concentrated in the inner-city area, the Catholic University should give emphasis to efforts that attempt to assist these people to fulfill their potential and to successfully move into the American mainstream. We should do our best to actively recruit low-income African-American students and to enhance financial aid and academic supportive services to assist them to graduate.

The Catholic university response to social justice and poverty in the United States should focus not only on poverty that is external to the University community but also that which is internal. We should do our best to make sure that all full-time employees (including both employees and people working on campus for outside contractors) receive wages and benefits that permit them and their families at a minimum to meet their needs for essential goods and services. Probably one of the most admirable features of Loyola Marymount University is that, in comparison to many other employers in the United States today, all employees are provided with a set of benefits including: health care, a pension program, and tuition remission for full-time employees, their spouses, and their children. The tuition-remission benefit is a particularly important concrete means which the University utilizes to directly further social justice. Hopefully, for as long as Loyola Marymount University is in existence, the children of the clerical staff, painters, electricians, secretaries, custodians, and gardeners, as well as the children of the faculty and administrators, will be able to attend college because of the tuition-remission program. The Catholic University should make sure the same benefits the high-wage employees receive are extended to the low-wage employees. For instance, efforts to promote social justice within the university community could be enhanced by expanding eligibility for participation in the home-ownership program to all full-time employees.

Conclusions

Three enduring world views that have distinctly different conceptualizations of social justice and equality have been examined in this paper: classical conservatism, classical liberalism, and socialism/progressive liberalism. The discussions, presentations, and readings that were elements of the President's Institute on the Catholic Character of Loyola Marymount University suggest to me that the socialist/progressive liberal commitment to the promotion of social justice through the expansion of equal opportunity, political equality, and equality of material conditions would find a comfortable home in a modern Catholic University.

Steven Privett, S.J., in his paper, "The University and the Struggle for Justice," contends that a humanistic Catholic education must offer students:

a profound understanding of and sensitivity to the plight of those whom Franz Fanon named "the wretched of the earth." This understanding and sensitivity opens the minds and hearts of the truly educated and strengthens their resolve to engage somehow in the global struggle for human development. (Privett, 2000, p. 56)

While the Catholic university community should be concerned with the struggle for human development that is taking place in the disadvantaged communities throughout the world, the efforts to promote social justice will have the most immediate and concrete impacts within the local community and within the university itself. Through our teaching, scholarship, and community service activities we should concentrate on attempting to expand equal opportunity, political equality, and equality of material conditions in the several inner-city neighborhoods with high levels of urban blight and concentrated poverty. Our commitment to advance social justice should also direct us to be particularly attentive to the needs of our low-wage employees. Helping the employees and their families to meet both their lower-order physiological needs and higher-order self-esteem/self-actualization needs should be a high priority of a Catholic institution with a "preferential option for the poor."

References

Engh, M.E., S.J. (2000). Just ones past and present at Loyola Marymount University. In M.K. McCullough (Ed.), *The just one justices: The role of justice at the heart of Catholic higher education* (pp. 21–36). Scranton, PA: University of Scranton Press.

Privett, S., S.J. (2000). The university and the struggle for justice. In M.K. McCullough (Ed.), *The just one justices: The role of justice at the heart of Catholic higher education* (pp. 44–58). Scranton, PA: University of Scranton Press.

Wilson, W.J. (1987). *The truly disadvantaged: The inner city, the underclass and public policy.* Chicago, IL: University of Chicago Press.

Wilson, W.J. (1996). *When work disappears: The world of the new urban poor.* New York, NY: Alfred A. Knopf.

DO WE DARE SPEAK OF LOVE? WOMEN'S VOICES AND THE MISSION OF JESUIT HIGHER EDUCATION

Barbara J. Busse

Each day, we observe artifacts which reveal that all kinds of organizations seem to be talking about "mission." These signs of our times are everywhere: protected under Plexiglas at the auto shop, printed on the backs of menus in fast-food joints, mounted discretely on the walls of mortuaries, done up artistically by calligraphers for the hallways of schools and hospitals, emblazoned like sacred script in glossy annual reports.

It is easy to be skeptical about mission statements since there often seems to be a chasm between platitude and practice. Skeptics conclude that strategic planning processes leading to mission statements are a waste of time at best. Those who are more optimistic believe that systematic processes of self-analysis are critical if an organization is to explain itself clearly to its internal and external audiences, envision what it can and ought to do, and help organizational members strategize about how best to engage their collective efforts. If "mission talk" fulfills these latter purposes, organizations increase the likelihood that they can realize their goals and objectives. Most strategists agree that the results of strategic planning conversations about an organization's mission will be only as good as the process which produced it. This paper explores the possibility that mission conversations within Jesuit colleges and universities might be enhanced substantially by including the perspectives of women.

Regular inquiry into and clarification of an organization's aims is especially important if a significant number of newcomers join the organization on a regular basis and if the organization wishes its members to identify strongly with the organization and its values (Bullis & Tompkins, 1989). Jesuit colleges and universities have both transient populations (students) and an institutional commitment to values they hope to communicate to members in order to transform their lives (the encouragement of learning and the promotion of social justice).

Many organizational theorists believe that if members do not understand and identify with the values and assumptions of an organization, a sense of community cannot truly develop (Bullis & Tompkins, 1989;

Tompkins & Cheney, 1985). If creating a sense of community is an especially important characteristic of Jesuit higher education, it is obviously important for organizational members to understand the values on which the organization's identity depends. The organization's values are not images created by the organization for commodity value; rather, an identity is the character of an organization that can be inferred by observation of its practices. The ways the organization's values are made obvious to newcomers, therefore, involve much more than making claims about itself; values also are revealed in observable actions of organizational members.

Persons committed to Jesuit higher education have a special interest in communicating and living their mission. For the Jesuits themselves, education is not merely a centuries-old family enterprise; "education is an apostolate, a continuation of the work of the Apostles . . . which means helping in some way to establish God's reign" (Genovesi, 1998, p. 5). Consequently, the conversation about Jesuit education is at the center of Jesuit reflection about how to conduct the work of the society. Fueling the conversation is the realization that Jesuits will be increasingly dependent on lay collaborators in order to staff their schools, colleges, and universities (*Documents*, 1995). As a result of this realization, the Jesuits must forge agreements about mission not merely through discussions among themselves, but they must engage the support of lay collaborators for the work they intend to accomplish, as well as discover ways to make their organizational values accessible to the constant stream of newcomers (entering students, new faculty and staff) to their colleges and universities. Since many of these collaborators are women and since a significant portion of the students at Jesuit colleges and universities are women, this author assumes it is especially important to include women's voices prominently in the conversation, an assumption implicitly and strongly affirmed by the Jesuit's decree on women (*Document*, 1995), which also addresses the "universal reality" of discrimination against women. It is also imperative to investigate the possibility that men and women may understand the mission of Jesuit education differently because of differences in gender role socialization and different life experiences. Since institutional identification requires that existing members of an organization are able to explain the values, meanings, and expectations to new members in order to maintain a sense of organizational community, it would be important to know what existing members actually believe to be true about their organization's central characteristics.

The rich conversation about Jesuit education, characterized by both breadth and depth, cannot be reviewed completely here. Instead this paper uses selected themes developed in Stephen Privett's (2000) "The University and the Struggle for Justice" as the basis for three questions and some tentative thoughts about each. These questions were suggested in a more general form by Frank H.T. Rhodes's keynote address at "Assembly 89." The questions are still ripe for discussion: "Is there unanimity on a 'Jesuit' position on what constitutes social justice and how it should be promoted? Are there alternative models for the mission of Jesuit education? And if outstanding professional preparation is your mission, how do Jesuit trained alumni differ from those who have graduated from other institutions?" (Rhodes, 1989, p. 57).

In order to respond to Privett's presentation, I have transformed Rhodes's general queries into the following three questions:

Question One: Is Privett's understanding of justice consistent with an "ethic of care" (Gilligan, 1982) or other feminist critique models (Larrabee, 1993)?

Question Two: Is Privett's understanding of sacrifice consistent with "constructive self sacrifice" (Golden, 1998)?

Question Three: How can conversations about mission be translated into the just action Privett describes?

In responding to these questions, it should become clear that if women's voices are not prominent in conversations about the mission of Jesuit higher education, an opportunity for informative and equitable dialogue will be lost. In the spirit of good conversation, these questions are meant to provoke that dialogue. This spirit is consistent with Privett's own commitment to ongoing dialogue and debate about the Catholic and Jesuit tradition (Privett, 2000). Prior to discussion of the particular questions, several segments of Privett's paper will be highlighted.

The Jesuit University

Privett's central theme is explicit: There is a performative aspect to justice without which all manner of academic deliberations may be judged sterile (Privett, 2000). Privett identifies both personal and global dimensions of justice, and consistent with the Jesuit preferential option for the poor, gives numerous examples of justice to underserved populations. Throughout his paper, Privett cites examples of a variety of "just ones," including some "notable contemporary exemplars" (Privett, 2000, p. 49), many of whom sacrificed their lives for just causes. Privett's cited examples of self-giving run the gamut from common decency (greeting students as persons) and "looking through the lenses of conscience and compassion" in an internship project to "direct experiences with underserved populations" (Privett, 2000, p. 57). This breadth of scope does weaken

Privett's clear and passionate commitment to "the two-thirds of the world who are hungry, illiterate, homeless" (Privett, 2000, p. 55). Instead it intensifies the sense that to be a "just one" involves a way of living one's entire life, not merely engaging in particular caring acts to underserved populations.

Question One

While Privett does not specify a definition of the term "justice," he clearly is not speaking about a narrowly-defined sense of social obligation, but about action motivated by a religious vision of the dignity of each human being. He recalls the Patristic maxim, "*Gloria Dei homo vivens*"—God's glory is the human person fully alive (Privett, 2000, p. 52). He describes a form of justice compelled by "sensitivity and responsiveness to human suffering" which "opens the minds and hearts of the truly educated" (Privett, 2000, p. 54). Privett demonstrates, through the language he uses and the illustrations he suggests, that his concept of Jesuit mission moves beyond the kind of justice typically ascribed to Kohlberg or Rawls. In describing a course he is teaching, Privett notes several "fundamental premises" of a television series, premises which seem entirely consistent with his own beliefs: "the human is the divine, if only we can see it; when push comes to shove, mercy is justice; and there is a chosen people and they are everyone" (Privett, 2000, p. 52). Indeed, although Privett never uses the word "love" in his paper, his descriptions of justice appear much more closely aligned to the "self-gift" of "agape—purely other-directed love" described so powerfully in Michael Himes's (1995) work. In short, in thinking about justice as Privett does, those interested in Jesuit mission must be committed to qualifying justice with love. Consequently, since we are called to love and serve others, justice is not merely an intellectual orientation to fair and just treatment, but requires that we move "beyond justice" to love.

Feminist critique related to conceptions of justice offers potentially useful ways to make conversations about justice more inclusive and rich. For example, Annette Baier (1993) in seeking to discover a "key concept, or guiding motif, [which] might hold together the structure of a moral theory" (p. 21), asks the following provocative question:

What would be a suitable central question, principle, or concept, to structure a moral theory which might accommodate those moral insights women tend to have more readily than men, and to answer those moral questions which, it seems worry women more than men? (Baier, 1993, p. 21)

In exploring the question, Baier suggests blending theories based on obligation ("justice" narrowly defined) with theories based on "the ethic of love" in a new concept she calls "appropriate trust" (Baier, 1993, p. 27).

As Carol Gilligan (1982) famously suggested:

> What we need now is a marriage of the old male and newly articulated female insights in order to temper considerations of justice with considerations of care. We may be unable to create a voice of moral authority to which both men and women will powerfully respond unless we articulate these moral imperatives in languages which speak compellingly to both male and female life experience. (p. 174)

Although the "ethic of care" conversation is rarely conducted on theological grounds, it is arguable that its vision of virtue is closely aligned with the concept of "agape." Similarly, Baier's concept of "appropriate trust" might be close to what is meant by "social justice" in the mission statements of Jesuit institutions. Why are these connections important? It is because these commonly held notions of what the words "mean" will influence how a variety of different audiences will understand "justice" and on what grounds they will be compelled to act justly.

Baier argues, for example, that while "one of the great strengths of Rawls' theory is the careful attention given to the question of how just institutions produce the conditions for their continued support, across generations, and in particular of how the sense of justice will arise in children" (Baier, 1993, p. 23), Rawls takes for granted that "the parents . . . love the child, and in time the child comes to love and trust the parents" (Rawls, 1971, p. 463).

Baier concludes appropriately that Rawls's form of justice would not persist beyond the next generation were it not for the existence of what Rawls takes for granted—namely the love of a parent capable of teaching a child how to love. Arguing that "a decent morality will *not* depend for its stability on forces to which it gives no moral recognition" (Baier, 1993, p. 25), Baier rejects a conception of justice which is not based on love as well as what she calls "appropriate trust" (Baier, 1993, p. 27), a mosaic which blends the ethic of obligation and the ethic of love. Regardless of one's stance on the seminal argument introduced by Gilligan (1982), it is undeniable that her claims about the value of women's experiences have been welcomed by many women seeking a more expansive definition of morality than "duty and obligation." This may be understandable given women's subordination in many cultures, including our own. The significant response to her work confirms broad interest in Gilligan's claims. While Gilligan expressly denies that the "different voice" of moral reasoning she describes is *necessarily* a woman's response, she argues consistently that women's life experiences often tend to produce a particular kind of human connectedness that makes women more likely to act "beyond justice" in choosing to care about and care for others. As is the case with other gender-linked characterizations, great caution must be exercised in particularizing these characteristics to women as opposed to men. We must resist simplistic responses that would lead to a limiting kind of biological determinism that locks men and women into restricted moral roles. As one of Gilligan's many respondents notes, "Care involves a way of responding to other persons and does not merely provide standards for evaluation of agents" (Blum, 1993, p. 64). If the "territory" Blum mentions is often accessible to women, however, they might be useful guides to others struggling to make moral choices not clearly motivated by the abstract principles of justice.

Baier claims that the kind of moral philosophy "as done by men following in the footsteps of the great moral philosophers (all men)" is "different in tone and approach" from the contributions of women (Baier, 1993, p. 19). Similarly, if it follows that an approach to "good action" is motivated by a woman's orientation of self to other, we ought to study that orientation for clues to what creates and animates it.

The most thoughtful investigation of the implications of this bold claim is necessary: Do most women attend differently to other people and consequently learn to care about others in a different way than most men? If so, what are the implications for educators committed to motivating women and men to act justly, motivated by love?

Question Two

As he recently returned from concelebrating the funeral liturgy for assassinated Bishop Gerardi, it is understandable that Privett ponders the question of sacrifice, i.e., what motivates someone "to live and die for something that flatly contradicted their own self interest" (Privett, 2000, p. 49). Similarly, he notes that "real people 'justice' at great personal cost to themselves" (Privett, 2000, p. 49).

The implied sense of sacrifice which seems to be suggested by Privett involves self-denial: a cost to one's self. If correctly interpreted, this implication may signal an understanding of sacrifice familiar to many—that sacrifice means giving up something that you value. This interpretation of sacrifice is challenged in a thoughtful new book by Stephanie Golden (1998) which discusses self-sacrifice as a Christian virtue, "the first principle of the moral world" (p. 7). She claims that "women's propensity for self-sacrifice is so well-known it's a cliche" (Golden, 1998, p. 12). She argues that, especially for women, sacrifice is often linked to suffering, that some women are "too good for their own good" and that sacrifice often carries with it burnout, ineffectiveness, and the distorting emotions of anger, guilt, and a sense of self-righteousness (Golden, 1998, p. 15).

Instead of rejecting sacrifice as an ideal, Golden proposes a re-appropriation of "the original, empowering meaning of sacrifice as an expansive and self-fulfilling act" which completes what she identifies as a "sacred circuit" (Golden, 1998, pp. 280–283).

How is this understanding relevant to Jesuit higher education? If we are asking students to move beyond narrow self-interest and learn to love and care for others, personally and globally, we will necessarily be engaged in discussing and modeling the sacrifices just/loving action requires. Motivating people to sacrifice may be impossible, or worse, destructive, unless we find the vocabulary and the models to create a more fulfilling vision of sacrifice.

Golden posits an orientation to sacrifice which is "life-giving," "transformative and not maiming" (Golden, 1998, p. 265). The key to this transformation is a revisioning of the self—learning to view the self expansively, interconnected to all people and the natural universe which supports humankind. She argues that women are "particularly equipped to invent an effective balance between holding on to personal selfhood and recognizing the selfhood of others," thus "expanding the circuit of what is made sacred" (Golden, 1998, p. 283). It is self-evident that this search is spiritual and resonates clearly with Ignatian spirituality.

It would be irresponsible of Jesuit educators to presume that forming "men and women with and for others" does not require intelligent and informed conversations (incorporating the viewpoints of women and men) about the implications of that sacrifice. Absent this element of service learning, we deny students the "exquisite luxury of being able to help people," understanding "when one gives, one gets back much more than one gives" (Golden, 1998, p. 255). Replacing this understanding for the sense of what one loses inoculates the self-giver from the anger, guilt, despair, self-righteousness, and ineffectiveness Golden poignantly describes in people struggling to do good without an intellectual and spiritual framework for valuing the self-gift *and* the giver.

Question Three

There is a common suspicion that developing a mission statement is often an exercise whose only tangible result is a piece of calligraphy under Plexiglas on a wall in the president's suite. Bridging the gap between words and deeds is a persistent concern, expressed by Privett thusly: There is a performative aspect to justice, without which all manner of academic deliberations may be judged sterile (Privett, 2000). Talking about mission in an organization committed to social justice is especially complex because, according to Peter Drucker (1993), there is a temptation to be content with the goodness of the cause and to substitute good intentions with good results. Not only do such organizations have to be committed to a cause, they have to have a mission and be imbued with passion (Drucker, 1993). Perhaps these three characteristics (cause/mission/passion) begin to shape a response to the question How did they (the just ones) come by the wherewithal to take their stands? (Privett, 2000). According to Drucker (1993), the extent to which any organization achieves its mission should be evaluated by the results it creates, an approach completely consistent with the Gospel standard Privett highlights: by their fruits you will know them" (Privett, 2000). For Privett, the central question is "How and who do we want our graduates to be in this world?" (Privett, 2000, p. 54), a question which must focus all Catholic universities on outcomes not necessarily tested by traditional discipline-bound assessment within the university, but tested by the real world consequences of what they choose to do with the greatest two gifts any human can offer—love and work. "Are they becoming the people we wanted them to become?" and "Are they making the differences we prepared them to make?" would become the pivotal assessment concerns of student-centered Jesuit university educators. Bridging what Drucker calls the chasm between good intentions and performance, requires will and work, but does not require miracles (Drucker, 1993).

How effectively are Jesuit universities translating their intentions into performance? Are Jesuit schools forming men and women so committed to just action that they have a profound understanding of and sensitivity to the plight of the "other 99" Privett describes? (Privett, 2000). This observer is without a clear answer and there are few indications that the foundational "leavening" claim is being tested in any systematic way. Academic appraisal seems to be focused narrowly on academic competence, alumni outreach on fundraising. Despite more examples of student involvement in particular mission-related initiatives such as service-learning projects, various observers still note the need to translate talk into action (Genovesi, 1998; Privett, 2000).

Among women there are particular concerns about how women can make optimal use of their distinctive gifts and a profound suspicion that women's gifts will continue to be devalued, despite the hopeful language of the Jesuit's recent decree on women (Mayeski, 1993; Stinson, 1995). The aim of Jesuit educational enterprise has always been clear: "the glory of God and the common good of humanity" (*Documents*, 1995). This aim leads us back to a question central to making the promotion of justice a lived reality: By what means can a Catholic University create a coherent system of educational practices that will assist its students to freely choose to live justly, even if that choice involves enormous "self-giving"?

Privett proposes a comprehensive humanism which would develop humane sensitivities and provide tools by which the human condition can be thoughtfully addressed (Privett, 2000). He urges the development of a curriculum intentionally aimed at "who we want our graduates to be in this world," a curriculum which clearly "embodies our educational goals and objectives" (Privett, 2000, p. 54). He advocates immersion experiences in developing countries or inner cities as "powerful means for 'acting' faculty and staff into new ways of thinking about their disciplines and their responsibilities to and for the academy" and, by implication, to the global community (Privett, 2000, p. 57).

Privett may be right that if students (and faculty and staff) could appropriate a "profound understanding of and sensitivity to the plight of those Franz Fanon named 'the wretched of the earth,'" that the change "opens the minds and hearts of the truly educated and strengthens their resolve to engage somehow in the global struggle for human development" (Privett, 2000, p. 56). In addition to these issues, Privett broadens the scope of the Jesuit educational mission by tracing the history of the Society of Jesus from its original commitment to "do any service that may be for the greater glory of God and the common good" (*Documents*, 1995). Jesuit education was to assist "men and women struggling to realize their full human potential through the pursuit of the truth" (Privett, 2000, p. 52). Privett also claims that, "Theology names that ultimate truth, God, and the pursuit of truth is, at its core, the pursuit of God" (Privett, 2000, p. 52). The central Mystery of God is love. Development of these themes in this way is entirely familiar to those who have scrutinized Jesuit ministries. Placing Privett's distillations in broader context may prove useful, as he seems to implicitly acknowledge when he identifies the "hoped-for outcome of a Jesuit education" as "a skilled and knowledgeable person who lives a fully human life" (Privett, 2000, p. 53).

Privett's address does not, however, address the particular focus of this paper—what women's insights may contribute to conversations about social justice, especially as they relate to women and the "universal reality" of discrimination against women that manifests itself in a variety of ways. The "feminization of poverty" and the "feminine face of oppression" are not accidental consequences of life, but the result of a "legacy of systematic discrimination against women" that is "embedded within the economic, social, political, religious, and even linguistic structures of our societies" (*Documents*, 1995). Not only have the Jesuits described the problem, they have begun to develop an agenda for addressing this huge human need. Now it is time to ask how our colleges and universities can address these and other issues in concrete terms.

The Jesuits have done an especially good job of explaining the necessity for communication in their decree on the situation of women. "We invite all Jesuits to listen carefully and courageously to the experience of women. Listening, in a spirit of partnership and equality, is the most practical response we can make and is the foundation for our mutual partnership to reform unjust structures" (*Documents*, 1995, Decree 14). Listening should entail more than just hearing the voices of individual women express their concerns; it should entail deep engagement of some of the questions this paper introduces: Does the lived experience of women create a different kind of moral reasoning? Does women's experience of sacrifice teach us something useful about just and loving action? Does discrimination against women in any form make it less likely that half of humankind can realize full human potential?

Several elements of Decree 14 could be used as models of approaches to any marginalized group. First and perhaps most importantly, there is an assumed respect for the other that permeates the message. Second, the Jesuits identify themselves as willing to learn from women themselves what the "real concerns" are. Third, the difficulty of listening to another is not underestimated. Finally, the Decree acknowledges what another observer notes as the practical reality of the world:

All too often, the picture of the planet we carry around with us—a picture formed of our own experiences and the stream of information from the mass media—is at odds with what is real and important. The world is much more diverse, sorrowful, and splendid than the white-washed and overwhelmingly present stereotypes many of us have in our heads. And it is much more female—there's a whole half of the world that is waiting to be heard from. Throughout history, the challenges, the courage, the oppression of women—the majority of people on Earth—have been kept out of sight. Now, the hidden is coming into view. It reminds us forcefully of a lesson that can never be repeated enough: there is overwhelming drama and value in each and every human life, no matter how profoundly these lives are ignored. These are the lives upon which the well-being of the world depends. (Wolf, 1996, p. 9)

Long before "hiring for mission" became a widely discussed objective, some administrators appreciated that accomplishment in an academic discipline was a necessary but not sufficient justification for hiring a faculty member. Loyola Marymount University's current Academic Vice President, Joseph Jabbra, is among those administrators. At a faculty gathering Jabbra recounted a conversation which took place during the hiring process of a faculty member for the history department. The AVP asked the candidate what he had to offer to the students he taught. Damazo Dut Majak Kocjak, with a characteristic smile, replied without hesitation, "I will love them, of course." Damazo's simple response captured with clarity and grace the central mission of Catholic education: to love. There is no doubt that Damazo was hired because of his solid academic credentials, but also because he was the kind of man to whom we were willing to entrust our students' education. We discovered poignantly after Damazo's untimely death how profound his love was. As his son revealed later, as Damazo's terminal illness progressed, he was so ill that he could do little other than get to his classes—where he would engage his students in questions of human significance—and love them. Still, he persisted until very near his death. Returning to paraphrase Privett's query, "How did he come by the wherewithal to take his stand?" It would be hard to imagine a sense of professional duty sufficiently strong to motivate such personal sacrifice: it was love.

Perhaps the most challenging part of the careful examination of institutional conscience, a good mission conversation about Jesuit higher education would necessarily involve Privett's final, essential challenge: How do we weave together the three characteristic strands of religious perspective, comprehensive humanism, and firm resolve to move against the unjust and inhumane?

If love is at the heart of our educational enterprise, the distinctive character of Catholic colleges and universities can be elaborated by probing the meanings and expectations we have about the mystery we call "love." In a culture bent on trivializing the word, reappropriating a particular meaning for "love" and explaining it in the context of the complex work of a university will be challenging. Addressing the challenge is a worthy endeavor, however, because such an effort may afford an opportunity to weave together the central strands Privett identifies as characteristics of Catholic and Jesuit higher education.

As Privett's 2000 address persuasively and ably demonstrates, the problems facing humanity currently are complex and urgent. The list of concerns overwhelms: hunger, poverty, illiteracy, oppression, war. More immediate concerns related to justice may be present both on our campuses and in the world at large. One problem highlighted here is the problem of injustice to women and the need to include women's voices prominently in conversations about how justice and love may be practiced and taught. It seems self evident that the world's many injustices will require the best thinking and the most concerted action by the largest possible number of people, women and men, working together. What flows from this self-evident claim? Nothing less than the most rigorous and compassionate education can motivate the action our world now requires.

References

Baier, A .C. (1993). What do women want in a moral theory? In M.J. Larrabee (Ed.), *An ethic of care: Feminist and interdisciplinary perspectives* (pp. 19–32). New York, NY: Routledge.

Blum, L. (1993). Gilligan and Kohlberg: Implications for moral theory. In M.J. Larrabee (Ed.), *An ethic of care: Feminist and interdisciplinary perspectives* (pp. 49–68). New York, NY: Routledge.

Bullis, C., & Tompkins, P. (1989). The forest ranger revisited: A study of control practices and identification. *Communication Monographs, 56*, 287–306.

Documents of the Thirty Fourth General Congregation of the Society of Jesus (1995). St. Louis, MO: Institute of Jesuit Sources.

Drucker, P.F. (1993). *Managing in turbulent times*. New York, NY: Harper Collins.

Genovesi, V.J., S.J. (1998, May 23). Is Jesuit education fulfilling its mission? *America, 178* (18), 5–6.

Gilligan, C. (1982). *In a different voice: Psychological theory and women's development*. Cambridge, MA: Harvard University.

Golden, S. (1998). *Slaying the mermaid: Women and the culture of sacrifice*. New York, NY: Harmony.

Himes, M. (1995, Fall). Living conversation: higher education in a Catholic context. *Conversations on Jesuit Higher Education*.

Larrabee, M.J. (Ed.) (1993). *An ethic of care: Feminist and interdisciplinary perspectives*. New York, NY: Routledge.

Mayeski, M. A. (1993, Summer). *Vistas*, 3–7. Los Angeles, CA: Loyola Marymount University.

Pauly, J.J. (1997, Fall). Mission talk and the bugaboo of modernity. *Conversations, 12*, 24–29.

Privett, S.A., S.J. (2000). The university and the struggle for justice. In M. K. McCullough (Ed.), *The just one justices: The role of justice at the heart of Catholic higher education* (pp. 49–67). Scranton, PA: University of Scranton Press.

Rawls, J. (1971). *A theory of justice*. Cambridge, MA: Harvard University Press.

Rhodes, F.H.T. (1989, August 5). The mission and ministry of Jesuits in higher education. *America, 161*, 54–60.

Stinson, K.M. (1995, Winter). Through the looking glass. *Xavier Magazine, 2*, 16–19.

Tompkins, P. & Cheney, G. (1985). Communication and unobtrusive control in contemporary organizations. In R. McPhea, & P. Tompkins (Eds.), *Organizational communication: Traditional themes and new directions*. Beverly Hills, CA: Sage.

Wolf, N. (1996). Preface. In F. D'Aluisio, & P. Menzel, *Women in the material world*. San Francisco, CA: Sierra Club Books.

HOW MUCH SHOULD AND COULD THE CATHOLIC UNIVERSITY JUSTICE?

Herbert A. Medina

The thirty-fourth General Congregation of the Society of Jesus reaffirmed the society's commitment to the promotion of justice and argued for an "ever fuller integration of the promotion of justice into our lives of faith, in the company of the poor and many others who live and work for the coming of God's kingdom" (Privett, 2000, p. 50). As a Catholic university, Loyola Marymount University understands and declares its purpose to be: the encouragement of learning, the education of the whole person, the service of faith, and the promotion of justice (*Mission, Goals and Objectives*, 1990). Thus it is clear that Loyola Marymount University's overarching philosophy is completely consistent with and commits to engaging in one of the cornerstones of the Society of Jesus: the promotion of justice.

Today, the two greatest spiritual and philosophical challenges for Loyola Marymount University and other Catholic universities are (a) defining its degree of commitment to social justice; and (b) finding and carrying out concrete and tangible actions with which to carry out this commitment.

The View of Stephen A. Privett, S.J.

Stephen A. Privett, S.J., argues in favor of a very strong commitment to the promotion of social justice at modern Catholic universities and attempts to interpret what this commitment could mean at such institutions. Fr. Privett's opinion that the commitment to social justice should be an integral part of every Catholic university is articulated very well in his statement: "Sensitivity and responsiveness to human suffering and a consequent passion for justice are essential elements of a contemporary humanism and, as such, these concerns must have a place in the curriculum of a Catholic and Jesuit university" (Privett, 2000, p. 54). He goes on to state that suffering millions must be a part of our conversation about the mission of the university and the goals of Jesuit education (Privett, 2000). Both of these statements suggest that Fr. Privett believes a Catholic university cannot exist without engaging in a concerted effort to fight

81

injustice and promote justice. Because a university primarily is composed of people —students, faculty, administrators, and staff—it is implicit in these statements that Fr. Privett believes the individuals who make up a Catholic university must be engaged in fighting injustice and promoting justice.

Fr. Privett also sheds some light on the types of activities that could constitute part of this commitment. For example, he states "[Jesuit education] must offer students a profound understanding of and sensitivity to the plight of those whom Franz Fanon named 'the wretched of the earth'" (Privett, 2000, p. 56). He also recommends that, "Immersion experiences in developing countries or our own inner cities are powerful means for 'acting' faculty and staff into new ways of thinking about their disciplines and responsibilities to the academic community" (Privett, 2000). However, as is evident in his philosophically stimulating and non-specific concluding sentence, Fr. Privett also does not have many other concrete ideas as to how a Catholic university could implement its commitment to social justice: "The challenge and the mission of Catholic education is to weave into the warp and woof of academic life the concerns and values of the Catholic tradition and thereby leaven society for good and offer a vibrantly distinctive pattern to American academic life" (Privett, 2000, p. 57).

As mentioned above, Fr. Privett is short on the specifics of what activities constitute engagement in the promotion of social justice, but he does offer examples of the types of attitudes and activities that certainly are consistent with this activity. For example, he states, "Civil engineers everywhere are taught how to construct bridges, dam rivers, and lay highways. Is it important for them to also learn how decisions are made about where and how such structures are built and whose interests they serve?" (Privett, 2000, p. 53). He is implying that a Catholic university education must go well beyond the technical training of a discipline. He implies that it must explore existential and spiritual issues related to the individual being educated when he writes, "The central curricular issues should not revolve around 'how much' English, Theology, Social Studies, Philosophy or Natural Science but how and who do we want our graduates to be in this world" (Privett, 2000, p. 54). These statements, supported on "the education of the whole person," another pillar of Jesuit education, warn about the types of educational traps modern universities (some Catholic ones included) have fallen into and which cannot be part of their structure if a Catholic university is to be engaged in the promotion of justice.

Loyola Marymount University's Commitment to Social Justice

Fr. Privett is not alone among prominent individuals in Catholic education who believe a strong commitment to social justice is central to the mission of Catholic universities. For example, Monika K. Hellwig, Professor of Theology at Georgetown University and Executive Director of the Association of Catholic Colleges and Universities, writes, "Catholicism in a Catholic university setting . . . should involve opportunities for students to become aware of those less fortunate than themselves, to develop compassion and a strong sense of social justice, and to come to accept the social responsibilities commensurate with their privileges" (Hellwig, 1995, p. 18). Another example comes from Peter-Hans Kolvenbach, S.J. (1985), Superior General of the Society of Jesus:

> Instead of seeing the promotion of justice in the name of the gospel as a threat to the educational sector, this apostolic priority that we have received from the Church should be seen as a pressing commitment to reevaluate our institutions, our teaching priorities, our programs and the people we attract to our schools. A university which does not see the necessity of that evaluation should not be surprised if it is left in splendid isolation, without anything very worthwhile to offer the world and the people of today. (Kolvenbach, 1985)

Views such as those presented herein lead to the conclusion that many individuals who have the authority to influence Catholic higher education believe that commitment to social justice should be strong.

Furthermore, one of the cornerstones of the university is its commitment to the Jesuit tradition. Historically, Jesuit institutions have taken their commitment to social justice very seriously. One can look at the rigorous analysis and calls for reform of the economic and political structures by Ignacio Ellacuría and other Jesuits and lay faculty at the Universidad Centroamericana (UCA) in El Salvador during the 1980s, and the admission of Jewish students by Loyola Law School in Los Angeles during the 1920s, as recent examples of this tradition (Engh, 2000). Thus, if Jesuit universities are to continue the Jesuit tradition of higher education, they must continue to work on the promotion of social justice.

Finally, arguably even more important than the views of well-respected individuals involved in Catholic higher education and the Jesuit tradition is one of Loyola Marymount University's goals and objectives: "Fostering a just society through a commitment to social justice and service" (*Mission, Goals and Objectives*, 1990). One can conclude that Loyola Marymount University cannot be a Jesuit institution of higher education and cannot be

faithful to its mission, goals, and objectives without a very strong commitment to the promotion of social justice.

Fulfilling its Commitment to Social Justice

Having established that Catholic higher education and Loyola Marymount University's commitment to social justice must be very strong, I will
address the challenge of finding and carrying out concrete and tangible
actions with which to carry out this commitment. The list presented herein
mainly will address policy the administration set so as to fulfill its goal of
promoting social justice. No specific examples of actions by students and
faculty that promote social justice are given because the activities that do
so number in the millions and should be chosen by individuals to match
interests, highlight strengths, maximize spiritual and educational growth,
and improve the world in which we live.

1.   An evaluation process of faculty that addresses contributions to the
Mission, Goals and Objectives of the University: Each year and at the time
of application for tenure and promotion, faculty members prepare a self-
evaluation that is used as the basis for assessing their performance as a
faculty member. This evaluation should require the faculty member to
address one simple question: How has your work contributed to the
Mission, Goals and Objectives of Loyola Marymount University?
Requiring each faculty member to contribute to the Mission of the
University and to the Society of Jesus is one of the educational ideals of St.
Ignatius Loyola: "In a Jesuit university, any faculty can function as long as
it contributes to the Society's general purpose" (Ganss, 1970). Having an
evaluation procedure in which each faculty member is required to describe
her/his contribution to the Mission is a necessity if the University indeed is
to have a faculty that contributes to the Society's general purpose.

2.   A program that awards faculty, on a competitive basis, LMU Summer
Social Justice Grants: The University already has a well-established and
very competitive internal summer research grant program. Using
endowment money given by the Rains Family, this program awards roughly
forty LMU faculty $3,500 grants to carry out research during the summer.
The positive impact the program has had on the University's academic
environment has been significant. Indeed, although it is difficult to get
precise statistics, Dr. Joseph Jabbra, Vice President for Academic Affairs,
reports each year, an increase in the number of scholarly publications and
presentations at professional forums by LMU faculty.
      If the University established a similar program where the focus was
work on issues of social justice instead of scholarly publication, it is clear

that it would motivate faculty to engage in activities that promote social justice. The opportunities for such work in the Los Angeles area are many, and designing a competitive grant process for taking advantage of these opportunities would be simple as there are many faculty on campus that could take the lead in designing the program.

The skeptic might argue that working on social justice issues is an activity that is motivated not by monetary support but by sincere interest and dedication. While this is most certainly true, today's economic demands on faculty are very real, and compensating faculty for fulfilling the University's Mission is not in contradiction with sincere interest and dedication. It in fact compliments it. One parallel example is compensating faculty for conducting research. Should faculty engage in research for monetary compensation or because of sincere interest and dedication? Compensating faculty for conducting research compliments their interest and desire to do so and has proven very successful already at Loyola Marymount University. It is a blueprint that easily could be adapted to promote work on social justice issues. Most likely, because of restrictions on the endowment, the Rains money could not be used to fund these social justice grants, but the University could prioritize finding a donor to make these funds available.

3.   Faculty sabbaticals to work on issues of social justice: As already pointed out, Privett suggests that faculty at Jesuit institutions could engage in immersion experiences in developing countries or our own inner cities with the aim of promoting social justice (Privett, 2000). Loyola Marymount University has a non-competitive sabbatical policy that allows faculty to take sabbaticals to engage in research/scholarly activity. The program relieves faculty, for one semester at full pay or one year at half pay, of their teaching responsibilities every seventh year so that they may work exclusively on an approved research project. The program could be expanded to allow faculty the possibility of taking sabbaticals to engage in work that promotes social justice. The administration could establish a procedure for approval of sabbatical social-justice projects similar to the one already in place. There would be no cost for this expansion of the current sabbatical program.

4.   A social-justice internship requirement for graduation: Some LMU academic departments require their majors to complete a community internship. For example, the Chicano Studies Department requires all its majors to complete Chicano Studies 485, Community Research Internship. Because of this requirement, Chicano Studies majors have worked in Latino/Chicano community organizations that are the pillars of their community and that work to promote social justice on a full-time basis.

The University administration could provide guidelines and incentives so that all academic departments institute a similar graduation requirement. Fr. Privett implies the necessity of engaging every undergraduate in social justice work, in the performative aspect to justice, without which all manner of academic deliberations may be judged sterile (Privett, 2000). A graduation requirement to perform community/social-justice work, tailored to each academic discipline, would be a means of "acting" students to understand and live out the guiding principles of the Thirty-Fourth General Congregation of the Society of Jesus and Loyola Marymount University's Mission.

5. Embarking on a concerted plan to lower tuition: In the sixteenth century, above the door of the Collegio Romano in Rome, one of the first Jesuit educational institutions, hung the famous inscription "School of Grammar, Humanities, and Christian Doctrine, Free." While the economic realities of our time make it nearly impossible to conceive a university that did not charge tuition, it is necessary that Jesuit institutions lower tuition if they truly are not going to "perpetuate the present division between the privileged and the excluded" (Kolvenbach, 1985).

The tuition and fees for an undergraduate entering Loyola Marymount University in the fall semester of 1998 were $17,208; and the budget for that student if s/he lived on campus was more than $24,000. For 1998, the United States Department of Health and Human Services defined that a family of four is "living in poverty" if their yearly household income below $16,450 (*Federal Register*, 1998, pp. 9235–9238). Thus, even if 100% of the income of a family of four living in poverty were to be used for tuition and fees, that family could not afford to send a child to Loyola Marymount University. (In this discussion, I do not take into account student financial aid.) The cost for one student to attend the university and live on campus is roughly 150% of the household income for a family of four living in poverty. Perhaps this would not be such a huge concern if the number of Americans living in poverty were insignificant. Unfortunately, this is not the case. For example, during 1997 the percentages of Latinos and African-Americans living in poverty were 27.1% and 26.5% respectively (Report CB–175, 1998). This means that for over one fourth of the Latino and African-American families in this country, not even 100% of their household income could pay for tuition and fees at Loyola Marymount University. The U.S. Census Bureau (1998) also reports that in 1997, 19.9% of all children in the country were living in poverty; this figure certainly implies that in the near future a college education at Loyola Marymount University is not a realistic option for about one-fifth of all people in this country.

In fact, an education at Loyola Marymount University is beyond the economic means of not just those living in poverty and not just those from specific ethnic groups. For example, the median household incomes in 1997 for African-Americans and Latinos were $25,050 and $26,628 respectively (Report CB–175, 1998). That is, 100% of the household income for an "average" African-American or Latino household barely would cover the budget for one student to attend Loyola Marymount University. The situation is not much better for the general population. The 1997 median household income in the United States was $38,972 (Report CB–175, 1998). After paying for one student to live on campus, a family at this economic level would have less than $15,000 for all other expenses.

This situation is unacceptable. Loyola Marymount University must set as a goal lowering tuition to a level such that an education at this institution, with the help of financial aid, is feasible to *any* student in the country. It is doubtful this goal will be achieved within the next few years (or even decades); nevertheless it should be one of the goals of the University if it is truly an institution that claims to be fighting for social justice. If an education at Loyola Marymount University is not within the economic means of the majority of the country, then the institution is itself perpetuating the present division between the privileged and the excluded.

Concluding Remarks

Loyola Marymount University is a Jesuit Marymount institution of higher education and as such must work to fulfill the mission and goals of the Society of Jesus and the Religious of the Sacred Heart of Mary. Among these goals is the promotion of social justice. The University has committed to promoting social justice in its *Mission, Goals and Objectives* but has yet to implement policy and programs that will do so. The concrete policy changes and programs that I offer in this paper can be a small part of the University's future endeavors in the promotion of social justice.

References

Engh, M.E., S.J. (2000). Just ones past and present at Loyola Marymount University. In M.K. McCullough (Ed.), *The just one justices: The role of justice at the heart of Catholic higher education* (pp. 21–36). Scranton, PA: University of Scranton Press.

Federal Register, Volume 63, No. 36. U.S. Government. Washington, D.C. (1998, February 24).

Ganss, G.E., S.J. (Ed.) (1970). *The constitutions of the Society of Jesus*. St. Louis, MO: The Institute of Jesuit Sources.

Hellwig, M. K. (1995, Fall). The best of times, the worst of times. *Conversations in Jesuit Higher Education*, 15–19.

Kolvenbach, P.H., S.J. (1985, November 5). Address to the directors or presidents of Jesuit institutions. *Acta Romana Societatis Jesu.*

Mission, Goals and Objectives (1990). Loyola Marymount University. Los Angeles, CA.

Privett, S., S.J. (2000). The Jesuit university and the struggle for justice. In M.K. McCullough (Ed.), *The just one justices: The role of justice at the heart of Catholic higher education* (pp. 49–58). Scranton, PA: University of Scranton Press.

Report CB–175. U.S. Census Bureau. Washington, D.C. (1998).

JUSTICE IN A DIFFERENT VOICE

Ellen Marie Keane, R.S.H.M.

The topic "Justice in a Different Voice" allows me the freedom to present this important topic in a conversational style, which will integrate my research interests with the dialogue of the Institute participants. The topic is an attempt to explore some of the questions in Ethics and Epistemology which have fascinated and engaged me since the late 1970s when I became acquainted with the feminist philosophies. By feminists I refer to people who attempt to change the social order in an attempt to create a more egalitarian society. Fisher (1988) provides the following definition of feminism:

> . . . a vision of life emphasizing inclusion rather than exclusion, connectedness rather than separateness and mutuality in relationships rather than dominance and submission. Feminism also entails the conviction that full individual development can take place only within a human community that is structured in Justice. And so, feminism works for social change. (p. 2)

The topic of feminism is also relevant to the Loyola Marymount University community which, as a former Trustee, I know to be resolutely student centered, and currently boasting a student enrollment which is 60% female. I am also heartened by the pledge the Jesuits made at their 1995 General Congregation to listen attentively to the voices of women and be receptive to feminist critiques in all disciplines. With each contributor to this volume I am committed to the value of Catholic Higher Education as a catalyst for the promotion of justice in a most practical way. What we really need to promote justice are people who live justice—not just talk about it. As Hopkins (1995) writes in his poem, "As Kingfishers Catch Fire," the just one justices, "I say more: the just man justices; Keeps grace: that keeps all his goings graces" (p. 115).

The title, "Justice in a Different Voice," is borrowed from the groundbreaking work of Carol Gilligan (1982), *In a Different Voice*, in which she listens to, records, and analyzes the voices of women as they struggle with moral decisions. Gilligan's work grew out of her discovery that the moral development studies conducted by Lawrence Kohlberg

(1981) were systematically conducted on men. Gilligan, a clinical psychologist, looked at the socialization process that encourages humans to act in different ways. She does not say that women and men are innately different, but that women generally undergo a developmental moral decision-making process which is distinct, yet parallel to that of men. Gilligan discovered that women add to the notion of justice a notion of care.

> In her articles and in her book, *In a Different Voice*, Gilligan has distinguished a morality of rights and formal reasoning, which she now labels the "justice perspective," from a morality of care and responsibility, the "care perspective." (Kittay & Meyers, 1987, p. 3)

The morality of rights described in the above passage is embodied in the familiar liberal tradition of Locke, Kant, and in recent times, Rawls. The morality is characterized by an autonomous moral agent who discovers and employs a set of fundamental rules through abstract reasoning. Carol Gilligan believes women are socialized to value an alternate set of moral concerns which form a morality of care described in the following passage:

> Here, the central preoccupation is a responsiveness to others that dictates providing care, preventing harm, and maintaining relationships. Gilligan believes that what we have here are two distinct domains of moral concern empirically linked to a gender difference. (Kittay & Meyers, 1987, p. 3)

Gilligan suggests that the morality of rights and formal reasoning typically dominates the moral development of men, as outlined in the research of Kohlberg (1981). Gilligan's discovery of the morality of caring adds to and eclipses the descriptions of moral development held previously. Correcting for this bias toward the male moral development calls for what is popularly known as a paradigm shift. According to Thomas Kuhn (1962), a paradigm shift is generated when an old way of thinking no longer accounts for the facts of experience; and this is what is currently happening in Philosophy. The paradigm shift, which calls for a shift from isolated learning to a connected learning, is also applicable to the work of this Institute as we think about the moral implications of Justice issues.

Questions about Justice have been a central focus on Western Philosophy and Theology. Like most Philosophy students, I was introduced to a serious discussion on Justice in Plato's *Republic*. For Plato, and Aristotle after him, the essential virtue for us, as social animals, is Justice. While students search in vain for a clear, unequivocal definition of Justice in Plato, what is immediately clear is what it is *not*. In one of the classic early exchanges in *The Republic*, the philosophical thug, Thrasymachus, argues the ultra-cynical line that justice always serves the interest of the rulers of the society, "the advantage of the stronger" (Hamilton, 1961). If you are an ordinary person, you are only hurting yourself by trying to live in accordance with justice.

This shocking thesis of the advantage of the stronger is refuted by Socrates: right is properly distinguished from mere might, and Thrasymachus walks off in a huff. In Thrasymachus's abandoned place, Glaucon suggests a more modest hypothesis, that justice is ultimately just a matter of self-interest, and people adhere to its conventions only to avoid punishment. Socrates takes this suggestion much more seriously, but he ultimately insists that justice is not merely a matter of convention and, in the vulgar sense intended, it is not a matter of self-interest either. Then Socrates spends the rest of the *Republic* taking us through a whirlwind of philosophical considerations as he speculates about metaphysics and human nature, praises some of the political ideals of ancient Greece, and introduces his own rather radical republicanism to show that justice must be counted as desirable for its own sake. He further insists that justice is harmony in the state, that justice is the rule of reason and, finally, that justice even "pays off" in the end, for the just man can ultimately suffer no harm, at least to his soul. However, given the definitions of justice Socrates does relay, what do we not get? What is it we thought we would get that we do not? We do not get anything like an adequate criterion concerning what sorts of considerations we should use in evaluating this or that social arrangement or rule.

The disconcerting reality is that so many of Plato's and Aristotle's questions still face us today. Are the current standards of justice ultimately in the interests of the stronger, more established and most powerful citizens? Answering this question presumes, of course, that there is an adequate answer to the original question of what justice is in the first place. Is it fairness? Is it equal treatment? It is getting one's due? Does justice depend on a particular content, social goals, or conventions? Is justice something bigger and more universal?

The question of justice is still on center stage in contemporary moral philosophy. In 1971, Harvard philosopher, John Rawls, published his epochal book, *A Theory of Justice*, and the old Socratic question has never been more alive. Following in the footsteps of Locke and Kant, the contemporary discussions about justice follow a social contract model and uphold the ideal of personal liberty. In this tradition, individual autonomy has two main dimensions: moral autonomy and personal autonomy. The individual is self-governing and thus still free, even when subject to regulations. Locke's list of natural rights, life, liberty, and property, though variously interpreted through the years, captures a constant of what Gilligan

(1982) calls, "the Justice tradition." People are entitled to noninterference. As a community of individuals searching for a common good, the bottom line is "do no harm."

As a branch of the broader liberal social contract tradition, Rawls also connects with Mill's Utilitarianism, when the greatest happiness of the greatest number comes into play. As Kittay and Meyers (1987) see it, both Mill and Mary Wollstonecraft's questions about women's equality are properly placed within this traditional justice tradition. This placement is close to the topic of "justice in a different voice" because Kohlberg's theories of moral development reverse this line of thought and call into question the maturity of women's moral judgment.

In Kohlberg's (1981) scheme, women test out as morally inferior to men because they tend to see moral problems as embedded in a contextual frame that eludes abstract, deductive reasoning. For many of the women studied by Gilligan (1982), making moral decisions required not so much a deductive employment of general principles, but a strategy that aimed to maintain ties where possible without sacrificing the integrity of the self. The question becomes one of discerning whether this connective approach is a moral deficiency or perhaps simply a different approach of commensurate moral worth. Theorists who follow Gilligan usually refer to their position as illustrative of a perspective of care as distinguished from the Rawlsian justice perspective.

Without enumerating the intricate arguments which Rawls advances, it is important to point out that his theory begins as all contract theories do, by construing society as an association of equals, conceived as individuals who are more or less equal in their ability to compete for the benefits of social cooperation. However, "all persons" would include the formerly disenfranchised, such as women and all people of color. It would also include people with special needs, who are dependent in basic ways, such as children, the disabled, and the frail elderly. In traditional Western Philosophy, the rights and needs of these classes of dependent persons are generally dealt with as a private, domestic issue, and therefore, not properly part of the public, political domain. This private venue sometimes renders their position and needs virtually invisible to those who determine public policy.

The individualism championed in the theory of rights and political liberties creates a conceptual illusion that dependents do not exist, or at least are not a political matter. As some writers point out, this makes it appear that the extension of equality to all, not only to heads of households, is an easy matter. Simply treat everyone equally. To create a level playing field sounds like an easy solution. This seemingly simple matter depends entirely on who the "everybody" includes.

The Ethics of Justice holds that we should blindfold ourselves, as Rawls suggests, by donning a "veil of ignorance." In other words, one is to resolve moral conflict without considering who the people actually are or what roles they might occupy in reality. In this way, decisions will not be swayed by inequalities, self-interest, and/or personal relationship that might give any one person undue advantage over another.

While this ingenious scheme speaks eloquently to the ideal of treating all people fairly, it does not answer another set of questions: Equal to whom? Who sets the standard? Who decides what is deviant? What about the people standing in the shadows? It is these questions that Annette Baier (1994) addresses in her book *Moral Prejudices*. In Chapter 2, "The Need for More Than Justice," she compares the two perspectives of "justice" and "care." Baier points out, and I agree, how easy it is to exaggerate the differences between the two approaches, and how she wants to avoid doing this. The goal is to be inclusive, and build a good moral theory which places care on an equal footing with justice.

Merging the ethic of justice with the ethic of care gives us two good perspectives to put on moral issues. The liberal orthodoxy in moral theory presents its adherents with many challenges, four of which are pointed out by Baier (1994):

1.   A focus on individualism, where noninterference sometimes leads to neglect and the justification of exploitation and oppression (p. 24).
2.   A habit of inattention to relations of inequality. How do I relate to those not equal in power? What is the need for attention to relations of inequality and dependence in society (p. 28)?
3.   An exaggeration of the scope of choice in moral decision making. The paradigm of contrasting ideas of love and commitment (p. 29).
4.   A practice of excessive rationalism and denigration of the role of emotion. A need to add the role of emotion and affect into moral decision making (p. 30).

Conclusion

As Baier concludes her article with a plea for the marriage of the justice and care perspectives, so do I. I am convinced that separating justice from care and love diminishes both. Justice without care can become cold and harsh. Care without justice is easily sentimentalized and trivialized. Indeed we see social workers today calling for "tough love," clearly a combination of these two approaches. We also see women calling for a combination of an ethic of justice and an ethic of care through feminism.

Justice and care are different but complementary aspects of morality. Each has instinctive aims that deal with issues not well covered by the other. The so-called "rights" mode, for example, provides principles for treating people as if they were equals, while the "responsibility" mode outlines principles for supporting individuals' development so that they might become capable of participation in society on an equal basis. Both are needed by all of us. We will suffer from fewer blind spots if we move back and forth, like a reversing figure-ground picture, between the two. Any institution or relation, no matter how public or private, can be judged from the perspectives of justice and of care. Each approach illuminates different aspects of the issues in very different and interesting ways. If the combination of these two perspectives formed our tradition, would it have taken so long to see "domestic violence" as much more than just a "private" spat that the public authorities should ignore?

Finally, my dream is that in learning to integrate these two approaches or voices, we may begin to move toward a future less individualistic and violent and more interdependent. No movement goes forward without the radicals. The first phase of the feminist movement, typical of most revolutions, set up as the goal: independence and autonomy. Now that at least some of us have achieved this goal, we need to turn our attention toward building a world where mutuality and interdependence become the norm. According to Baier (1994), "The best moral theory has to be a cooperative product of women and men, has to harmonize justice and care" (p. 118). We are talking about a huge transformation of society as we know it.

References

Baier, A. (1994). *Moral prejudices*. Cambridge, MA: Harvard University Press.

Belenky, M. F., Clinchy, B. M., Goldberger, N. R., & Tarule, J. M. (1966). *Women's ways of knowing*. New York, NY: BasicBooks, Inc.

Belenky, M. F., Clinchy, B. M., Goldberger, N. R., & Tarule, J. M. (1997). *A tradition that has no name*. New York, NY: BasicBooks, Inc.

Byrne, P, (1995, Spring). Paradigms of justice and love. *Conversations*.

Fisher, K. (1988). *Woman at the well* (E. Rabkin, Ed.). New Jersey: Paulist Press.

Glaspell, S. (1912). Trifles. In E.S. Rabkin (Ed.) (1993), *Masks and other works*. Ann Arbor: The University of Michigan Press.

Gilligan, C. (1982). *In a different voice: Psychological theory and women's development*. Cambridge, MA: Harvard University Press.

Goldberger, N. R., Belenky, M. F., Clinchy, B. M., & Tarule, J. M. (1996). *Knowledge, difference, and power*. New York, NY: BasicBooks, Inc.

Haughay, J. (1977). *The faith that does justice*. New Jersey: Paulist Press.

Hamilton, E. (Ed.) (1961). *The collected dialogues of Plato: The Republic* (P. Shorey, Trans.). New Jersey: Princeton University Press.

Held, V. (Ed.) (1995). *Justice and care: Essential readings in feminist ethics*. Colorado: Westview Press.

Hopkins, G.M., S.J. (1995). As kingfishers catch fire. In C. Phillips (Ed.), *Gerard Manley Hopkins* (p. 115). New York, NY: Oxford University Press.

Kittay, E. F., & Meyers, D. (1987). *Women and moral theory*. Maryland: Rowman and Littlefield Publishers.

Kohlberg, L. (1981). *Essays in moral development*. New York, NY: Harper & Row.

Kuhn, T. (1962). *The structure of scientific revolution*. Chicago: University of Chicago Press.

Miller, J. B. (1976). *Towards a new psychology of women*. Boston, MA: Beacon Press.

Noddings, N. (1984). *Caring*. Berkeley, CA: University of California Press.

Okin, S. M. (1979). *Women in western political thought*. Princeton, NJ: Princeton University Press.

Okin, S. M. (1989). *Justice, gender and the family*. New York, NY: BasicBooks, Inc.

Osborne, M. L. (Ed.) (1979). *Women in western thought*. New York, NY: Random House.

Rawls, J. (1971). *A theory of justice*. Cambridge, MA: Harvard University Press.

Rawls, J. (1993). *Political liberalism*. New York, NY: Columbia University Press.

Schott, R. M. (1977). *Feminist interpretations of Immanuel Kant*. University Park, PA: Penn State Press.

Snow, N. (Ed.). (1966). *In the company of others*. MO: Rowman & Littlefield.

Solomon, R., & Murphy, M. (Eds.) (1990). *What is justice*. England: Oxford University Press.

Young, I. (1990). *Justice and the politics of difference*. Princeton, NJ: Princeton University Press.

TRIFLES

Susan Glaspell

Characters

GEORGE HENDERSON, County Attorney
MRS. PETERS
MRS. HALE
HENRY PETERS, Sheriff
LEWIS HALE, A Neighboring Farmer

SCENE

The kitchen in the now abandoned farmhouse of JOHN WRIGHT, *a gloomy kitchen, and left without having been put in order—unwashed pans under the sink, a loaf of bread outside the breadbox, a dish towel on the table— other signs of incompleted work. At the rear the outer door opens and the* SHERIFF *comes in followed by the* COUNTY ATTORNEY *and* HALE. *The* SHERIFF *and* HALE *are men in middle life, the* COUNTY ATTORNEY *is a young man; all are much bundled up and go at once to the stove. They are followed by two women—the* SHERIFF'S *wife first; she is a slight wiry woman, a thin nervous face.* MRS. HALE *is larger and would ordinarily be called more comfortable looking, but she is disturbed now and looks fearfully about as she enters. The women have come in slowly, and stand close together near the door.*

COUNTY ATTORNEY. [*Rubbing his hands.*] This feels good. Come up to the fire, ladies.

MRS. PETERS. [*After taking a step forward.*] I'm not—cold.

SHERIFF. [*Unbuttoning his overcoat and stepping away from the stove as if to mark the beginning of official business.*] Now, Mr. Hale, before we move things about, you explain to Mr. Henderson just what you saw when you came here yesterday morning.

COUNTY ATTORNEY. By the way, has anything been moved? Are things just as you left them yesterday?

SHERIFF. [*Looking about.*] It's just the same. When it dropped below zero last night, I thought I'd better send Frank out this morning to make a fire for us—no use getting pneumonia with a big case on, but I told him not to touch anything except the stove—and you know Frank.

COUNTY ATTORNEY. Somebody should have been left here yesterday.

SHERIFF. Oh—yesterday. When I had to send Frank to Morris Center for that man who went crazy—I want you to know I had my hands full yesterday, I knew you could get back from Omaha by today and as long as I went over everything here myself—

COUNTY ATTORNEY. Well, Mr. Hale, tell just what happened when you came here yesterday morning.

HALE. Harry and I had started to town with a load of potatoes. We came along the road from my place and as I got here I said, "I'm going to see if I can't get John Wright to go in with me on a party telephone." I spoke to Wright about it once before and he put me off, saying folks talked too much anyway, and all he asked was peace and quiet—I guess you know about how much he talked himself; but I thought maybe if I went to the house and talked about it before his wife, though I said to Harry that I didn't know as what his wife wanted made much difference to John—

COUNTY ATTORNEY. Let's talk about that later, Mr. Hale. I do want to talk about that, but tell now just what happened when you got to the house.

HALE. I didn't hear or see anything; I knocked at the door, and still it was all quiet inside. I knew they must be up, it was past eight o'clock. So I knocked again, and I thought I heard somebody say, "Come in." I wasn't sure, I'm not sure yet, but I opened the door—this door [*Indicating the door by which the two women are still standing.*] and there in that rocker—[*Pointing to it*] says Mrs. Wright.

[*They all look at the rocker.*]

COUNTY ATTORNEY. What—was she doing?

HALE. She was rockin' back and forth. She had her apron in her hand and was kind of—pleating it.

COUNTY ATTORNEY. And how did she—look?

HALE. Well, she looked queer.

COUNTY ATTORNEY. How do you mean—queer?

HALE. Well, as if she didn't know what she was going to do next. And kind of done up.

COUNTY ATTORNEY. How did she seem to feel about your coming?

HALE. Why, I don't think she minded—one way or other. She didn't pay much attention. I said, "How do, Mrs. Wright, it's cold, ain't it?" And she said, "Is it?"—and went on kind of pleating at her apron. Well, I was surprised; she didn't ask me to come up to the stove, or to set down, but just sat there, not even looking at me, so I said, "I want to see John." And then she—laughed. I guess you would call it a laugh. I thought of Harry and the team outside, so I said a little sharp: "Can't I see John?" "No," she says, kind o' dull like. "Ain't he home?" says I. "Yes," says she, "he's home." "Then why can't I see him?" I asked her, out of patience. "'Cause he's dead," says she. "*Dead?*" says I. She just nodded her head, not getting a bit excited, but rockin' back and forth. "Why—where is he?" says I, not knowing what to say. She just pointed upstairs—like that. [*Himself pointing to the room above.*] I got up, with the idea of going up there. I walked from there to here—then I says, "Why, what did he died of?" "He died of a rope round his neck," says she, and just went on pleatin' at her apron. Well, I went out and called Harry. I thought I might—need help. We went upstairs and there he was lyin'—

COUNTY ATTORNEY. I think I'd rather have you go into that upstairs, where you can point it all out. Just go on now with the rest of the story.

HALE. Well, my first thought was to get that rope off. It looked . . . [*Stops, his face twitches.*] . . . but Harry, he went up to him, and he said, "No, he's dead all right and we'd better not touch anything." So we went back downstairs. She was still sitting that same way. "Has anybody been notified?" I asked. "No," says she, unconcerned. "Who did this, Mrs. Wright?" said Harry. He said it businesslike—and she stopped pleatin' of her apron. "I don't know," she says. "You don't *know?*" says Harry. "No," says she. "Weren't you sleepin' in the bed with him?" says Harry. "Yes," says she, "but I was on the inside." "Somebody slipped a rope round his neck and strangled him and you didn't wake up?" says Harry. "I didn't wake up," she said after him. We must'a looked as if we didn't see how that could be, for after a minute she said, "I sleep sound." Harry was going to ask her more questions, but I said maybe we ought to let her tell her story first to the coroner, or the sheriff, so Harry went fast as he could to Rivers's place, where there's a telephone.

COUNTY ATTORNEY. And what did Mrs. Wright do when she knew that you had gone for the coroner?

HALE. She moved from that chair to this one over here [*Pointing to a small chair in the corner.*] and just sat there with her hands held together and looking down. I got a feeling that I ought to make some conversation, so I said I had come in to see if John wanted to put in a telephone, and at that she started to laugh, and then she stopped and looked at me—scared. [*The* COUNTY ATTORNEY, *who has had his notebook out, makes a note.*] I dunno, maybe it wasn't scared. I wouldn't like to say it was. Soon Harry got back, and then Dr. Lloyd came, and you, Mr. Peters, and so I guess that's all I know that you don't.

COUNTY ATTORNEY. [*Looking around.*] I guess we'll go upstairs first —and then out to the barn and around there. [*To the* SHERIFF] You're convinced that there was nothing important here—nothing that would point to any motive.

SHERIFF. Nothing here but kitchen things. [*The* COUNTY ATTORNEY, *after again looking around the kitchen, opens the door of a cupboard closet. He gets up on a chair and looks on a shelf. Pulls his hand away sticky.*]

COUNTY ATTORNEY. Here's a nice mess.

[*The women draw near.*]

MRS. PETERS. [*To the other woman.*] Oh, her fruit; it did freeze. [*To the* COUNTY ATTORNEY] She worried about that when it turned so cold. She said the fire'd go out and her jars would break.

SHERIFF. Well, can you beat the women! Held for murder and worryin' about her preserves.

COUNTY ATTORNEY. I guess before we're through she may have something more serious than preserves to worry about.

HALE. Well, women are used to worrying over trifles.

[*The two women move a little closer together.*]

COUNTY ATTORNEY. [*With the gallantry of a young politician.*] And yet for all their worries, what would we do without the ladies? [*The women do not unbend. He goes to the sink, takes a dipperful of water from the pail, and pouring it into a basin, washes his hands. Starts to wipe them on the roller towel, turns it for a cleaner place.*] Dirty towel! [*Kicks his foot against the pans under the sink.*] Not much of a housekeeper, would you say, ladies?

MRS. HALE. [*Stiffly.*] There's a great deal of work to be done on a farm.

COUNTY ATTORNEY. To be sure. And yet [*With a little bow to her.*] I know there are some Dickson County farmhouses which do not have such roller towels.

[*He gives it a pull to expose its full length again.*]

MRS. HALE. Those towels get dirty awful quick. Men's hands aren't always as clean as they might be.

COUNTY ATTORNEY. Ah, loyal to your sex, I see. But you and Mrs. Wright were neighbors. I suppose you were friends, too.

MRS. HALE. [*Shaking her head.*] I've not seen much of her of late years. I've not been in this house—it's more than a year.

COUNTY ATTORNEY. And why was that? You didn't like her?

MRS. HALE. I liked her all well enough. Farmers' wives have their hands full, Mr. Henderson. And—then—

COUNT ATTORNEY. Yes—?

MRS. HALE. [Looking about.] It never seemed a very cheerful place.

COUNTY ATTORNEY. No—it's not cheerful. I shouldn't say she had the homemaking instinct.

MRS. HALE. Well, I don't know as Wright had, either.

COUNTY ATTORNEY. You mean that they didn't get on very well?

MRS. HALE. No, I don't mean anything. But I don't think a place'd be any cheerfuler for John Wright's being in it.

COUNTY ATTORNEY. I'd like to talk more of that a little later. I want to get the lay of things upstairs now.

[*He goes to the left, where three steps lead to a stair door.*]

SHERIFF. I suppose anything Mrs. Peter does'll be all right. She was to take in some clothes for her, you know, and a few little things. We left in such a hurry yesterday.

COUNTY ATTORNEY. Yes, but I would like to see what you take, Mrs. Peters, and keep an eye out for anything that might be of use to us.

MRS. PETERS. Yes, Mr. Henderson.

[*The women listen to the men's steps on the stairs, then look about the kitchen.*]

MRS. HALE. I'd hate to have men coming into my kitchen, snooping around and criticizing.

[*She arranges the pans under the sink which the* COUNTY ATTORNEY *had shoved out of place.*]

MRS. PETERS. Of course it's no more than their duty.

MRS. HALE. Duty's all right, but I guess that deputy sheriff that came out to make the fire might have got a little of this on. [*Gives the roller towel a pull.*] Wish I'd thought of that sooner. Seems mean to talk about her for not having things slicked up when she had to come away in such a hurry.

MRS. PETERS. [*Who has gone to a small table in the left rear corner of the room, and lifted one end of a towel that covers a pan.*] She had bread set.

[*Stands still.*]

MRS. HALE. [*Eyes fixed on a loaf of bread beside the breadbox, which is on a low shelf at the other side of the room. Moves slowly toward it.*] She was going to put this in there. [*Picks up loaf, then abruptly drops it. In a manner of returning to familiar things.*] It's a shame about her fruit. I wonder if it's all gone. [*Gets up on the chair and looks.*] I think there's some here that's all right, Mrs. Peters. Yes—here; [*Holding it toward the window.*] this is cherries, too. [*Looking again.*] I declare I believe that's the only one. [*Gets down, bottle in her hand, goes to the sink and wipes if off on the outside.*] She'll feel awful bad after all her hard work in the hot weather. I remember the afternoon I put up my cherries last summer.

[*She puts the bottle on the big kitchen table, center of the room. With a sigh, is about to sit down in the rocking—chair. Before she is seated, realizes what chair it is; with a slow look at it, steps back. The chair which she has touched rocks back and forth.*]

MRS. PETERS. Well, I must get those things from the front room closet. [*She goes to the door at the right, but after looking into the other room, steps back.*] You coming with me, Mrs. Hale? You could help me carry them.

[*They go in the other room; reappear,* MRS. PETERS *carrying a dress and skirt,* MRS. HALE *following with a pair of shoes.*]

MRS. PETERS. My, it's cold in there.

[*She puts the clothes on the big table, and hurries to the stove.*]

MRS. HALE. [*Examining her skirt.*] Wright was close. I think maybe that's why she kept so much to herself. She didn't even belong to the Ladies Aid. I suppose she felt she couldn't do her part, and then you don't enjoy things when you feel shabby. She used to wear pretty clothes and be lively, when she was Minnie Foster, one of the town girls singing in the choir. But that—oh, that was thirty years ago. This all you was to take in?

MRS. PETERS. She said she wanted an apron. Funny thing to want, for there isn't much to get you dirty in jail, goodness knows. But I suppose just to make her feel more natural. She said they was in the top drawer in this cupboard. Yes, here. And then her little shawl that always hung behind the door. [*Opens stair door and looks.*] Yes, here it is.

[*Quickly shuts door leading upstairs.*]

MRS. HALE. [*Abruptly moving toward her.*] Mrs. Peters?

MRS. PETERS. Yes, Mrs. Hale?

MRS. HALE. Do you think she did it?

MRS. PETERS. [*In a frightened voice.*] Oh, I don't know.

MRS. HALE. Well I don't think she did. Asking for an apron and her little shawl. Worrying about her fruit.

MRS. PETERS. [*Starts to speak, glances up, where footsteps are heard in the room above. In a low voice.*] Mr. Peters says it looks bad for her. Mr. Henderson is awful sarcastic in a speech and he'll make fun of her sayin' she didn't wake up.

MRS. HALE. Well, I guess John Wright didn't wake when they was slipping that rope under his neck.

MRS. PETERS. No, it's strange. It must have been done awful crafty and still. They say it was such a—funny way to kill a man, rigging it all up like that.

MRS. HALE. That's just what Mr. Hale said. There was a gun in the house. He says that's what he can't understand.

MRS. PETERS. Mr. Henderson said coming out that what was needed for the case was a motive; something to show anger or—sudden feeling.

MRS. HALE. [*Who is standing by the table.*] Well, I don't see any signs of anger around here. [*She puts her hand on the dish towel which lies on the table, stands looking down at the table, one-half of which is clean, the other half messy.*] It's wiped to here. [*Makes a move as if to finish work, then turns and looks at loaf of bread outside the breadbox. Drops towel. In that voice of coming back to familiar things.*] Wonder how they are finding things upstairs. I hope she had it a little more red-up up there. You know, it seems kind of *sneaking*. Locking her up in town and then coming out here and trying to get her own house to turn against her!

MRS. PETERS. But Mrs. Hale, the law is the law.

MRS. HALE. I s'pose 'tis. [*Unbuttoning her coat.*] Better loosen up your things, Mrs. Peters. You won't feel them when you go out.

[MRS. PETERS *takes off her fur tippet, goes to hang it on hook at back of room, stands looking at the under part of the small corner table.*]

MRS. PETERS. She was piecing a quilt.

[*She brings the large sewing basket and they look at the bright pieces.*]

MRS. HALE. It's log cabin pattern. Pretty, isn't it? I wonder if she was goin' to quilt it or just knot it?

[*Footsteps have been heard coming down the stairs. The* SHERIFF *enters followed by* HALE *and the* COUNTY ATTORNEY.]

SHERIFF. They wonder if she was going to quilt it or just knot it!

[*The men laugh; the women look abashed.*]

COUNTY ATTORNEY. [*Rubbing his hand over the stove.*] Frank's fire didn't do much up there, did it? Well, let's go out to the barn and get that cleared up.

[*The men go outside.*]

MRS. HALE. [*Resentfully.*] I don't know as there's anything so strange, our takin' up our time with little things while we're waiting for them to get the evidence. [*She sits down at the big table smoothing out a block with decision.*] I don't see as it's anything to laugh about.

MRS. PETERS. [*Apologetically.*] Of course they've got awful important things on their minds.

[*Pulls up a chair and joins* MRS. HALE *at the table.*]

MRS. HALE. [*Examining another block.*] Mrs. Peters, look at this one. Here, this is the one she was working on, and look at the sewing! All the rest of it has been so nice and even. And look at this! It's all over the place! Why it looks as if she didn't know what she was about! [*After she has said this, they look at each other, then start to glance back at the door. After an instant,* MRS. HALE *has pulled at a knot and ripped the sewing.*]

MRS. PETERS. Oh, what are you doing, Mrs. Hale?

MRS. HALE. [*Mildly.*] Just pulling out a stitch or two that's not sewed very good. [*Threading a needle.*] Bad sewing always made me fidgety.

MRS. PETERS. [*Nervously.*] I don't think we ought to touch things.

MRS. HALE. I'll just finish up this end. [*Suddenly stopping and leaning forward.*] Mrs. Peters?

MRS. PETERS. Yes, Mrs. Hale?

MRS. HALE. What do you suppose she was so nervous about?

MRS. PETERS. Oh—I don't know. I don't know as she was nervous. I sometimes sew awful queer when I'm just tired. [MRS. HALE *starts to say something, looks at* MRS. PETERS, *then goes on sewing.*] Well, I must get these things wrapped up. They may be through sooner than we think. [*Putting apron and other things together.*] I wonder where I can find a piece of paper, and string.

MRS. HALE. In that cupboard, maybe.

MRS. PETERS. [*Looking in cupboard.*] Why, here's a birdcage. [*Holds it up.*] Did she have a bird, Mrs. Hale?

MRS. HALE. Why, I don't know whether she did or not—I've not been here for so long. There was a man around last year selling canaries cheap, but I don't know as she took one; maybe she did. She used to sing real pretty herself.

MRS. PETERS. [*Glancing around.*] Seems funny to think of a bird here. But she must have had one, or why would she have a cage? I wonder what happened to it.

MRS. HALE. I s'pose maybe the cat got it.

MRS. PETERS. No, she didn't have a cat. She's got that feeling some people have about cats—being afraid of them. My cat got in her room and she was real upset and asked me to take it out.

MRS. HALE. My sister Bessie was like that. Queer, ain't it?

MRS. PETERS. [*Examining the cage.*] Why, look at this door. It's broke. One hinge is pulled apart.

MRS. HALE [*Looking too.*] Looks as if someone must have been rough with it.

MRS. PETERS. Why, yes.

[*She brings the cage forward and puts it on the table.*]

MRS. HALE. I wish if they're going to find any evidence they'd be about it. I don't like this place.

MRS. PETERS. But I'm awful glad you came with me, Mrs. Hale. It would be lonesome for me sitting here alone.

MRS. HALE. It would, wouldn't it? [*Dropping her sewing.*] But I tell you what I do wish, Mrs. Peters. I wish I had come over sometimes when she was here. I—[*Looking around the room.*]—wish I had.

MRS. PETERS. But of course you were awful busy, Mrs. Hale—your house and your children.

MRS. HALE. I could've come. I stayed away because it weren't cheerful—and that's why I ought to have come. I—I've never liked this place. Maybe because it's down in a hollow and you don't see the road. I dunno what it is, but it's a lonesome place and always was. I wish I had come over to see Minnie Foster sometimes. I can see now—[*Shakes her head.*]

MRS. PETERS. Well, you mustn't reproach yourself, Mrs. Hale. Somehow we just don't see how it is with other folks until—something comes up.

MRS. HALE. Not having children makes less work—but it makes a quiet house, and Wright out to work all day and no company when he did come in. Did you know John Wright, Mrs. Peters?

MRS. PETERS. Not to know him; I've seen him in town. They say he was a good man.

MRS. HALE. Yes—good; he didn't drink, and kept his word as well as most, I guess, and paid his debts. But he was a hard man, Mrs. Peters. Just to pass the time of day with him—[*Shivers.*] Like a raw wind that gets to the bone. [*Pauses, her eye falling on the cage.*] I should think she would a wanted a bird. But what do you suppose went with it?

MRS. PETERS. I don't know, unless it got sick and died.

[*She reaches over and swings the broken door, swings it again. Both women watch it.*]

MRS. HALE. You weren't raised 'round here, were you? [MRS. PETERS *shakes her head.*] You didn't know—her?

MRS. PETERS. Not till they brought her yesterday.

MRS. HALE. She—come to think of it, she was kind of like a bird herself—real sweet and pretty, but kind of timid and—fluttery. How—she —did—change. [*Silence; then as if struck by a happy thought and relieved to get back to everyday things.*] Tell you what, Mrs. Peters, why don't you take the quilt in with you? It might take up her mind.

MRS. PETERS. Why, I think that's a real nice idea, Mrs. Hale. There couldn't possibly be any objection to it, could there? Now, just what would I take? I wonder if her patches are in here—and her things. [*They look in the sewing basket.*]

MRS. HALE. Here's some red. I expect this has got sewing things in it. [*Brings out a fancy box.*] What a pretty box. Looks like something somebody would give you. Maybe her scissors are in here. [*Opens box. Suddenly puts her hand to her nose.*] Why— [MRS. PETERS *bends nearer, then turns her face away.*] There's something wrapped up in this piece of silk.

MRS. PETERS. Why, this isn't her scissors.

MRS. HALE. [*Lifting the silk.*] Oh, Mrs. Peters—it's—

[MRS. PETERS *bends closer.*]

MRS. PETERS. It's the bird.

MRS. HALE. [*Jumping up.*] But, Mrs. Peters—look at it! Its neck! Look at its neck! It's all—other side *too.*

MRS. PETERS. Somebody—wrung—its—neck.

[*Their eyes meet. A look of growing comprehension, of horror. Steps are heard outside.* MRS. HALE *slips box under quilt pieces, and sinks into her chair. Enter* SHERIFF *and* COUNTY ATTORNEY. MRS. PETERS *rises.*]

COUNTY ATTORNEY. [*As one turning from serious things to little pleasantries.*] Well, that's interesting, I'm sure. [*Seeing the birdcage.*] Has the bird flown?

MRS. HALE. [*Putting more quilt pieces over the box.*] We think the—cat got it.

COUNTY ATTORNEY. [*Preoccupied.*] Is there a cat?

[MRS. HALE *glances in a quick covert way at* MRS. PETERS.]

MRS. PETERS. Well, not *now*. They're superstitious, you know. They leave.

COUNTY ATTORNEY. [*To* SHERIFF PETERS, *continuing an interrupted conversation.*] No sign at all of any one having come from the outside. Their own rope. Now let's go up again and go over it piece by piece. [*They start upstairs.*] It would have to have been someone who knew just the—[MRS. PETERS *sits down. The two women sit there not looking at one another, but as if peering into something and at the same time holding back. When they talk now it is in the manner of feeling their way over strange ground, as if afraid of what they are saying, but as if they cannot help saying it.*]

MRS. HALE. She liked the bird. She was going to bury it in that pretty box.

MRS. PETERS. [*In a whisper.*] When I was a girl—my kitten—there was a boy took a hatchet, and before my eyes—and before I could get there—[*Covers her face an instant.*] If they hadn't held me back I would have—[*Catches herself, looks upstairs where steps are heard, falters weakly.*]—hurt him.

MRS. HALE. [*with a slow look around her.*] I wonder how it would seem never to have had any children around. [*Pause.*] No, Wright wouldn't like the bird—a thing that sang. She used to sing. He killed that, too.

MRS. PETERS. [*Moving uneasily.*] We don't know who killed the bird.

MRS. HALE. I knew John Wright.

MRS. PETERS. It was an awful thing was done in this house that night, Mrs. Hale. Killing a man while he slept, slipping a rope around his neck that choked the life out of him.

MRS. HALE. His neck. Choked the life out of him.

[*Her hand goes out and rests on the birdcage.*]

MRS. PETERS [*With rising voice.*] We don't know who killed him. We don't *know*.

MRS. HALE. [*Her own feeling not interrupted.*] If there'd been years and years of nothing, then a bird to sing to, it would be awful—till, after the bird was still.

MRS. PETERS. [*Something within her speaking.*] I know what stillness is. When we homesteaded in Dakota, and my first baby died—after he was two years old, and me with no other then—

MRS. HALE. [*Moving.*] How soon do you suppose they'll be through, looking for the evidence?

MRS. PETERS. I know what stillness is. [*Pulling herself back.*] The law has got to punish crime, Mrs. Hale.

MRS. HALE. [*Not as if answering that.*] I wish you'd seen Minnie Foster when she wore a white dress with blue ribbons and stood up there in the choir and sang. [*A look around the room.*] Oh, I *wish* I'd come over here once in a while! That was a crime! That was a crime! Who's going to punish that?

MRS. PETERS. [*Looking upstairs.*] We mustn't—take on.

MRS. HALE. I might have known she needed help! I know how things can be—for women. I tell you, it's queer, Mrs. Peters. We live close together and we live far apart. We all go through the same things—it's all just a different kind of the same thing. [*Brushes her eyes; noticing the bottle of fruit, reaches out for it.*] If I was you, wouldn't tell her her fruit was gone. Tell her it *ain't*. Tell her it's all right. Take this in to prove it to her. She—she may never know whether it was broke or not.

MRS. PETERS. [*Takes the bottle, looks about for something to wrap it in; takes petticoat from the clothes brought from the other room, very nervously begins winding this around the bottle. In a false voice.*] My, it's a good thing the men couldn't hear us. Wouldn't they just laugh! Getting all stirred up over a little thing like a dead canary. As if that could have anything to do with—wouldn't they *laugh*!

[*The men are heard coming downstairs.*]

MRS. HALE. [*Under her breath.*] Maybe they would—maybe they wouldn't.

COUNTY ATTORNEY. No, Peters, it's all perfectly clear except a reason for doing it. But you know juries when it comes to women. If there was some definite thing. Something to show—something to make a story about —anything that would connect up with this strange way of doing it—

[*The women's eyes meet for an instant. Enter* HALE *from outer door.*]

HALE. Well, I've got the team around. Pretty cold out there.

COUNTY ATTORNEY. I'm going to stay here a while by myself. [*To the* SHERIFF.] You can send Frank out for me, can't you? I want to go over everything. I'm not satisfied that we can't do better.

SHERIFF. Do you want to see what Mrs. Peters is going to take in?

[*The* COUNTY ATTORNEY *goes to the table, picks up the apron, laughs.*]

COUNTY ATTORNEY. Oh, I guess they're not very dangerous things the ladies have picked out. [*Moves a few things about, disturbing the quilt pieces that cover the box. Steps back.*] No, Mrs. Peters doesn't need supervising. For that matter, a sheriff's wife is married to the law. Ever think of it that way, Mrs. Peters?

MRS. PETERS. Not—just that way.

SHERIFF. [*Chuckling.*] Married to the law. [*Moves toward the other room.*] I just want you to come in here a minute, George. We ought to take a look at these windows.

COUNTY ATTORNEY. [*Scoffingly.*] Oh, windows!

SHERIFF. We'll be right out, Mr. Hale.

[HALE *goes outside. The* SHERIFF *follows the* COUNTY ATTORNEY *into the other room. Then* MRS. HALE *rises, hands tight together, looking intensely at* MRS PETERS, *whose eyes make a slow turn, finally meeting* MRS. HALE's. *A moment* MRS. HALE *holds her, then her own eyes point the way to where the box is concealed. Suddenly* MRS. PETERS *throws back quilt pieces and tries to put the box in the bag she is wearing. It is too big. She opens box, starts to take bird out, cannot touch it, goes to pieces, stands there helpless. Sound of a knob turning in the other room.* MRS. HALE *snatches the box and puts it in the pocket of her big coat. Enter* COUNTY ATTORNEY *and* SHERIFF.]

COUNTY ATTORNEY. [*Facetiously*.] Well, Henry, at least we found out that she was not going to quilt it. She was going to—what is it you call it, ladies?

MRS. HALE. [*Her hand against her pocket*.] We call it—knot it, Mr. Henderson.

CURTAIN

THE JUST MAN/WOMAN:
A (SELFISH) PERSPECTIVE OF CARE

Linda Bannister

Ellen Marie Keane's presentation "Justice in a Different Voice" at the 1998 President's Institute on the Catholic Character of Loyola Marymount University focuses on feminine ethics and epistemology. She contrasts a morality of rights, formal reasoning, autonomous individuals, and unconnected isolated learning (a masculine paradigm) with a morality of care, intuition/emotion, relationships, and learning communities (a feminine paradigm). Keane argues that this feminine epistemology focuses on "providing care and maintaining relationships," going far beyond the patriarchal (Lockeian) "right to life, liberty and property" theory of justice, one we still laud in contemporary Western society. Keane rightfully points out that safeguarding the rights of the individual results in a widespread ethic of non-interference, not particularly helpful in building a common good.

Keane contrasts non-interference with the feminine tradition of selfless involvement. This feminine tradition is best expressed by two utterances: (a) I'm here to serve others and (b) My needs are not important (Keane, 2000). Not surprisingly, Keane suggests that this tradition is rather incomplete. Though care and connection are worthy human occupations, ignoring the self can result in the ultimate injustice. The feminine tradition of care can leave the caregiver standing in the shadows of self-sacrifice, never equal, disempowered, and finally, disconnected—disconnected because the self has been lost.

Keane is really asking for, it seems to me, a man-womanly or (woman-manly) ethic, an androgynous justice, if you will. It seems a simple point, but Keane advocates a collaborative ethic, a melding of the feminine and masculine justice traditions to the betterment of both.

Keane hopes for a justice of care that I call "androgynous," an idea based on my own work with classical rhetoric and the early feminist theory of Virginia Woolf. In her epic essay, *A Room of One's Own*, Woolf posits an androgynous creative consciousness in response (I think) to gender bias.

Gender bias in the concept of creativity and genius is a very old idea. The rhetoric of creativity has operated for centuries by excluding women— only men are capable of producing true art. But this rhetoric is also fraught with contradictions. As critic Christine Battersby argues, "It is hard to think through the implications of the fact that 'feminine'—generally used as a sneer-word in reference to art-works by women—takes on much more positive connotations when applied to males" (Battersby, 1989, p. 7). The myth of the bisexual androgyne was integral to the Romantics' account of true genius; but as Virginia Woolf noted in *A Room of One's Own* (1929) when a writer like Coleridge insisted that the mind of the great artist is androgynous, he certainly did not mean that such a mind has any "special sympathy with women, a mind that takes up their cause or devotes itself to their interpretation" (p. 108). Nor did he mean that a great creative artist is female. His advice to young authors in *Biographia Literaria* (1817) makes that quite clear. The Romantics' androgyne has male genital organs; it is only his soul that is "feminine." In other words, the great artist is a feminine male.

The roots of the androgynous aesthetic (which *fuses* male and female) has permeated our culture, and may be traced as far back as Plato and Ovid. In Plato's *Symposium*, Aristophanes explains that man's original nature was dual, consisting of two bodies united into one perfectly round being. The two bodies joined were either two males, two females, or one male and one female—an androgyne. In Plato's myth, the dual state was a privileged one. These joined beings were more than the sum of their two parts. They were, as critic Kari Weil (1985) says, "manifestations of perfect plenitude, evidenced by their spherical shape" (p. 5). These powerful, dualistic beings dared to rival their god. Angered by their impudence, Zeus split them into two separate bodies. Profound incompleteness resulted; desire was born; each separated being was forever in search of his or her other half. The androgyne has been the focus of the fascination with Plato's myth, while the two homosexual couples are largely ignored—a significant exclusion. The androgyne has been identified as an ideal state of being, a state of wholeness, a state of total love. Plato's primordial androgyny is also problematic however, because it hides an unstable binary hierarchy. Weil points out that, "Aristophanes' explanation of human desire, for example, is a celebration of male homosexual love, seen as the one relationship which most fully reproduces the wholeness that soul and spirit desire. Women are said to limit the nature of love to base physical necessity and to procreation" (Weil, 1985, p. 6). Again, women get the aesthetic and mythic sneer.

Plato's androgyne existed at the *origin*, before division, before desire. Ovid's hermaphrodite is the result of a *transformation* where two beings are metamorphosed into one. In the *Metamorphoses*, Ovid tells the story of Hermaphroditus (son of Hermes and Aphrodite) and a beautiful nymph, Salmacis, who is so smitten with him she wishes for an inseparable union. The gods comply, and the two are grafted together into one dual-sexed being. Both Plato's androgyne and Ovid's hermaphrodite call to mind the endless human desire for self-completion and creative fulfillment, for wholeness.

In *A Room of One's Own*, Virginia Woolf defines the truly creative imagination as a unity, a marriage of the male and female in the mind. Woolf speaks of an "androgynous mind . . . resonant and porous," able to "transmit emotion without impediment" and "naturally creative, incandescent and undivided" (Woolf, 1957, p. 108). The integrity of vision Woolf describes is the necessary quality of the true artist. Creative genius is possible only when there is a unity of mind within the artist, a unity that is then transferred to the work of art. The androgynous mind transcends the two individual sexes, is a marriage of opposites. Woolf says, "It is when this fusion takes place that the [artist's] mind is fully fertilized and uses all its faculties. Perhaps [she suggests], a mind that is purely masculine cannot create, any more than a mind that is purely feminine" (Woolf, 1957, p. 108). Woolf goes on to say how hard it is to attain such a harmonious condition where the two sexual/spiritual/creative forces cooperate utterly. When Woolf posits two sexes in the mind, she also posits that perhaps "in the man's brain, the man predominates over the woman, and in the woman's brain, the woman predominates over the man . . . but the *fully developed* mind does not think specially or separately of sex" (Woolf, 1957, pp. 107–108).

Woolf's ideas about the ideal creative mind are decidedly more Platonic than Ovidian, more androgynous than hermaphroditic. She envisions the artist as a being with clearly defined sexual organs, but with a *psychic bisexuality*. In fact, I'd suggest that for Woolf, the ideal creative act is facilitated by the freely symbiotic androgynous consciousness; no barriers separate the two sexes of the mind. They flow *in* and *out* and *around* one another perfectly, completely.

Woolf's idea of an androgynous creative imagination is explored most fully in her 1928 novel *Orlando*. A mock biography spanning 400 years, *Orlando* features an androgynous protagonist who is transformed from a man into a woman, allowing Woolf to explore a variety of topics, including gender roles, masculinity, femininity, androgyny, and their relationship to the creative life. Orlando is a frustrated poet who begins to truly grow as a writer after his sexual transformation, after he has become a physical woman. When the novel begins, we are told in no uncertain terms that Orlando is a *he*; indeed Woolf writes, "There could be no doubt of his sex, though the fashion of the time did something to disguise it" (Woolf, 1956, p. 13). When the novel ends, Orlando, now a woman, has produced an epic poem which has gone into no less than seven editions. Orlando is transformed from a man into a woman, from a daydreamer and a dabbler into a writer. His physical transformation is the outward sign of an inward marriage, a mental collaboration. Woolf is careful to let us know that Orlando had become a woman—there is no denying it. But in every other respect, Orlando remained as he had been. "The change of sex, although it altered *their* future, did nothing whatever to alter *their* identity" (Woolf, 1956, p. 14). Woolf uses the plural pronoun pointedly here, jangling the reader who expects to hear "he" or even "she," but is stopped short by "they." Orlando's masculine consciousness and feminine consciousness are fused; the mental collaboration Woolf finds crucial to the creative act is now possible. Neither man nor woman can prevail in the truly creative imagination; neither half can create true art separately.

Like Woolf, Keane implicitly argues that neither man nor woman can prevail in a truly "just" society. Nor can any ethical system which ignores the (feminine) philosophy of care flourish. What Keane seems to be asking for is an androgynous ethical system, one which unites the masculine and feminine traditions, one which combines "the right to life" with the "duty to serve" (Keane, 2000). This new androgynous justice is both selfish and selfless. It honors the act of caregiving, but also acknowledges the need to nurture the self. Thus Keane truly advocates "justice in a different voice," a voice that is neither masculine nor feminine, though *her* title implies a feminine perspective. This different voice is that of the just man/woman (or the fully human justice): one which advocates a selfish perspective of care.

References

Battersby, C. (1989). *Gender and genius: Towards a feminist aesthetics.* Bloomington, IN: Indiana University Press.

Coleridge, S. (1817). *Biographia literaria.* London, England: J.M. Dent & Co.

Keane, E.M., R.S.H.M. (2000). Justice in a different voice. In M. K. McCullough (Ed.), *The just one justices: The role of justice at the heart of Catholic higher education* (pp. 89–95). Scranton, PA: University of Scranton Press.

Weil, K. (1985). The aesthetics of androgyny in Balzac and Woolf, or the difference of difference. *Critical matrix, 1.*

Woolf, V. (1956). *Orlando.* San Diego, CA: Harcourt Brace & Company.

Woolf, V. (1957). *A room of one's own.* New York, NY: Harcourt Brace Jovanovich.

AND WHO IS MY NEIGHBOR? AUTONOMY VALUE, THE ETHIC OF CARE, AND FULL INCLUSION FOR PEOPLE WITH MENTAL DISABILITIES

Jan C. Costello

Professor Ellen Marie Keane, in "Justice in a Different Voice," invites us to build a good moral theory which places care on an equal footing with justice (Keane, 2000). She identifies two approaches to discussions of justice: the traditional social contract model whose dominant value is individual autonomy, and the "ethic of care," which places the highest value on connectedness and preserving relationships with others. Professor Keane summarizes the social contract/autonomy justice tradition, the basis for most Western moral philosophy, as "People are entitled to noninterference. As a community of individuals searching for a common good, the bottom line is 'do no harm'" (Keane, 2000, p. 92). This justice tradition values liberty and the individual's right to self-governance. It has been and continues to be used by disenfranchised persons and groups seeking civil and political liberty under a theory of "equality." However, in Keane's view this justice perspective is flawed because: (a) noninterference sometimes leads to neglect and the justification of exploitation and oppression; (b) it ignores or oversimplifies issues of inequality; (c) it exaggerates the scope of choice in moral decision making; and (d) it excessively values rationalism and denigrates the role of emotion. She therefore urges us to be "inclusive" in our vision of social justice, to work toward "building a world where mutuality and interdependence become the norm" (Keane, 2000, p. 94).

Commentators were asked to explore the ideas raised in Professor Keane's paper in the context of our own faith tradition and professional field of expertise. Accordingly, I disclose that I am a Roman Catholic and have been since my baptism in 1950. I am a lawyer and law professor with a special area of expertise in mental disability law. Before becoming a full-time academic, I represented people with mental disabilities in civil and criminal proceedings; I continue to serve as a consultant and board member for two organizations which provide legal services to people with mental

117

disabilities. It may also be of use to readers to know that I am a woman and a feminist.

Professor Keane's paper raises for me several interesting questions: Are autonomy values and relationship values really such polar (and, to some extent, gender-identified) opposites? Is the "ethic of care" the same as the call to "be a neighbor" set out in the parable of the Good Samaritan? How does the existing law affecting people with mental disabilities reflect the limitations of both autonomy value and the ethic of care? How can law reflect a view of people with disabilities as "neighbors"?

The Ethic of Care, Women and Relationships

Professor Keane in using the term "ethic of care" refers to psychologist Carol Gilligan's groundbreaking research (1982) suggesting that women are more likely than men to embrace such an ethic. Gilligan postulated that men and women develop moral and ethical values somewhat differently. Women feel a moral imperative to care for others, and base decisions on "not hurting anyone" and meeting the needs of all parties. Men develop a more logical, rule-based ethic which places highest value on "fairness" and "protecting the rights" of all parties.

Gilligan's "different voice" metaphor is helpful in defining an "ethic of care" which emphasizes preserving relationships and meeting others' needs. However, it is harmful to identify such an ethic solely with women, or to hold it up as morally superior to an ethic concerned with autonomy. Although she emphasized that *both* approaches to moral reasoning were valuable, "This point was lost on many of Gilligan's adherents, who delightedly replaced the male bias in moral-development studies with a female bias" (Tavris, 1992, p. 80). Separating the "autonomy" and "care" moral perspectives into two gender-specific camps is not supported by either Gilligan's original work or the subsequent research testing her thesis. That research has tended to show that men and women use *both* care-based and rights-based reasoning, that "people make moral decisions not only according to abstract principles of justice, but also according to principles of compassion and care" (Tavris, 1992, p. 85). Ultimately labeling the "ethic of care" as "women's way" unfairly and unnecessarily polarizes men and women and undermines the goal of meaningful exchange about social justice.

That said, it is hardly surprising if women place great value upon the preservation of relationships. As a general rule, women's social status and economic security are crucially based upon their relationships—with parents, husband, children, and in-laws. Depending on the culture, a woman's obligations to her mother, as opposed to her mother-in-law, for example, may vary, but preserving family relationships is most likely to ensure the survival of both the woman and her children. Women who may spend much of their childbearing years either pregnant, recovering from childbirth, or nursing may need to be protected and supported during such vulnerable states. That means pleasing and being of importance to someone in the position to provide support—whether it is a husband, in-law, parent, or other relative. A woman's security in old age (or upon the end of a marriage by death or divorce) similarly may depend upon her relationship with her adult children.

Women's concern for preserving relationships may only seem greater when compared to the individualistic, autonomy values of a (highly hypothetical) dominant white male Western philosopher. In any relationship of unequal power, the less powerful individual is more apt to value the relationship because he needs it more. The less powerful person will also be more skillful in "intuiting" the needs of the more powerful, and in meeting those needs. Even in the United States, men who belong to less powerful groups—immigrants, racial minorities, unskilled laborers—certainly value and rely upon relationships to survive. A man may get a job through a family, church, military veteran, or social club connection, and keep it because of a good relationship with his employer or on-the-job supervisor. Men and women who belong to disadvantaged groups may value and promote "autonomy" not so much of the individual as of the group or tribe. The ultimate expression of autonomy value may be the American ideal of a young man who is free to "invent himself"—to keep the language, values, religion, customs of his parents, or to reject them in favor of assimilation into the larger dominant culture. Yet such assimilation has usually not been available to people of color or women—possibly why members of these comparatively disenfranchised groups have tended to value preservation of relationships within their group.

In short, for less powerful individuals or groups, following "an ethic of care" may simply mean acting to promote relationships beneficial to them. A dependent person will only succeed in being cared for to the extent he or she is valued by the dominant individual or group. Understanding this helps avoid the easy error of misidentifying autonomy value with selfishness and the ethic of care with altruism. The "ethic of care" Gilligan identified may indeed be an important corrective and counterweight to the autonomy perspective. But how does it compare to the "love of neighbor" which both Judaism and Christianity consider a fundamental commandment?

The Good Samaritan and the Ethic of Care

There was a scholar of the law who stood up to test him, and said, "Teacher, what must I do to inherit eternal life?" Jesus said to him, "What is written in the law? How do you read it?" He said in reply, "You shall love the Lord, your God, with all your heart, with all your being, with all your strength, and with all your mind, and your neighbor as yourself." He replied to him, "You have answered correctly; do this and you will live."

But because he wished to justify himself, he said to Jesus, "And who is my neighbor?" (*New American Bible*, Luke 10:25–37)

This exchange always sounds very familiar to me as a lawyer (twenty-two years) and law professor (fifteen years). I can so easily imagine it taking place in a law school classroom or at an academic conference. Why does the legal scholar need to "justify" having asked Jesus a question? Perhaps because that particular question—"What must I do to inherit eternal life?"—is one which is already satisfactorily answered in the written law. Jesus' response "What is written in the law?" is comparable to a professor in class telling the student to refer back to a treatise which sets out well-established principles or "black letter" law. (It's something of a re-proof, suggesting that the questioner has not done his homework.) The questioner recites the "black letter law" here, and Jesus tells him the answer is correct.

If the legal scholar's question was really about the "black letter law"—the language of the rule itself—there would have been no need to inquire of Jesus, since the rule was "written in the law" and readily accessible. Indeed, since the black letter law was on such an important subject ("what . . . [to] do to inherit eternal life") any competent scholar of the law would already know it. The questioner thus needs to "justify" his question by showing that he was fully aware of the "black letter law"; his question to Jesus was rather a more sophisticated one about the interpretation or "application" of the rule.

The questioner accepts that he has a duty to love his "neighbor," but asks for a clear definition of that term. Such a definition is critical, since eternal life is at stake. The scholar wants to make sure that he does not fail to fulfill his duty to anyone whom the law regards as his "neighbor." A good definition will have the additional benefit of avoiding giving love unnecessarily to "non-neighbors." While a non-lawyer in a generous mood might say, "Oh what the heck. Let's just love everybody, neighbor or not!" such reasoning is utterly foreign to a legal scholar. As a good lawyer, therefore, the questioner was probably hoping for a helpful definition such as: someone who lives in your village, or belongs to your tribe, or shares your nationality or religion. Jesus, however, does not cooperate. Rather than define "neighbor," he tells the familiar story of the Good Samaritan.

Jesus replied, "A man fell victim to robbers as he went down from Jerusalem to Jericho. They stripped him and beat him and went off leaving him half-dead. A priest happened to be going down that road, but when he saw him he passed by on the opposite side. Likewise a Levite came to the place, and when he saw him, he passed by on the opposite side. But a Samaritan traveler who came upon him was moved with compassion at the sight. He approached the victim, poured oil and wine over his wounds and bandaged them. Then he lifted him up on his own animal, took him to an inn and cared for him. The next day he took out two silver coins and gave them to the innkeeper with the instruction, 'Take care of him. If you spend more than what I have given you, I shall repay you on my way back.' 'Which of these three, in your opinion, was neighbor to the robbers' victim?' He answered, 'The one who treated him with mercy.' Jesus said to him 'Go and do likewise.' (Luke 10: 30–37)

Jesus does not say, What a terrific lawyer the Samaritan was. He looked at the victim and realized that this was a neighbor from his hometown. He realized that he had a duty to care for this neighbor, and so did his duty. The parable describes the victim merely as "a man," giving no suggestion about whose "neighbor" he might be. The priest and Levite of course know the "black letter law" and presumably would have stopped to rescue a "neighbor" to whom they owed a duty of care. Since they did not stop, perhaps it was because they identified the victim as a "non-neighbor."

By contrast, the Samaritan stops and cares for the victim, not because he recognizes and fulfills a legal duty, but because he is "moved with compassion at the sight." The Samaritan acts not out of duty but in response to the victim's need. The parable makes it clear that the Samaritan did not expect to see the wounded man again. He was on his way to Jerusalem and told the innkeeper he'd pay any additional expenses incurred in caring for the victim on his way back. Yet although the Samaritan and the victim had no previous relationship and may not meet again, because of the Samaritan's act, they have become "neighbors."

Jesus asks the questioner, "Which . . . was neighbor to the robbers' victim?" The scholar replies, "The one who treated him with mercy." This is different from the one who did his duty. Jesus has changed the issue from, Who is my neighbor (That is, whom must I care for?) to How do I show myself to be a neighbor? "Neighbor" is not a limited category of those who are entitled to our love. It is a potentially limitless category in which we by our actions can earn membership. If we all follow the injunction, "Go and do likewise," eventually we will all become neighbors.

Mental Disability Law Limitations of the Autonomy Value and the Ethic of Care

In this section, I will describe how law affecting people with mental disabilities reflects the limitations of the autonomy value and the ethic of care. Over the past twenty-five years, courts and legislatures have been willing to acknowledge autonomy rights of mentally disabled persons but less so to recognize rights to care and treatment. In practice this has meant that people with disabilities have not received the programs and services which could either improve the quality of their lives within institutions or enable them to live outside of institutions and in the community. Two decisions of the United States Supreme Court, *O'Connor v. Donaldson* (1975) and *Youngberg v. Romeo* (1982), well illustrate this problem.

First, a little background: In the United States, as in English common law, the traditional approach was to equate mental disability with legal incompetence. Persons who were "lunatics" (mentally ill) or "idiots" (developmentally disabled or impaired because of organic brain damage) could not marry, make valid contracts or wills, vote or exercise other civil rights. They might be cared for by their family or in private or state institutions. Commitment to such an institution could be lifelong and was typically accomplished with few or no legal protections (Perlin, 1994). However, care within the family did not necessarily guarantee either greater autonomy or superior care for mentally disabled persons. As Professor Keane recognized, "In traditional Western philosophy, the rights and needs of these classes of dependent persons is generally dealt with as a private, domestic issue, and therefore, not properly part of the public, political domain. This private venue sometimes renders their position and needs virtually invisible to those who determine public policy" (Keane, 2000, p. 92).

The modern movement to establish rights for people with mental disabilities began in the late 1960s and early 1970s. Building upon legal precedents establishing civil rights for racial minorities and women, advocates for mentally disabled people generally advanced two types of "rights" claims: (1) autonomy rights and (2) rights to care or treatment. Autonomy claims are grounded in the rights to liberty and privacy, and include the right not to be wrongly institutionalized or subjected to involuntary treatment. Treatment rights include the right to appropriate treatment (for mentally ill persons) or habilitation services (for developmentally disabled individuals) either within an institution or in the community.

Autonomy rights are often characterized as due process rights: under the Due Process clauses of the Fifth and Fourteenth Amendments to the United States Constitution, no state can deprive a person of life, liberty, or property "without due process of law." When the state acts to confine a mentally disabled person in an institution, or to subject the person to involuntary treatment, the Due Process clause applies. To satisfy "substantive" due process, the state must show an interest strong enough to justify the proposed deprivation of liberty. Courts have long recognized that such substantive interests included the state's *parens patriae* authority to act as "parent" on behalf of children or adults incapable of caring for themselves, and the *police power* to confine dangerous persons. To satisfy "procedural" due process, the state must provide the person with procedures adequate to guard against erroneous deprivation of liberty. For example, in the civil commitment context, state and federal courts have found that procedural due process includes, at a minimum, notice of the proposed commitment and a hearing before a neutral decision maker at which the state must prove that the person satisfies the legal criteria for involuntary confinement or treatment (Perlin, 1994).

The underlying assumption of autonomy rights is that a person has the right to act without government interference. This principle—"the right to be left alone"—was famously expressed in Justice Brandeis's dissenting opinion in *Olmstead v. United States* (1927). "The right to be left alone" presumes an individual's ability to be fully autonomous: the government must leave such a person alone because he or she "can take care of myself." The state cannot exercise its *parens patriae* power over an individual who is self-sufficient.

Right to care and treatment claims first focused on conditions of confinement in state institutions. Advocates sought to improve both the basic custodial care provided—food, clothing, shelter, and medical care—and to require the state to offer individualized treatment for the residents' mental disability. For some individuals, the goal of such treatment would be to increase the ability to function within the institution; for others, improvement to the point of eventual release to live in the community. Depending upon the ability and progress of the mentally disabled person, community living could mean residence in a halfway house or supervised apartment, while employed in a sheltered workshop; it could also mean a "normal" life of residence and employment identical to those of people without mental disabilities. As the mental health care professions made significant advances in treatment of mental illness and developing habilitation programs, this vision of "normalization" and "community integration" seemed tantalizingly within reach.

But did mentally disabled people have a "right" to treatment and services? In other words, did the state have a duty to provide appropriate treatment and services to mentally disabled individuals? Advocates pursued three lines of argument, all grounded in substantive due process. The first relied upon the principle that the state does have a duty of care to persons in its custody, whether prisoners in a state correctional facility or children in a foster home. The state has a "special relationship" with such individuals, and must provide for their basic needs of food, clothing, shelter, and medical care. Advocates hoped to establish that mentally disabled persons in state custody were entitled to at least the same level of basic care as prisoners.

But what about a right to treatment and services beyond such "custodial care"? Advocates developed a *quid pro quo* rationale, arguing that because the state has deprived institutionalized mentally disabled persons of their liberty, it "owes" them appropriate treatment or habilitation in return. Since institutional residents were not criminals but had been civilly committed, they were entitled to more than the basic care given to prisoners, in return for having forfeited their liberty. A final and stronger substantive due process argument, citing the language of a Supreme Court decision called *Jackson v. Indiana* (1972, p. 738), was that "the nature and duration of confinement must bear some reasonable relation to the state's purpose in confining" the individual. Thus, advocates argued, if the state's justification for commitment was that an individual was mentally disabled and needed treatment or habilitation, the individual had a constitutional right to receive (and the state a duty to provide) it. A related principle of substantive due process was that, where a fundamental liberty interest was at stake, the state must use the "least drastic means" to accomplish its purposes. Advocates used this principle to argue for a "right to treatment in the least restrictive alternative." This meant that the state had a duty to provide community-based care if the individual could safely and appropriately be treated outside of an institutional setting.

In the early 1970s, adopting one or more of these rationales, several federal courts ruled that mentally ill or mentally retarded residents of state institutions had a right to treatment or habilitation services. The courts then ordered sweeping reforms of institutional conditions and in some cases established panels of experts to establish standards of care and treatment and to monitor compliance with court orders. This kind of judicial oversight of state institutions was similar to that done in earlier cases where federal judges (or monitors or panels) ended up supervising desegregation of public schools and overhauling of prison conditions. It was (and continues to be) controversial, denounced by critics as impermissible interference with state self-governance; defended by advocates as the only way to force states to provide adequate care for a population largely unrepresented when policies are decided and budgets are drawn up. Among the critics of this "judicial activism" was Chief Justice Warren Burger, who earlier in his career, when he served on the United States Court of Appeals for the District of Columbia, had strongly opposed his Chief Justice David L. Bazelon's rulings finding that mentally disabled people had a right to treatment.

In 1975, a case called *O'Connor v. Donaldson* was on appeal to the United States Supreme Court. The facts of the case were compelling. In 1957, Kenneth Donaldson had been committed to a Florida mental hospital because of paranoid delusions. He stayed in the state hospital for 15 years, during which time he repeatedly, but unsuccessfully, demanded his release, claiming that he was dangerous to no one, that he was not mentally ill, and that, at any rate, the hospital was not providing treatment for his supposed illness. Friends periodically offered to let him live with them, or to give him a job, but Dr. O'Connor, the hospital superintendent, refused to release Donaldson. Finally Donaldson sued for violation of his civil rights under federal law, claiming that O'Connor had intentionally and maliciously deprived him of his constitutional right to liberty. At trial the jury returned a verdict against O'Connor for both compensatory and punitive damages. Dr. O'Connor appealed to the United States Court of Appeals for the Fifth Circuit, which ruled for Donaldson (*Donaldson v. O'Connor*, 1974). The Fifth Circuit not only found that Donaldson's liberty rights had been violated, but declared a sweeping right to treatment: "a person involuntarily committed to a state mental hospital has a constitutional right to receive such individual treatment as will give him a reasonable opportunity to be cured or to improve his mental condition. . . . Where, as in Donaldson's case, the rationale for confinement is the *parens patriae* rationale that the patient is in need of treatment, the due process clause requires that minimally adequate treatment be in fact provided" (*Donaldson v. O'Connor*, 1974, p. 521).

When the United States Supreme Court agreed to hear the *Donaldson* case, mental disability rights advocates worried about the possibility of an adverse decision. There was good reason to believe that Chief Justice Burger would write a sweeping majority opinion which would reject the whole right to treatment concept and stymie further litigation to improve institutional conditions or to force states to develop community-based treatment programs. Knowing this, attorneys for Donaldson made a critical strategic decision: they changed the "right to treatment" into a "right to liberty" case. Ken Donaldson didn't want treatment, they told the Court, he just wanted to be left alone. In language carefully tailored to follow the facts of Donaldson's own situation, they urged the Court to uphold the right to liberty of the "nondangerous mentally ill capable of surviving safely in freedom alone or with help of willing family or friends" (Woodward & Armstrong, 1979, p. 376).

Given this option, a majority of justices signed on to the "right to liberty" holding. The majority opinion written by Justice Potter Stewart explained why the case presents only a narrow question:

There is no reason now to decide whether mentally ill persons dangerous to themselves or others have a right to treatment upon compulsory confinement by the State, or whether the State may compulsorily confine a non-dangerous, mentally ill person for the purpose of treatment. As we view it, this case raises a single, relatively simple, but nonetheless important question concerning every man's constitutional right to liberty. The jury found that Donaldson was neither dangerous to himself nor dangerous to others, and also found that, if mentally ill, Donaldson had not received treatment. (*O'Connor v. Donaldson*, 1975, p. 573)

The Court went on to suggest constitutional limits on the State's ability to interfere with the autonomy of mentally ill persons:

A finding of "mental illness" alone cannot justify a State's locking a person up against his will and keeping him indefinitely in simple custodial confinement. Assuming that that term can be given a reasonably precise content and that the "mentally ill" can be identified with reasonable accuracy, there is still no constitutional basis for confining such persons involuntarily if they are dangerous to no one and can live safely in freedom. (*O'Connor v. Donaldson*, 1975, p. 575)

This part of the Donaldson opinion reflects the law's respect for individual autonomy: if people are not dangerous and are able to function independently, the State cannot force care on them just because it is for their own good. Therefore, even if Donaldson was indeed mentally ill, O'Connor had no right to confine him. Donaldson's right to liberty trumps the State's interest in providing treatment. Chief Justice Burger, concurring, shared the majority's autonomy rationale to an extent, saying that the theory that a State could "confine an individual simply because it is willing to provide treatment, regardless of the subject's ability to function in society . . . raises the gravest of constitutional problems" (Burger concurring opinion, *O'Connor v. Donaldson*, 1975, p. 585).

O'Connor v. Donaldson was an important victory in recognizing the autonomy rights of people with mental disabilities. But what about the right to treatment issue? Chief Justice Burger ultimately voted with the majority in *O'Connor v. Donaldson*, but right to treatment wrote a separate concurring opinion rejecting strongly a constitutional right to treatment. He emphasized that historically mentally disabled people had been cared for by their families, not the State. Where the State did act *parens patriae* to commit, until recently this had been primarily for custodial care, not treatment. Mentally disabled individuals who are dependent on their families or who cannot survive outside an institution cannot truly be said to trade their liberty for treatment when they are confined by the State. Moreover, some forms of mental illness and disability are not treatable. Therefore, the *quid pro quo* argument for a constitutional right to treatment fails.

Burger's concurrence pinpointed the weakness of both the special relationship and *quid pro quo* arguments. The law assumes that a "normal" individual is autonomous—intellectually competent and physically strong enough to provide for his or her own care and protection. Thus, the "special relationship" duty of care attaches only when a person is in state custody because the state has removed from the individual the ability to meet his or her own basic needs.

A mentally disabled person like Kenneth Donaldson, who values autonomy more than the care available in the institution, is free to refuse state custody—so long as he or she is capable of surviving safely in freedom. But what if the individual is not autonomous and cannot function outside an institution without assistance? The state may simply say, "You in effect have no liberty to lose or trade. Your dependency upon the state means you get basic custodial care, but you are not entitled to any treatment or habilitation."

Burger intended his concurrence as a message to the lower courts, discouraging them from finding a right to treatment in future cases (Woodward & Armstrong, 1979), and it was certainly read that way by many courts and commentators. Still advocates continued to litigate in lower courts federal and state law claims to treatment or habilitation in institutions and in the community during the late 1970s and early 1980s. Then the Supreme Court agreed to decide the case of *Youngberg v. Romeo* (1982).

Nicholas Romeo, like Kenneth Donaldson, was a sympathetic plaintiff. He was profoundly retarded, and at age thirty-three had the mental capacity of an eighteen-month-old child with an I.Q. between eight and ten. He could not talk and lacked the most basic self-care skills. Until he was twenty-six, Romeo lived with his parents in Philadelphia. But after the death of his father, Romeo's mother was unable to care for him at home and he was committed to Pennhurst, the Pennsylvania state facility for the mentally retarded, on a permanent basis. At Pennhurst he was injured on at least sixty-three occasions "both by his own violence and by the reactions of other residents to him" (*Youngberg v. Romeo*, 1982, p. 311). His mother filed a complaint against state officials, originally alleging that they knew, or should have known, that Romeo was suffering injuries and that they failed to protect him. The complaint was later amended to add that the defendants were restraining Romeo (tying him to a bed or chair) for prolonged periods on a routine basis, and claiming damages for the failure to provide Romeo with "appropriate treatment or programs for his mental retardation" (p. 311). The United States Court of Appeals for the Third Circuit found that the Due Process Clause of the Fourteenth Amendment gave Romeo a liberty interest in "minimally adequate habilitation" designed to treat his mental retardation (*Youngberg v. Romeo*, 1981, pp. 164–170).

At the same time Nicholas Romeo's individual case was proceeding through the courts, so was a class action on behalf of all the residents at Pennhurst (*Halderman v. Pennhurst State School and Hospital*, 1978). The class action claimed that the conditions of confinement at Pennhurst violated the rights of the mentally disabled residents to freedom from harm under the Eighth Amendment (the same basic right possessed by a state prisoner) and to adequate treatment or habilitation under the Fourteenth Amendment. The class action sought both improvement of conditions at Pennhurst and assessment of residents to see if they could appropriately be placed and treated in less restrictive, community-based programs. The United States Supreme Court had not ruled on the constitutional claims in *Pennhurst*, but had earlier sent the case back on remand to the lower courts on various other grounds (*Pennhurst I*, 1981; *Pennhurst II*, 1984). Certainly the justices were well aware of the breadth of the claims involved in this companion case, and not inclined to affirm such a broad right to treatment, especially one that would result in lower courts closing state institutions and ordering the building of community-based programs (Perlin, 1994).

As in *Donaldson*, therefore, attorneys for Nicholas Romeo narrowed their claim in his individual case. They asserted, and the Supreme Court found, only a narrow "right to minimally adequate treatment or habilitation" within the state institution. Justice Powell, writing this time for the majority, stated: "This case does not present the difficult question whether a mentally retarded person, involuntarily committed to a state institution, has some guaranteed constitutional right to training *per se*, even when no type or amount of training would lead to freedom" (*Youngberg v. Romeo*, 1982, p. 318). At oral argument, Romeo's counsel explicitly disavowed any claim that Romeo was constitutionally entitled to such treatment as would enable him "to reach his maximum potential" (a claim made at trial), and conceded that he could not function outside an institution. (Ironically, years later, when the Pennhurst class action was settled, Nicholas Romeo actually was placed in a community living arrangement.) The majority was reassured that "the self-care programs he seeks are needed to reduce his aggressive behavior" and "he seeks only training related to safety and freedom from restraints" *(Youngberg v. Romeo*, 1982, p. 318). Therefore, the Court narrowly held only that "respondent's liberty interests require the State to provide minimally adequate or reasonable training to ensure safety and freedom from undue restraint" (*Youngberg v. Romeo*, 1982, p. 319). The Court did not require that the training be "the least restrictive" or "least intrusive" of Romeo's liberty; so long as a qualified professional decided on a program or treatment, it would pass constitutional muster.

The *Youngberg* majority opinion made an explicit connection between Nicholas Romeo's limited autonomy rights and his right to "minimally adequate" training or habilitation. Literally, he was only entitled to such training as would help him to preserve and exercise what little autonomy he had left. As concurring justices Blackmun, Brennan, and O'Connor poignantly put it, "For many mentally retarded people, the difference between the capacity to do things for themselves within an institution and total dependence on the institution for all of their needs is as much liberty as they ever will know" (*Youngberg v. Romeo*, 1982, p. 327).

Chief Justice Burger, again concurring, agreed with the majority that "Some amount of self-care instruction may be necessary to avoid unreasonable infringement of a mentally retarded person's interests in safety and freedom from restraint" (*Youngberg v. Romeo*, 1982, p. 330). However, Burger:

> . . . would hold flatly that respondent has no constitutional right to training, or "habilitation," *per se.* The parties, and the Court, acknowledge that respondent cannot function outside of the state institution, even with the assistance of relatives. . . . Under these circumstances, the State's provision of food, shelter, medical care, and living conditions as safe as the inherent nature of the institutional environment reasonably allows, serves to justify the State's custody of respondent. The State did not seek custody of respondent; his family understandably sought the State's aid to meet a serious need. (p. 329)

For Burger, Romeo's inability to function autonomously outside the institution precluded any right to training or services beyond the custodial care which the state conceded it would give him. His "serious need" for assistance did not create an entitlement to services. On the contrary, his total dependency upon the state meant that he had no liberty left to "trade" under a *quid pro quo* rationale.

Post-*Youngberg*, advocates explored, with limited success, other legal bases for right to treatment claims: for example, combining federal constitutional claims with state laws (Costello & Preis, 1987), or interpreting state constitutions to provide broader rights than the United States Constitution (Perlin, 1987). However, the sweeping vision of a federal constitutional right to treatment, both inside institutions and in the community, was gone (Perlin, 1994).

The Supreme Court in *O'Connor* and *Youngberg* primarily embraced the autonomy value, saying that the state has no right to interfere with mentally disabled people so long as they are autonomous. It acknowledged a duty of care with respect to only a limited number of mentally disabled individuals—those who are in state custody. Moreover, that duty of care is triggered by a "special relationship" of dependency, rather than any inherent right of the mentally disabled person. And the duty extends only to providing "minimally adequate" treatment or habilitation to protect mentally disabled persons within an institution—not programs designed to maximize their ability to function, and perhaps ultimately to live as full members of the community.

The *O'Connor* and *Youngberg* decisions show the limits of autonomy value and the ethic of care (at least as applied in legal terms) as a basis for mentally disabled people's rights to treatment and habilitation in institutions or in the community. The consequence of institutional confinement historically has been stigmatization and separation from the community. Relinquishing autonomy in order to receive "minimally adequate" care thus continues to be too high a price for many people with mental disability to pay. Yet mentally disabled individuals who exercise their "right to be left alone" may avoid institutional confinement, but still suffer from the symptoms of their untreated condition as well as from society's ignorance and prejudice. Is there a third legal approach which can be more successful in respecting mentally disabled people's autonomy while providing them with treatment and services needed to function fully in the community?

The Americans with Disabilities Act (ADA) and the Full Integration Mandate

The federal Americans with Disabilities Act (1990), which applies to both mental and physical disabilities, has established a right to full integration in the community. In passing the ADA, Congress found that:

Historically, society has tended to isolate and segregate individuals with disabilities, and, despite some improvements, such forms of discrimination against individuals with disabilities continue to be a serious and pervasive social problem. (sec. 12101, a, 2)

To correct this injustice, the ADA provides that:

The Nation's proper goals regarding individuals with disabilities are to assure equality of opportunity, **full participation,** independent living, and economic self-sufficiency for such individuals. (sec. 12101, a, 8)

This is sometimes referred to as the "full participation" or "full integration" mandate of the ADA. Using this mandate, people with mental and physical disabilities have begun to receive the treatment or habilitation services they need to reclaim their place in the community (Bird, 1998).

One case, *Helen L. v. DaDario* (1995), illustrates the remarkable difference in both the approach and the result, when compared to the constitutionally based autonomy and right to treatment claims. *Helen L.* involved a woman in a nursing home who was ready for discharge but could not go home because there were no home-care attendant services for her. Idell S. (one of several original plaintiffs in the case) was age forty-two and the mother of two children ages twenty-two and fourteen. She was paralyzed from the waist down by meningitis in her mid-thirties, and had been living in a nursing home for five years. Although she needed help with certain activities of daily living (bathing, laundry, shopping, getting in and out of bed, and housecleaning), she could function in her home with assistance. The problem was that her state, Pennsylvania, like many other states, didn't have a home-care or attendant-care program. The state had opted to spend Medicaid funds for nursing home care but not for in-home services. The effect of this administrative policy decision was that a woman with a disability was unnecessarily confined in a nursing home and separated from her family.

Did Idell S. have a "right" to receive care services in her own home? Under the reasoning of *O'Connor v Donaldson* (1975) and *Youngberg v. Romeo* (1981), the answer would have been no. True, the parties agreed that Idell S. "is not so incapacitated that she needs the custodial care of a nursing home" (*Helen L.*, 1995, p. 328). But there is no help for Idell S. in autonomy value alone—under the *O'Connor* reasoning it would only mean she had a right to be left alone by the state. If she wanted to leave the nursing home and strike out on her own, the state certainly had no power to commit her. But she could not care for herself without assistance, so in practice the state's willingness to respect her autonomy was meaningless. Did Idell S. have a right to in-home services under an ethic of care? The parties also agreed that, "Idell S. is not capable of fully independent living" (p. 328). Therefore, Idell S. is in a "special relationship" to the state, and the state acknowledged a duty to care for her. But because she concededly is dependent, under *Youngberg*, if the state chooses to provide for her only in a nursing home, she has no right to receive services in a less restrictive setting, such as her own home.

Crucially, the United States Court of Appeals for the Third Circuit ruled that Pennsylvania was required to spend its funds to care for Idell S.

in her own home—not under the United States Constitution, but under the ADA. The court quoted the "full participation" language of the ADA integration mandate and equated segregation of people with disabilities in nursing homes as prohibited discrimination. It explained that toward the end of the 1980s, the United States Senate and the House of Representatives both recognized that then current laws were "inadequate" to combat "the pervasive problems of discrimination that people with disabilities are facing" (p. 330 citing S. Rep. No. 116, 101st Cong., 2d Sess. 47, 1990). Congress concluded that:

> There is a compelling need to provide a clear and comprehensive national mandate for the elimination of discrimination against individuals with disabilities and for the integration of persons with disabilities into the economic and social mainstream of American life. (p. 331, citing S. Rep. No. 116, 20, H.R. Rep. No. 485(II), 50)

Congress made an explicit connection between the historical practice of confining people with disabilities in institutions (thus segregating them from the community) and discrimination. The ADA "evolved from an attempt to remedy the effects of 'benign neglect' resulting from the 'invisibility' of the disabled" (*Helen L.*, 1995, p. 334). Its intent is "to insure that qualified individuals receive services in a manner consistent with basic human dignity rather than a manner which shunts them aside, hides, and ignores them" (p. 334). Thus, Idell S. was entitled to relief under the ADA the moment she proved that her confinement in the nursing home was unnecessary. "The ADA and its attendant regulations clearly define unnecessary segregation as a form of illegal discrimination against the disabled" (p. 332).

The Third Circuit emphasized that its decision under the ADA, based upon unnecessary institutional confinement, is completely different from earlier analyses based upon the Due Process Clause of the Fourteenth Amendment (*Helen L.*, 1995, p. 333). Idell S. is not asserting a right to community care or deinstitutionalization *per se*. She properly concedes that "[The state] is under no obligation to provide her with any care at all. She is merely claiming that, since she qualifies for [the state's] care program, [Pennsylvania's] failure to provide those services in 'the most integrated care setting appropriate' to her needs (without a proper justification) violates the ADA" (p. 336).

Helen L. demonstrates how the ADA represents a dramatically different approach to the "rights" of people with disabilities. (*Helen L.* involved physical disability, but courts have used similar reasoning on behalf of people with mental disabilities.) The full integration mandate of the ADA gives disabled individuals the right to assistance, enabling them to live and function in the community. It does not condition that right to assistance on disabled persons giving up their liberty and accepting institutional confinement. It does not restrict entitlement to services from the state to disabled individuals who are in a special relationship of total dependence. It declares an end to segregating people with disabilities from "normal" society: it recognizes that people with disabilities are in fact part of society.

Conclusion: People with Mental Disabilities As Neighbors

The ADA is of course a federal statute, not a biblical passage. But the ADA principle of full integration reflects the same vision as the parable of the Good Samaritan. It says that people with disabilities are our neighbors. That means that we have to live with them, learn about them, and ultimately value them. So to preserve their liberty and dignity they don't have to say: I'm completely autonomous, leave me alone. To get assistance they don't have to say: I'm in a special relationship, totally dependent, care for me. They need only say, We are your neighbors. This approach I think best responds to Professor Keane's call to be "inclusive" in our vision of social justice, to work toward "building a world where mutuality and interdependence become the norm."

References

Americans with Disabilities Act (1990), 42 U.S.C. sec. 1201 et seq.

Bird, M. (1998). The Integration of the ADA and the Problem of Deinstitutionalization, *31 Loyola Law Review, Rev.* 847, 851.

Catholic Study Bible/New American Bible (1990). Oxford University Press.

Costello, J. C., & Preis, J. J. (1987). Beyond least restrictive alternative: A constitutional right to treatment for mentally disabled persons in the community. *Loyola Law Review, Rev.* 1527, 20.

Donaldson v. O'Connor, 493 F. 2d 507 (5th Cir. 1974), *vacated*, 422 U.S. 563 (1975).

Gilligan, C. (1982). *In a different voice: Psychological theory and women's development.* Cambridge, MA: Harvard University Press.

Halderman v. Pennhurst State School and Hospital, 446 F. Supp. 1295 (E.D. Pa. 1978), *modified*, 612 F.2d 84 (3rd Cir., 1979), *rev'd*, 451 U.S. 1 (1981), *reinstated*, 673 F.2d 647 (3rd Cir. 1982), *rev'd*, 465 U.S. 89 (1984).

Helen L. v. DaDario, 46 F.3d 325 (3d Cir. 1995).

Jackson v. Indiana, 406 U.S. 715 (1972).

O'Connor v. Donaldson, 422 U.S. 563 (1975).

Olmstead v. United States, 277 U.S. 438, 478 (1927).

Pennhurst State School and Hospital v. Halderman, 451 U.S. 1 (Pennhurst I) (1981).

Pennhurst State School and Hospital v. Halderman, 465 U.S. 89 (Pennhurst II) (1984).

Perlin, M. L. (1987). State constitutions and statutes as sources of rights for the mentally disabled: The last frontier? *Loyola Law Review, Rev.* 1249, 20.

Perlin, M. L. (1994). *Law and mental disability*. Los Angeles, CA: Michie.
Tavris, C. (1992). *The mismeasure of woman*. New York, NY: Simon & Schuster.
Woodward, B., & Armstrong, S. (1979). *The brethren: Inside the Supreme Court*. New York, NY: Simon and Schuster.
Youngberg v. Romeo, 644 F 2d 147, 156 (3rd Cir.1981), *vacated*, 457 U.S. 307 (1982).
Youngberg v. Romeo, 457 U.S. 307 (1982).

PROMOTING JUSTICE: THE BUSINESS OF HIGHER EDUCATION?

Margaret O'Brien Steinfels

The discussion about Catholic Identity of Catholic Higher Education is a conversation that is going on all over the country. The first time I ever talked about the subject was in the mid 1980s, so this is a conversation that has been going on for more than ten years. And since I was not the first to speak about it, even longer.

There are issues that all Catholic schools have in common. Indeed there are issues that all schools with religious foundations, Protestant and Catholic, have in common. In many cases, Protestant schools moved away from those foundations early in the 1900s and some of them are now rethinking whether they gave up too much when they gave up mandatory chapel and a central place for religion and theology in their curricula. Yet in spite of the common character of the questions, most of the answers will prove to be local. That is, the response to the big question of the Catholic character of Catholic higher education here at Loyola Marymount University must reflect the particularities of the school itself, and so too for every college and university.

Now there are many people, including officials in the Vatican, who think that there is a big answer to this question and that big answer was set forth in *Ex Cordiae Ecclesiae*, an apostolic constitution on Catholic higher education. There are many useful things in that document and we should take them seriously. But I think the effort to implement *Ex corde* overlooks a major point: there can be no single big answer to this question of Catholic identity. Most colleges and universities are diverse institutions with a history and development of their own. The answer to Catholic identity is largely local and needs to be local, even when people draw on resources from the rich deposit of the Catholic tradition and from ideas and practices of other Catholic institutions. This is a task that cannot be carried out from above.

As institutions have explored this question of Catholic identity, I suppose that part of these conversations have produced or provided a chance to take a closer look at what we could call "markers" for Catholic identity. Inspired by Gerard Manley Hopkins, the 1998 President's Institute takes up the question: Is the promotion of justice a marker for Catholic identity?

Is justice, whatever we might mean by it, a quality that Loyola Marymount would hold up as a marker when it thought about itself and its Catholic character? This is a very complicated question. Many observers believe that justice should be central to higher education. It is one way of resolving the identity conundrum. Take up the banner of justice and announce that that is what is distinctive about us: We are a school that stands for justice. And the word *social* before the word justice certainly has a resonance, at least, in recent Catholic tradition. And usually it is social justice that people mean when they speak justice language. They point to the Jesuit Volunteer Corp, or students on spring break going to work with Habitat for Humanity, or having an immersion experience in a Central American country, or the inner city of Chicago or Los Angeles—doing social justice "out there."

But let's ask this question: Is promoting justice in this or in any other sense the business of higher education? And, if we think it is, how and why. Let me propose as a first point of consideration—and the readings were meant to press this question—shouldn't we consider the possibility that education, in effect, is a catalyst for injustice? Let me put it bluntly: Doesn't education promote and perpetuate injustice?

The Readings: Dickens, Coetzee, Sullivan, Hampl

Let's turn briefly to the readings as a way of exploring the question.

The opening pages of Charles Dickens's *Hard Times* (1854) suggest that one of the things that education does is to perpetuate the injustice of a society and its theories about how children should be educated. First, there is this wonderful diatribe about facts.

"Now what I want is, Facts. Teach these boys and girls nothing but Facts. Facts alone are wanted in life. Plant nothing else, and root out everything else." And Thomas Gradgrind very quickly sets an example by telling Sissy Jupe that she may not call herself Sissy because that's not a real name; in fact, her name is Cecilia. We then get the wonderful definition by Bitzer of "What is a horse, sir?" "'Quadruped. Graminivorous. Forty teeth, namely twenty-four grinders, four eyeteeth, and twelve incisive. Sheds coat in the spring; in marshy countries, sheds hoofs, too. Hoofs hard, but requiring to be shod with iron. Age known by marks in mouth.' Thus (and much more) Bitzer" (Dickens, 1854).

Their teacher, aptly named Mr. Choakumchild, who is new and who is being introduced by Mr. Gradgrind, "began in his best manner. He and some 140 other school masters had been lately turned at the same time in the same factory on the same principles like so many pianoforte legs. He had been put through an immense variety of paces, and had answered volumes of head-breaking questions." More facts (Dickens, 1854).

Those of us who have had children know that theories abound; the first child may have been educated in an open classroom while the second did service in a closed classroom. Did either theory have anything to do with that child or what the child learned or needed to learn? Dickens is mocking primary school theories, but theories abound in high schools and in colleges as well. So, let us consider the possibility that theories about education may perpetuate a society's injustices, above all on children.

The second reading is from *Life and Times of Michael K* (1995) by J.M. Coetzee, a South African writer. The book is a wonderful, short, desperate, grim, sorry, sad book. I weep whenever I read it. It is a book about a man who is born with a hare lip, a cleft palate. Very early in his life he is given an education that will never allow him to transcend or to move beyond that disability. It will always be the mark by which people identify him. We could say that in some ways, schools are a form of injustice that separates the goats from the sheep; that separates children; that separates people from one another, and as you move up the educational ladder, you separate people out more and more until finally we get to people like yourselves who have Ph.D.s. You are at the pinnacle of this system in which people have been separated from all sorts of things.

Andrew Sullivan's *Virtually Normal* (1996) is another kind of reading. It too is a wonderful and interesting book. What struck me in this particular selection is Sullivan's description of his sense of himself as different in some sexual way. He describes what that meant to him as he passed through his childhood. What I want us to notice is how his education ended in separating him from himself in some profound way.

> No homosexual child, surrounded overwhelmingly by hetero-sexuals, will feel at home in his sexual and emotional world, even in the most tolerant of cultures. And every homosexual child will learn the rituals of deceit, impersonation and appearance. Anyone who believes political, social, or even cultural revolution will change this fundamentally is denying reality. This isolation will always hold. It is definitional of homosexual development. And children are particularly cruel. At the age of eleven, no one wants to be the odd one out; and in the arena of dating and hormones, the exclusion is inevitably a traumatic one. (Sullivan, 1996)

We all recognize that that experience of alienation from self is not necessarily exclusive to homosexual children—women feel it, people of different races, ethnic groups feel it—even white men may feel it! Sullivan's is a powerful example of the way in which education signals and pulls out people from coming to an understanding of themselves.

And now to the Patricia Hampl reading, *A Romantic Education* (1981). What struck me here is intergenerational injustice. In a society of immigrants, which most of us were or are, our educations have separated us from our parents, from our grandparents. The fact that we got an education, even if our parents worked very hard and sacrificed for it, still in very important ways made us different from our parents. Patricia Hampl writes here about her Czech grandmother who in many ways she adored.

What becomes clear in Patricia Hampl's story is that her grandmother is not a smart person. Her grandmother doesn't know anything, except as her aunt says, "She knows who she was." She means that the grandmother has an overarching sense of her being, but knowing nothing, not where she was born in Czechoslovakia, not what Prague really looked like. And there is a particularly nice capturing of this when Hampl writes:

> Sometimes she came to me with questions. I was the modern world and, as I got older and older and kept staying in school, she became both a little alarmed and mightily impressed. She had seen me coming, the family intellectual, and in her way had tried to nip it in the bud. Books were something she had suspicions about. The book was somehow an insult to the supremacy of human conversation and busy activity of any kind—cooking, gardening, home-permanenting of all female children, canning, preserving, cleaning, cleaning, cleaning. Reading was boring, it was annoying to others (herself), it was unhealthy and unnatural for a child (myself) to be curled up on the plush sofa under the picture of a voluptuous girl strumming a lute, to be reading the day away, reading when I could have been messing around outside. . . . (Hampl, 1981)

Now I don't generally make much of gender differences, but this is a chick experience here, I have to tell you! Every woman has been sitting on a couch in her mother's, or grandmother's, or sister's house and someone comes by with a vacuum cleaner. And we all know what that means! Time to close that book and do your part!

My point, once again: education separates us from one another, from our families, from our communities, sometimes even in Andrew Sullivan's very poignant description from our very own selves. Education throws things out of balance.

Whole institutions are in this business, perhaps without recognizing it. Let me tell a story. Not so long ago, we ran an article in *Commonweal* extolling the virtues of Catholic parish schools written by a young woman in her mid-thirties; she's a lawyer, she's a partner in a Cincinnati law firm, she has two children. She writes, "We must preserve the parish schools, this is the only hope for the future of a Catholic culture and a Catholic people." Soon thereafter, we had this letter from a reader:

> Whatever the benefits of the Catholic school system—and there have been many—I think Kathleen McGarvey Hidy [April 10] has idealized the system, while overlooking some important questions. If, as she says, "notions of stewardship, the common good, the responsibility of all Catholics in a community to rear the young have weakenend or disappeared," where were the graduates of Catholic schools while this was happening? As for the flight to the suburbs, many graduates of our schools fled to avoid integration. Catholics are now very well represented in the very echelons of business, where the values espoused are increasingly counter to the gospel. Do the graduates of our Catholic schools see any conflict here? Catholic charitable gifts, traditionally the lowest among Christian groups, have dropped further. What kind of faith formation is revealed by these examples? (Deidre Hetzler, letter to *Commonweal*, May 22, 1998)

Good question. This point could be applied to all levels of Catholic education. It raises a challenge to the Jesuit motto of men and women for others. Let's ask ourselves whether Catholic colleges and universities, in fact, haven't been turning out, I include myself, men and women for themselves? Hetzler's question puts the Catholic identity of Catholic higher education on the line. What makes us, or any school, any different from any other right-thinking, decent American college or university training people to get ahead in the world?

What exactly are we talking about when we talk about justice?

The *American Heritage Dictionary* says, "Justice is moral rightness, equity, honor, fairness, good reason, it means to approach with proper appreciation," that is, to do justice *to*. Philosophers and theologians and lawyers know there are many kinds of justice. There's commutative justice, distributive justice, social, retributive, redistributive, there is rough justice and easy justice, and as I am sure our law school professor would tell us, there is also dumb justice and cheap justice. All those adjectives should alert us to the ubiquitous nature of justice talk. Those adjectives always ought to be raising questions about what we really mean by justice.

There's the obvious question: Can you have justice without injustice? I mean, what is the point of insisting on justice, if there is not injustice abounding? And what is injustice? Is it the opposite of justice? An absence of all those qualities of equity, honor, righteousness? Is it moral turpitude? Inequity, dishonorableness, unfairness? Well we can be certain that no school would advertise itself as a proponent or practitioner of injustice, because those qualities of dishonorableness, unfairness, and turpitude are truly unattractive to us.

But I have another question, and that is the adjective that is implied in the Institute's title, and the adjective is *social* justice. Is that what Hopkins (1995) was talking about? I suspect Hopkins had something more personal and more immediate in mind, something that Hopkins reflected in so much of the rest of his poetry: a Creator everywhere and in *all ways* present. The wonderful line from another of his poems, "The world is charged with the grandeur of God." It is an incarnational sense. A Creator embedded everywhere; if we had to use a phrase for Hopkins's notion of justice, then I wonder if it would be something that would lead us into a discussion about virtue ethics, not one that I am capable of getting us into, but it seems to me that he may be pointing in that direction rather than in the direction of social justice. But in any case, I think his views would run against the idea of justice as a program or as a project. I think he is talking about justice as a way of life and as a way of being. Of seeing oneself rightly in creation and in relation to others.

When we talk about social justice as a marker for Catholic identity, don't we need to ask whether the emphasis on social justice is also wholly congenial to a secular, academic environment? What is distinctive for Christians in this? Furthermore, doesn't this emphasis on justice avoid one of the most bothersome and for many people troubling religious issues, especially a belief in a transcendent reality? Doesn't saying we're in favor of justice avoid the tensions and struggles that we ought to deal with between that transcendent reality and the reigning academic ethos of naturalism which rises from the natural and social sciences with its disposition to a materialistic set of propositions? Are we or are we not more than genes or gender?

I have raised all these questions not to exclude justice as a marker of Catholic identity, but to ask what would be distinctive for Catholic identity if you espouse this?

I take it that the primary marker has to be education itself: imparting information, introducing neophytes to facts, to data, to ideas, to expressing those ideas in speech and writing as well, introducing them, the students, into a discipline and its traditions, training people in certain skills; cogitating, mulling, actually thinking, thinking critically, arguing, we talked about debating, hypothesizing, and synthesizing; writing, rewriting, reconsidering, editing, and rewriting again. This is what any college or university is primarily about; what everybody should be doing and what, in fact, justice in the first instance requires that you do.

Presumably Catholic education would honor in all of these activities some expression of the Catholic tradition, its history, theology, its aesthetic, its virtues, and we would hope not too many of its vices. It would give a particular shape or tone or color to that education. This Catholic tradition would be supported by a community who feels responsible for imparting it to the next generation. That too is a justice question.

Markers for Catholic Education

Let me now explore the kinds of categories people are looking at when they talk about markers for Catholic identity in higher education. There are three I want to look at with their accompanying subcategories.

1. The first thing that's needed is a critical mass of faculty, administrators, and interested others, and by interested others I mean people who care about this school. Parents, alumni, donors, community leaders. I think that there has to be a group of people who have a coherent and workable plan for maintaining Catholic identity, whatever the group, whatever the community comes to mean by that. And I think it can mean many things. This is the work of a community, not of a single person or a single department, such as the theology or philosophy department. There has to be a group of people who want to do it. Adults, who care about this issue, who not only care about it and talk about it but who know how to strategize in ways that carefully examine and will carry out a plan that offers a serious version of whatever you want to call it, Catholicity, Catholicism, Catholic Tradition to the university. But I don't think this is the only story. Contrary to the fears of many people, this cannot be an exclusionary process. (There are a few schools that think it can be exclusionary. I don't think most places can do it and I don't think they should do it. One of the great events following Vatican II was the sense that Catholics got out of their own world and began to think along with all sorts of other people, Jews and Protestants primarily, but the rest of the world as well. I don't think there's any going back on that.)

This question of critical mass is in most schools at a critical juncture because of the loss of clergy and religious. The Jesuit Community, the Marymount Sisters, the Madams of the Sacred Heart, the Benedictines, are all shrinking bit by bit. These were the people who single-mindedly dedicated themselves to the mission of Catholic higher education. However well or badly they did their work, and many of them did it very well indeed, they were in a sense the embodiment of Catholic identity. The rest of us didn't have to worry. Now this task falls or ought to fall to Catholic lay people, but I don't think it is just a Catholic lay person's job. It is the work of a community that is not necessarily made up solely of Catholics. The question is, are these people willing to work at Catholic identity? Are they ready to do it? That is what a lot of places struggle with and it is by no means clear that people are ready, willing, and able to do this.

2. The second thing that I think people look at when they're looking at Catholic identity is curricular matters. Curricular developments reflect an effort to maintain or construct or reconstruct a Catholic identity. Now we all I am sure have strong opinions about this and my opinion is totally dictated by my own experience. I went to a Jesuit college, I got a great education, it was totally dictated to me from freshman to senior year. I took a philosophy course every semester; I took a theology course every semester; everyone graduated from Loyola University in Chicago in 1963 with minors in philosophy and theology.

Now the theology courses were not great. On the other hand, we knew a lot of stuff. What were great were the philosophy courses. Whatever anyone thinks about what philosophy should do, etc., I think it is a process by which people learn how to think and think critically and think about the big questions and the questions that make us know that our own experience is not the whole world. That's my candidate for how you think about curricular development here.

The other issue that comes up when we talk about curriculum is uniculturalism. Do we have to give up on multiculturalism? Does talking about Catholic identity mean one set of ideas, one notion about culture? I believe by definition Catholicism *is* multicultural if we all understand it in the proper sense. The arguments about multiculturalism seem to me to raise false issues. But, obviously they raise important political issues, and how people deal with that while they're dealing with the Catholic identity question is probably critical in many places for how these matters are resolved.

Some schools are doing very specific things that are outside of the range of curricular revision. There are schools talking about Catholic studies programs. You locate what you want to do about Catholic identity in a program. These are usually interdisciplinary programs with history and literature and theology and philosophy. Do these programs create a ghetto within the school? That is an important question to be examined. One great plus seems to be that people sure want to give money to these programs. I recently got in the mail an announcement from Loras College in Dubuque, Iowa, which has gotten ten million dollars to start a Catholic studies program. And so too, St. Thomas in St. Paul, Minnesota. Rich people who care about Catholic identity may be ready to pay for it. A variation on this is an honors program. Although the Catholic identity question is not necessarily central, it can be an arena in which some of these issues get worked out and worked through a group of the best students.

3. Then the third thing that is a focus of discussion is the common life of the university. And what do I mean by that? The life of the university is usually seen through the life of the students because they are here, they have dorms, they are residents, they control a lot of territory, and everybody else is here for their benefit. But the university is, or should be, a community of the whole. It has its everyday life. It has its civic life (most universities are only a little larger than the Greek city/states). More people should be paying more attention to life in the public square, recognizing that this community should reflect the whole university and not simply the students and dorm life. That is, students should not dominate the culture and the everyday life of the university. That means that there has to be a "normal" way in which faculty, administrators, and all those other interested adults are present in the community. Significant numbers of them should be present in ways that validate, give reality to, the intellectual, the philosophical, the spiritual or religious mission of the university. I want to think here about this in terms of the social construction of reality. What do people talk about? What do they see on the walls? What do the film festivals have? Who do students run into? What kind of spontaneous and intelligent conversations are possible. All of that needs intelligent shaping in light of what anybody would be doing, thinking about in terms of Catholic identity.

Now this cannot be an *in loco parentis* operation, but in terms of Paul Goodman's (1962) wonderful book, *A Community of Scholars*, a college or university has to be a community, a kind of *scola*. This raises questions about a spirit of civility and decorum, for example, what is dorm life like for a lot of kids in it. Is it the lowest common denominator that rules in many dormitories? Is that very hard on a lot of kids? What responsibility do adults have for doing something about that? Now that may not seem to be primarily an identity question, but a question about education and about learning and about the ability to study, etc. What about a civic life, that provides a sense of the aesthetic, the spiritual, the intellectual? Obviously liturgical practice is very important as well. Symbols of the schools' own religious tradition and founding community, the ugly statues that someone was offering to sell yesterday—those sorts of things can make statements, they can say things about identity and purpose.

I also think there are ways in which other religious traditions should be present and welcome on any Catholic campus. One of the highlights of my liturgical year is the Seder. I feel it is deeply connected to what I am about as a Catholic. And even though my Jewish friends see it in a totally other context, those rituals remind us of our own deepest beliefs. Ramadan and the fast of Ramadan should remind Christians and Catholics about the benefits, the virtues that flow from a truly good spirit in fasting.

Then there are all the obvious other things. The ACCU, the Association of Catholic Colleges and Universities, had a special meeting some years ago for people who do counseling and who are service providers in colleges and universities, such as pastoral counseling offices, which are often disconnected from the educational process. Are these part of the Catholic identity issue? What role do they play in the religious mission of the school? I am reminded of a counselor who I once met who worked in the pastoral counseling offices of a very large Catholic university. She had been a pediatric nurse, had gotten burnt out, but was a caring, loving person. She was telling me all about the state of student-hood at her place, and the terrible effect that divorce had on kids she was counseling. There's not only practical questions like where the kids are going to go for the holidays, but also a totally disrupted sense of a cohesive universe. She was really quite interesting and sophisticated in talking about all this. So I asked, "Well, what do you say to them? What do the kids do?" And she said, "Well sometimes I have to send them to someone who is more experienced in counseling." I said, "But you're a pastoral counseling office. Do they ever get any pastoral counseling?" And she said, "Well like what?" And I said, "Well I don't know. Do you ever suggest they pray about this or go to church?" She said, "Oh, I'd never impose that on them. That's just too personal!" But she'd impose Freud or Jung on them. I was just stunned and I realized that she saw her job as totally within the realm of counseling, psychotherapy, etc., and it had nothing to do with what most religious traditions would offer these students.

Service learning is another way to establish Catholic identity. It's the whole justice question come back. How are students exposed to a world that's not part of their world? They have to leave their white suburban enclaves and go to Chicago, etc. I'm always amused that at Notre Dame they go to Chicago when they could just go right to South Bend in Indiana itself and see far worse problems than I suspect they ever encounter in Chicago. Where people go for their service learning is in itself an interesting question.

Service learning that is not totally integrated into the educational life of the university is false service learning. I am reminded of an article we received at *Commonweal* from a student at a very fine university in the Midwest which began, "I don't read newspapers, I don't watch TV; I can't afford magazines, but two months ago I went to a social justice fair at my school, and I read a pamphlet that showed me that U.S. sanctions against Iraq were killing millions of women and children." I was absolutely horrified at the idea that this kid is finding out about Iraq and sanctions from a pamphlet at a social justice fair when he obviously has heard nothing about this in his political science course, his history course. He is becoming a great "social justice advocate" in a totally and absolutely ignorant manner! He doesn't have to afford magazines; he could go to his library and read them. There is a certain amount of attitude that if you are a social justice person and you are passionate, you don't have to be smart about being a social justice person. If people want to be social justice advocates, they can't be stupid. The question of integrated knowledge and action, of connecting what people to learn in their classrooms with what they do outside, is critically important. Turning out stupid social justice advocates cannot be the endpoint of a university education.

Conclusion

These are some of the things I see people talking about as markers of Catholic identity. I have tried to suggest that these discussions can go in a whole different set of directions. I do not think there are univocal answers to these questions. It is very important for places like Loyola Marymount University to meditate and reflect on its own tradition, its own history. As it answers these questions, it must look not only to the great Catholic tradition, but also within this community for people, for possibilities, and for direction.

This is a work of construction and not destruction. It does not mean destroying the excellence that people have worked so hard to build, nor is it dismantling the ecumenical interfaith spirit so many schools possess. It is not destroying things. And it is not restoring anything. We are trying to do something we have never really done before. In a reflective and wholehearted way, we are grappling with the question of how to be and become a Catholic institution in this incredibly diverse, difficult and often unjust world.

References

Coetzee, J. M. (1995). *Life and times of Michael K*. New York, NY: Viking Press.

Dickens, C. (1854). *Hard times*. London: Bradbury & Evans.

Goodman, P. (1962). *A community of scholars*. New York, NY: Random House.

Hampl, P. (1981). *A romantic education*. Boston, MA: Houghton Mifflin.

Hopkins, G. M. (1995). As kingfishers catch fire. In C. Phillips (Ed.), *Gerard Manley Hopkins* (p. 115). New York, NY: Oxford University Press.

Sullivan, A. (1996). *Virtually normal: An argument about homosexuality*. New York, NY: Viking Press.

SOCIAL JUSTICE OR INJUSTICE?

Diane D. Glave

Sixteen years ago, I witnessed an assault by a homeless man against a young woman. I was in Downtown Manhattan, near the Staten Island Ferry, with the summer sun slipping behind me. I increased my pace because Wall Street becomes a bleak, hard place after dusk. Up ahead, I noticed a homeless man dressed in dark greasy brown clothing. I moved swiftly, slipping around him. Looking defensively over my shoulder, I confirmed he was not in pursuit. A well-coifed woman styled in a short blunt cut, her slim body buttoned down in a pearl grey suit and white silk blouse, her manner business-like, moved toward the man. Swiftly, the homeless man embraced, dipped, and kissed her. Seconds later, he released the woman. She stumbled backward—mortified, aghast, and furious—wiping her smudged lipstick from her face with the palm of her French manicured hand. I caught this, still moving toward the "E" train to Queens, filing this crime under: "Reasons Why I Strongly Dislike Homeless People."

As a home-loving, clean, middle-class African-American woman, the kiss is visceral for me. Such feelings justify the neat comfortable categories we create: the homeless are undeserving and stockbrokers are upscale chic. As such, people remain divided: the rich versus the poor, the educated versus the illiterate, men versus women, children versus adults, African Americans versus whites, and the list continues. Social injustice becomes more common than social justice. Our quirks, attitudes, and experiences shape how we judge those worthy or unworthy of equality in society. I am certainly guilty, having judged homeless people, based on a jumble of big-city experiences: arm-to-arm homeless combat to verbal assaults.

The leaders and participants in the President's Institute attempt to define social justice at the university, particularly concerning students. After discussing the validity of social justice issues for women or staff at Loyola Marymount University, we ultimately focus on our students and their role in social justice. We agree students should volunteer, rather than be recruited, for any community service in the arena of social justice.

Margaret O'Brien Steinfels, the editor of *Commonweal*, presents her ideas to the group during the Institute. She argues that higher education, one of those dividing lines, creates a standard that "promotes and perpetuates injustice," separating the educated from the less educated. She adds,

"Moving up the educational ladder, separates people out more and more until finally, people like yourselves who have Ph.D.'s, are at the pinnacle of this system in which people have been separated from all sorts of things" (Steinfels, 2000). Loyola Marymount University, like universities across the country, certainly perpetuates class divisions, created by varying degrees of education on- and off-campus. Conversely, Loyola Marymount University creates opportunities for social and economic mobility for under-, lower-, and working-classes, which Ms. Steinfels neglects to mention.

Consider Ms. Steinfel's argument concerning the definition of social justice. Social relates to human society, "interaction of the individual and the group, or welfare of human beings as members of society as the contact or relationship with a companion or friend" (WWWebster, 1999). Essentially, one is friendly, pleasant, convivial, and congenial when social. In addition, justice is the administration of law; "the establishment of rights according to the rules of law or equity" (WWWebster, 1999). Numerous words apply: impartial, fair, truth, right, honorable, correct, and righteous. Such a social relationship requires that we treat one another as equals. I would add that social justice becomes mere charity without political and grassroots elements.

The governing body of the Society of Jesus, the Jesuits, focuses on some theoretical ideals concerning social justice. The Society of Jesus says in "Our Mission and Justice: Decree Three" in the *Documents of the 34th General Congregation of the Society of Jesus* (1995):

> In response to the Second Vatican Council, we, the Society of Jesus, set out on a journey of faith as we committed ourselves to the promotion of justice as an integral part of our mission. That commitment was a wonderful gift of God to us, for it put us into such good company—the Lord's surely, but also that of so many friends of his among the poor and those committed to justice. As fellow pilgrims with them towards the Kingdom, we have often been touched by their faith, renewed by their hope, transformed by their love. As servants of Christ's mission, we have been greatly enriched by opening our hearts and our very lives to "the joys and the hopes, the griefs and the anxieties of the men and women of this age, especially those who are poor or in any way afflicted.

In theory, the Jesuits' central and biblical mission charges Christians to do as Jesus did, a Christian perspective and theology.

Loyola Marymount University identifies these same strands in the Mission Statement (1990): "Loyola Marymount University understands and declares its purpose to be: the encouragement of learning, the education of the whole person, the service of faith and the promotion of justice" (*Mission, Goals, Objectives*, 1990). In the Jesuit tradition, Loyola Marymount University sends "its members—faculty, administration and staff—into the community to learn, to teach, to minister, to labor, to participate in and lead efforts to create a more rational, faith-filled, just society" (*Mission, Goals, Objectives*, 1990). The University certainly has a number of programs, including De Colores directed by Campus Ministry, as part of the Jesuit tradition. The De Colores program sends LMU students to volunteer in the Hogar Infantile Orphanage in Tiajuana, Mexico, seven times a year. They also work in the surrounding community, painting, mixing concrete, digging dirt, moving bricks, and building playgrounds (De Colores Program, 1999).

Does Loyola Marymount University fulfill its promise of social justice in programs like this across the campus? First, this work fits two categories: charity and volunteerism. A political component part of the definition of social justice is missing. Second, Ms. Steinfels challenges Catholic universities that do not fulfill their promises. She argues that education perpetuates and reinforces injustice, ". . . in some ways, schools are a form of injustice that separates goats from the sheep; that separates children; that separates people from one another and as you move up the educational ladder" (Steinfels, 2000, p. 137). She adds, "Education throws things out of balance, and creates disorder rather than order" (Steinfels, 2000).

This is certainly true. Yet education benefits individuals, arguably an aspect of social justice. Disadvantaged people, including the poor, minorities, and women, create their own social justice versus mass social movements for equality. These individuals achieve a new social, economic, and political mobility, while diminishing distinctions among the classes. Once poor, some return to impoverished neighborhoods or their own countries, contributing once again to the process of social justice.

I am a faculty member in the African-American Studies Department at Loyola Marymount University, a Jesuit institution. As such, I am concerned about social justice for these groups and individuals: African-American students, faculty, and the community. I also embrace a more universal form of social justice in Colossians 3:11–14 from the *Holy Bible* (King James Version):

Where there is neither Greek nor Jew, circumcision nor uncircumcision, Barbarian, Scythian, bond nor free: but Christ is all, and in all. Put on therefore, as the elect of God, holy and beloved, bowels of mercies, kindness, humbleness of mind, meekness, longsuffering; Forbearing one another, and forgiving one another, if any man have a quarrel against any: even as Christ forgave you, so also do ye. And above all these things put on charity, which is the bond of perfectness.

In addition, love is a central theme in social justice in I Corinthians 13:3–7: "And though I bestow all my goods to feed the poor, and though I give my body to be burned, and have not charity, it profiteth me nothing. Charity suffereth long, and is kind; charity envieth not; charity vaunteth not itself, is not puffed up. Doth not behave itself unseemly, seeketh not her own, is not easily provoked, thinketh no evil; Rejoiceth not in iniquity, but rejoiceth in the truth; Beareth all things, believeth all things, hopeth all things, endureth all things." In Colossians 3:14 (New International Version), the word love is used instead of charity, which is central to social justice: "And over all these virtues put on love, which binds them all together in perfect unity." Committing these verses to memory, particularly the section on love, I ask, "What would Jesus do?" a catchphrase on many a Baptist's bracelet or pin.

Some twelve years later, returning to my homeless vignettes in Los Angeles, a friend asked me to visit her job at the Union Rescue Mission. I immediately refused, based on my experiences with the homeless in New York City. After much negotiation, I finally relented and visited the mission. My conceptualization of the homeless was quickly tested. As I moved from the Mission garage to the elevator, I felt convicted in the Baptist tradition. You see, on the wall to the left of the elevator, I noticed a passage from Ecclesiastes 4:9–10 (New International Version): "Two are better than one, because they have a good return for their work: If one falls down, his friend can help him up. But pity the man who falls and has no one to help him up!" When I returned home, I read the chapter in Ecclesiastes, noting the first verse: "I looked and saw all the oppression that was taking place under the sun: I saw the tears of the oppressed—and they have no comforter; power was on the side of their oppressors—and they have no comforter."

As a result of my visit and these verses, I was forced to re-evaluate the homeless, treating them with love as individuals and not a collective. In the seconds by the elevator, I understood that social justice begins with individuals on the politicized grassroots level. If not, the work is simply charity. In addition, the divisions we create can be shattered by love. Though I was and am appalled by the homeless because of the dirt and odor, I realized—no I was convicted—that each homeless person should be treated as an individual, ultimately the consumers and the seeds of social justice.

So I ask in the context of my singular revelation at the Union Rescue Mission:

- How can a Jesuit institution share in social justice without politics?
- Do we press past our prejudices to implement social justice rather than charity?
- What motivates us?
- Are the recipients of social justice receptive to, ambivalent toward, or indignant by our gestures of social justice?
- Have we asked them what they want or need?
- Do they perceive our efforts as a parent to a child?
- Would they like to attend to their own affairs, while we provide assistance in the form of money and time upon request?

I ask more questions than supply answers. We should persist in asking these questions in love to promote social justice.

References

De Colores Program, Loyola Marymount University (1999). Retrieved March 2, 1999, from the World Wide Web: http://www.lmu.edu/ministry/descolor.html.

Documents of the Thirty-fourth General Congregation of the Society of Jesus (1995). St. Louis, MO: Institute of Jesuit Sources. Retrieved March 2, 1999, from the World Wide Web: http://web.lemoyne.edu/~bucko/c34_03.html.

Mission, Goals, Objectives (1990). Loyola Marymount University, Los Angeles, CA. Retrieved March 2, 1999, from the World Wide Web: http://www.lmu.edu /mission/LMU_Mission.html.

Stenifels, M. O. (2000). Promoting social justice: The business of higher education? In M K. McCullough (Ed.), *The just one justices: The role of justice at the heart of Catholic higher education* (pp. 135–145). Scranton, PA: University of Scranton Press.

WWWebster Dictionary (1999). Retrieved March 2, 1999, from the World Wide Web http//www.m-w.com/cgi-bin/dictionary.

PROMOTING JUSTICE THROUGH INCLUSION

Victoria L. Graf

What is the purpose of higher education in a Catholic university? Is it to educate students or to promote other values such as social justice? Should its purpose be different from secular universities such as those funded by a state? Is the notion of promoting justice one way of resolving the identity conundrum for a lot of schools (Steinfels, 2000)? Who should answer these questions? These are some of the issues being explored by many universities which are either affiliated with a religious institution such as the Catholic Church, i.e., Georgetown University, or have a historical foundation based on a religious belief such as Methodism, i.e., Brown University.

These questions raised by Margaret O'Brien Steinfels, Editor of *Commonweal* magazine, are critical ones for those of us who are part of a university community such as Loyola Marymount University, which is associated with the Society of Jesus and the Religious of the Sacred Heart of Mary, and currently discussing our mission and identity. They are also important to me, personally, since I am a faculty member who is a Protestant in a Catholic university.

My Reaction

In reflecting upon Ms. Steinfels' presentation, I am struck by how thought-provoking yet reassuring it was. The critical questions raised in terms of the purpose of higher education are similar to the current discussion regarding the purpose of public education. In the book, *The Public Purpose of Education and Schooling* (Goodlad & McMannon, 1997), John Goodlad and others explore the connections between education and society by raising the following questions: "What is education? What purposes does it serve? How does it benefit the person being educated? How does it benefit society? . . . Do different levels of schooling (elementary, secondary, and postsecondary) have different purposes, or are they merely different parts of the continuum?" (McMannon, 1997, p. 1).

The answers to the questions regarding the purpose of both higher education and public education may have profound implications, according to McMannon (1997). He cites a quote from Lawrence Cremin. "When we ask such questions, we are getting at the heart of the kind of society we want to live in and the kind of society we want our children to live in" (McMannon, 1997, p. 14).

While these are very important issues to address, Ms. Steinfels challenges us with even more thought-provoking questions: "Shouldn't we consider the possibility that education, in effect, is a catalyst for injustice? Let me put it bluntly: Doesn't education promote and perpetuate injustice?" (Steinfels, 2000, p. 136). Since one usually thinks of education in terms of the benefits that can be gained from it, these questions were almost shocking when first heard. They made me realize how naive, accepting, and almost complacent one can be regarding one's practice. As I will discuss later in the paper, these two questions relate directly to my field of study, but I had not considered them within the context of higher education.

While the presentation was thought-provoking, it was also reassuring to me as a Protestant faculty member at a university which is grappling with its Catholic identity. The theme for Ms. Steinfels's discussion was the need for inclusion. One example of the presentation's inclusive nature was her emphasis on welcoming various religious traditions on a Catholic campus. This is encouraging to me since it was clear I was welcome to participate in the discussion regarding the Catholic identity of the university. This has often been a concern for me since one occasionally hears about the need to hire faculty in order to promote the mission and identity of the university. Does this mean that only Catholic faculty should be hired? What does this imply with regards to faculty at the university who are not Catholic? Who makes this decision—the Vatican, the Archdiocese, or the university? Ms. Steinfels encourages inclusion as she states, "The answers to Catholic identity are local and need to be local (Steinfels, 2000).

I am concerned that this positive message of inclusion of various religious traditions and local decision making at Catholic universities is not widespread even at the level of the local university. Non-Catholic and even some Catholic faculty members (tenured and non-tenured) are often hesitant to participate in discussions regarding the Catholic identity of universities out of concern for negative retribution by university administrators and other faculty members. Consequently, the audience for presentations such as this and subsequent discussions should include all members of the university community.

Relationship to the Discipline of Education

The presentation relates to the following three components of the field of education, which is my area of interest and expertise: (a) teacher education, (b) the role of justice in higher education, and (c) the inequities of education in practice.

The questions raised in the presentation remind us of the moral dimensions of higher education. How does this relate specifically to my field of study, teacher education, specifically, the education of teachers working with students with disabilities? Since the context in which these teachers work is primarily the public sector, issues of faith and religion are not discussed nor, typically, is the moral dimension of teaching. Instead, my field of teacher education emphasizes the preparation of teachers to be able to identify and assess students with disabilities as well as adapt curriculum so that students with learning disabilities, for example, can have access to the core curriculum. Rarely do teacher educators or graduates of teacher education programs ask or attempt to answer the questions raised by Steinfels (2000) or McMannon (1997).

An exception is the work of John Goodlad, Director of the Center for Educational Renewal at the University of Washington and co-editor of the book, *The Moral Dimensions of Teaching*. In a comprehensive study of the education of educators, John Goodlad and colleagues, Roger Soder and Kenneth Sirotnik, found the following:

> Relatively few teacher education programs offer courses addressing the role of the schools in a democratic society, the moral process of becoming humane, and some of the conflicts involved in squaring the educational needs of students with the special interests of the larger community. (Goodlad, Soder, & Sirotnik, 1990, p. xiv)

In contrast to these findings, these authors believe that "Education—a deliberate effort to develop values and responsibilities as well as skills—is a moral endeavor" (Goodlad, Soder, & Sirotnik, 1990, p. xii). Consequently, Goodlad (1994) has outlined a mission for teacher education which includes the following four components, all of which have a moral dimension: (a) enculturating the young in a social and political democracy; (b) providing access to knowledge for all children and youths; (c) teaching in a nurturing way; and (d) ensuring responsible stewardship of schools.

In an attempt to address the moral dimension of teaching, the development of a personal philosophy of teachers is viewed as critical to their practice. When individuals must ask themselves "What is good?" or "What is knowledge?" they begin to formulate the values that are important to them, which then influence the educational decisions they make. Having a personal philosophy assists teachers in addressing these moral questions regarding the purpose of education and the role of justice in education.

What should be the role of justice in higher education? Steinfels (2000) asks us to consider the various definitions of justice and injustice including the various forms of legal justice as well as social justice. Since the University and School of Education, with which I am affiliated, have a commitment to social justice because of the association with the Jesuit and Marymount traditions, I will focus on the role of social justice in higher education. According to Martin (1997), a commitment to social justice includes action. This action can include: "(1) modeling social justice in our interactions with students, colleagues, and the community; (2) incorporating social justice themes and analysis in our courses as appropriate; and (3) working for social justice in the community" (Martin, 1997, p. 1).

Higher education is grappling with its responsibility to social justice. In the Op-Ed section of the *Los Angeles Times*, two faculty members at Occidental College in the Los Angeles area write:

Colleges should be engaged in helping solve society's problems. In particular, four crucial, overlapping trends pose special challenges: widening economic and racial inequality; growing divisions between cities, suburbs and rural areas; persistent threats to our environment and public health; and the loss of community identities due to increasing globalization of economics and culture. (Dreier & Gottlieb, 1998, p. 9)

They go on to discuss how Occidental College has changed "from a cloistered and privileged environment to an institution that connects the campus and the community" (Dreier & Gottlieb, 1998, p. 9). They conclude the article by stating, "Connecting the campus to the community is not simply a service or an abstract proposition, but lies at the heart of the choices facing higher education" (Dreier & Gottlieb, 1998, p. 9). And so the debate over the mission of higher education has been going on for many years. Two major contributors to the debate were Robert Maynard Hutchins, President of the University of Chicago, and educational philosopher, John Dewey. Hutchins believed the undergraduate curriculum should emphasize "fixed truths" which, according to Hutchins, never change. Education should then be the same everywhere (Erlich, 1996; Morrison, 1997). In contrast to this philosophy, Dewey believed that Hutchins's views were dangerous since they went against democratic principles and were unrelated to practice and to solving the problems of society (Erlich, 1996). According to Erlich (1996), there has been a shift in higher education away from the thinking of Hutchins and toward the philosophy of Dewey.

This shift is due to several factors, according to Jacoby (1996). Students currently attending universities are committed to performing community service. This is due partially to the requirements of elementary and secondary schools for students to be involved in volunteer work. University students continue to participate in their communities and "are likely to express their lofty political and social impulses and practical desires to change the world through community service" (Jacoby, 1996, p. 4).

Support for Dewey's philosophy of connecting the mission of the university to solving the problems of society also comes from experts in higher education such as Ernest Boyer, who "urges colleges and universities to 'respond to the challenges that confront our children, our schools, and our cities, just as the land-grant colleges responded to the needs of agriculture and industry a century ago'" (Jacoby, 1996, p. 3).

To connect this desire to serve with academic learning, programs called service learning have emerged on college campuses. Jacoby defines service learning as "a form of experiential education in which students engage in activities that address human and community needs together with structured opportunities intentionally designed to promote student learning and development. Reflection and reciprocity are key concepts of service-learning" (Jacoby, 1996, p. 5). Steinfels (2000) cautions us about these programs which, if not integrated thoughtfully and rigorously into the academic life of the university, can result in social justice becoming a project rather than "a way of life and as a way of being" (Steinfels, 2000, p. 140).

Steinfels (2000) challenges us to consider the possibility that education can promote injustice. In her selection of readings and in her discussion, Steinfels illustrates how education can separate us from each other and sometimes from ourselves. My field of Special Education, the education of students with disabilities, evolved from this notion of separation.

Winzer (1993), in her book *The History of Special Education: From Isolation to Integration*, describes how intelligence was linked in the late nineteenth and early twentieth century to the notion of biological "goodness." Some groups of individuals were thought to have more or less intelligence as measured by intelligence tests and those with lower levels of intelligence were associated with delinquency and crime (Winzer, 1993). It became acceptable to stratify society on the basis of test results including immigrants from certain European countries. "The test results were used to prove irrefutably that certain areas of Europe produced genetically inferior stock" (Winzer, 1993, p. 256). This only encouraged stereotyping of individuals as well as racist attitudes.

The most dramatic and serious consequence of the practice of stratifying individuals was the eugenics movement. The purpose of this movement was to improve the human race through purposeful breeding which also included the restriction "of mating of the unfit" (Winzer, 1993, p. 284). This could be accomplished by education, legislation, segregation, and even sterilization, according to Winzer (1993). Eugenics continued as a widespread practice until the 1940s, although some states until recently continued using compulsory sterilization of individuals with mental retardation.

A less noxious form of stratification was the development of special education classes. Although the rationale for their development was well intended, abuses did result. In California in the early 1970s, it was observed that the majority of students in special education classes for the mildly retarded were either African-American or Latino. These students were over-represented in these classes in comparison to their percentage in the general school population. To address this inequity, lawsuits were filed, and as a result, the use of individual intelligence tests with African-American students was prohibited (*Larry P. v. Riles*, 1979) and more appropriate processes for placing Latino students in special education were to be developed (*Diana v. State Board of Education*, 1970).

Research into the benefits of special education classes over placement of students with disabilities in general education classes has been inconclusive as has the research into the effects of labeling and classifying a person as disabled (Hallahan & Kauffman, 1997). As Steinfels (2000) points out in her discussion of the readings, however, separation of individuals is unjust whether we can prove it or not. Inclusion of students with disabilities with students without disabilities, therefore, has become a goal for both general and special education.

Relationship to My Work

The points raised in Ms. Steinfels's presentation serve as a reminder of what should guide my practice as I interact with students and all members of the university community. I must ask myself often, "What is the purpose of my work?" Is it to educate students or to promote other values such as social justice? Does my practice promote injustice? How am I participating in the common life of the university? Am I, to paraphrase Gerard Manley Hopkins, acting in God's eye what in God's eye he is (Hopkins, 1995)?

I recently worked collaboratively with colleagues and students in the School of Education to develop a mission statement. In addition to the questions stated above, we were guided by the following goals from the mission statement: (a) to value and respect all individuals; (b) to promote cultural responsiveness and social justice; (c) to integrate theory and practice; (d) to develop moral, intellectual, and responsible leaders; and (e) to collaborate and share leadership across communities (School of Education Mission Statement, 1998). Fortunately, I have the support of my colleagues and students as I attempt to meet these goals.

My other source of guidance as I work with students is my own philosophy of teaching. Recently, I was asked to write my philosophy. Since I had never written or been asked to verbalize my own views about university teaching in almost 20 years of being in higher education, I spent a considerable amount of time thinking about what is important to me regarding my interactions with students. The following are the principles and values I hold: (a) all individuals can and should be successful learners, and age, religion or belief, socioeconomic status, gender, race, ethnicity, language, sexual orientation, disability, or any other human variation should not be seen as impediments but as positive contributions to the learner and the learning environment; (b) teaching is not the transmission of knowledge but is a means by which the learner is assisted in the process of constructing knowledge, ongoing self-discovery, critical inquiry, and reflection with the intent of serving others and transforming society; (c) teachers should serve as mentors, facilitators, guides, enablers, and role models; and (d) my mission is the encouragement of learning, the education of the whole person, the service of faith, and the promotion of justice.

As I think about Ms. Steinfels's presentation, the School of Education mission statement, and my own philosophy of teaching, I believe there are common goals shaping my work with students. First, I will reflect upon my practice regarding its intent. Second, I will value and respect each individual since each person is a child of God and I must act in God's eye what in God's eye He is. Third, I will act in a socially just manner.

Relationship to My Faith Perspective

I am a Protestant faculty member in a Catholic university, raised in the Lutheran Church–Missouri Synod, one of the most conservative synods of this denomination. While I have often had periods of doubt about my affiliation with this particular faith perspective, I have always considered myself to be a Christian. One of my personal issues has been the reluctance of the Church to question its practice. Ms. Steinfels' presentation reminds me there is a place in a Catholic university to question and discuss what the Catholic identity of a university should be, and that the answers can be found at the level of the individual university rather than coming from the Church hierarchy. As a result of not allowing dissension, the Lutheran Church–Missouri Synod experienced a very painful split between two factions of the Church due to differing beliefs regarding how the Bible should be interpreted. This resulted in many clergy being "exiled" by the hierarchy of the Church. Rather than trying to suppress reflection, questioning, and dissension, it appears to me that the discussion on the identity of the Catholic university can be inclusive rather than exclusive.

My other concern with my own faith perspective has been the minimal attention given to social justice by the Lutheran Church–Missouri Synod. Its beliefs are based on the teaching of Martin Luther which emphasize "Grace alone, Scripture alone and Faith alone" (Lutheran Church–Missouri Synod, 1998). While I do not disagree with these three principles, I also believe that one must put these principles into practice through action. I am in agreement with the Marymount and Jesuit traditions which "emphasize the importance of working for justice as a concrete way to respond to the stewardship relationship we have with our students. This takes the form of addressing injustice in our own lives and work, and also in the lives of our students" (Martin, 1997, p. 1).

Relationship to My Discipline, Work and/or Faith Life

While the presentation addressed many issues regarding the purpose of higher education and the discussion of the Catholic identity of universities, the readings for the Institute were specifically chosen to address Ms. Steinfels's concern that education may perpetuate injustice. As an educator of teachers, these readings were particularly significant, especially those from Charles Dickens and Andrew Sullivan.

Charles Dickens's *Hard Times* is particularly relevant to the questions raised by McMannon and discussed earlier in this paper. What is education? Is it as Mr. Gradgrind states, "Now, what I want is, Facts. Teach these boys and girls nothing but Facts. Facts alone are wanted in life" (Dickens, 1854, p. 3), or should it be "primarily a step toward employment, a means to achieve wisdom or something else entirely" (McMannon, 1997, p. 13).

Ms. Steinfels's choice of *Hard Times* is important in illustrating how students have typically been thought of as "little vessels, then and there arranged in order, ready to have imperial gallons of facts poured into them until they were full to the brim" (Dickens, 1854, p. 4). Do students come to the learning environment void of knowledge? Do teachers have all the knowledge and is it their job to transmit this knowledge? These questions elicited from the reading selection illustrate one of the current issues in the field of education regarding how knowledge is constructed. In contrast to the idea that students are empty vessels and that teaching and learning are unidirectional, the work of Lev Vygotsky (Wertsch, 1985) and Moll, Amanti, Neff, & Gonzalez (1992) provides evidence that knowledge is socially constructed and that students have "funds of knowledge" they bring to the learning environment. As Martin (1996) states, "The sociocultural theory of learning maintains that learning occurs in the interaction between the student, a teacher and the problem to be solved. Both the teacher and student bring something to the process, and the result of their interaction is the construction of knowledge" (p. 18).

The theme of feeling different, not belonging, and even being alienated from one's self as described in Andrew Sullivan's (1996) book, *Virtually Normal*, applies also to individuals with disabilities as well as to individuals who are homosexual. The challenge and question arising from this reading is, "How can we support people in their attempts to be true to themselves, to be real?" My field, in particular, has looked for differences in people, differences that distinguish them from what is socially viewed as "the norm," in an attempt to address individual needs. This has often resulted in students with disabilities being viewed as defective or deficient in some way. As the move toward including individuals with disabilities with those without disabilities progresses, we are shifting the focus from what separates us as human beings to what unites us. Ms. Steinfels's wisdom helps us in this endeavor.

References

Boyer, E.L. (1996). In B. Jacoby & Associates (Eds.), *Service-learning in higher education* (pp. 3–25). San Francisco, CA: Jossey-Bass Inc.

Cremin, L.A. (1997). In J.I. Goodlad & T.J. McMannon (Eds.), *The public purpose of education and schooling* (pp. 1–17). San Francisco, CA: Jossey-Bass Inc.

Diana v. State Board of Education. No. C–70–37 RFT (N.D. Cal. 1970).

Dickens, C. (1854). *Hard times.* London, England: Bradbury & Evans.

Dreier, P., & Gottlieb, R. (1998, August 14). Reconnecting campus and community. *Los Angeles Times*, p. 3.

Erlich, T. (1996). Foreword. In B. Jacoby & Associates (Eds.), *Service-learning in higher education* (pp. xi–xvi). San Francisco, CA: Jossey-Bass Inc.

Goodlad, J.I. (1994). *Educational renewal.* San Francisco, CA: Jossey-Bass Inc.

Goodlad, J.I., & McMannon, T.J. (Eds.) (1997). *The public purpose of education and schooling.* San Francisco, CA: Jossey-Bass Inc.

Goodlad, J.I., Soder, R., & Sirotnik, K.A. (Eds.) (1990). *The moral dimensions of teaching.* San Francisco, CA: Jossey-Bass Inc.

Hallahan, D.P., & Kauffman, J.M. (1997). *Exceptional learners: Introduction to special education.* Boston, MA: Allyn & Bacon.

Hopkins, G. M. (1995). As kingfishers catch fire. In C. Phillips (Ed.), *Gerard Manley Hopkins* (p. 115). New York: Oxford University Press.

Jacoby, B. (1996). Service-learning in today's higher education. In B. Jacoby & Associates (Eds.), *Service-learning in higher education* (pp. 3–25). San Francisco, CA: Jossey-Bass Inc.

Jacoby, B., & Associates (Eds.) (1996). *Service-learning in higher education.* San Francisco, CA: Jossey-Bass Inc.

Larry P. v. Riles, 495 F. Supp. 96 (N.D. Cal. 1979), *aff'd* (9th cr. no. 80–427. Jan. 23, 1984).

Lutheran Church–Missouri Synod (1998). *Belief and practice.* Retrieved August 16, 1998, from the World Wide Web: http://www.lcms.org/belief.shtml.

Martin. S. (1996). *Cultural diversity in catholic schools: Challenges and opportunities for Catholic educators.* Washington, DC: National Catholic Educational Association.

Martin, S. (1997). Conceptual framework: Sociocultural/constructivist theory. Unpublished manuscript, Loyola Marymount University.

McMannon, T.J. (1997). Introduction: The changing purposes of education and schooling. In J.I. Goodlad & T.J. McMannon (Eds.), *The public purpose of education and schooling* (pp. 1–17). San Francisco, CA: Jossey-Bass Inc.

Moll, L.C., Amanti, C., Neff, D., & Gonzalez, N. (1992). Funds of knowledge for teaching: Using a qualitative approach to connect homes and classrooms. *Theory Into Practice, 31*, 132–141.

Morrison, G.S. (1997). *Teaching in America*. Boston, MA: Allyn & Bacon.

School of Education Mission Statement (1998). Loyola Marymount University. Los Angeles, CA.

Steinfels, M.O. (2000). Promoting justice: the business of higher education? In M.K. McCullough (Ed.), *The just one justices: The role of justice at the heart of Catholic higher education* (pp. 135–145). Scranton, PA: University of Scranton Press.

Sullivan, A. (1996). *Virtually normal: An argument about homosexuality*. New York, NY: Viking Press.

Wertsch, J.V. (1985). *Vygotsky and the social formation of mind*. Cambridge, MA: Harvard University Press.

Winzer, M.A. (1993). *The history of special education: From isolation to integration*. Washington, DC: Gallaudet University Press.

CAN ITS COMMITMENT TO JUSTICE DISTINGUISH A CATHOLIC EDUCATION?

W. S. K. Cameron

Both in her Georgetown lecture and in her presentation at Loyola Marymount University, Margaret O'Brien Steinfels made a series of acute observations covering a wide range of issues. In what follows I will take up the question she highlighted here: Can a Catholic school's focus on justice distinguish it from secular colleges, or does it represent a common denominator of both approaches—and hence a factor which may dissolve a distinctively Catholic tradition? In Steinfels's (2000) provocative formulation:

> . . . whether the emphasis on social justice is also wholly congenial to a secular academic environment? What is distinctive for Christians in this? Furthermore, doesn't this emphasis on justice avoid one of the most bothersome and for many people troubling religious issues, especially a belief in a transcendent reality? Doesn't saying we're in favor of justice avoid the tensions and struggles that we ought to deal with between that transcendent reality and the reigning academic ethos of naturalism which rises from the natural and social sciences with its disposition to a materialistic set of propositions? (p. 140)

What, then, is the relation between a concern for justice that is clearly not exclusive to the Catholic tradition and that tradition's overall identity? In what follows I will take a brief look at the historical and philosophical contexts to see whether they provide any indications of an answer. My thesis: a justice focus is indeed common to both Catholic and secular traditions and thus at one level it cannot distinguish them. At Catholic schools—and I've chosen the generic term since the point holds of primary and secondary as well as of tertiary education—faculty can be grateful that the common theme of justice provides an external point of contact with secular schools and an internal link for those uncomfortable with the more distinctively Catholic aspects of their school's mission. Yet the focus on justice does in another sense provide a way to distinguish the two traditions precisely because it alone cannot specify the mission of a secular, much less that of a Catholic, school. One's theory of justice—and consequently any just practice—necessarily depends on one's broader account of the good. And that, in the Catholic tradition, must inevitably refer to bothersome religious issues, especially a belief in a transcendent reality (Steinfels, 2000).

Back to the first point then: Steinfels is clearly correct to suggest that while the theme of justice may be a necessary component of a Catholic education, it is not sufficient, at least at first sight, to identify that tradition uniquely. In fact, even secular accounts of the history of philosophy are usually generous enough to admit the reason: the modern universities—virtually all Christian at their foundation—had been stunningly successful at convincing educated people that they were obligated to seek justice for all. It was, in short, the *success* of the Catholic intellectual tradition which ensured that its focus on justice would not be unique. The core Enlightenment commitments to modern natural law and human rights affirmed, albeit in secular form, the Christian belief in the equality of all before God.

To be sure, there had been other, albeit less immediate and less unequivocal influences. Plato's major dialogues take justice as their theme, and his conviction of the centrality of virtue in the good life certainly shaped the subsequent development of Western philosophy. But while the Platonic tradition valued education in the service just government, its account of justice was not inherently universalist: one could, like Aristotle, distinguish those deserving justice—humans—from those who looked like humans but who were not—i.e., slaves. Stoicism, on the other hand, played an influential role in spreading the belief in the inherent dignity of all humans, but its encouragement of political quietism and the willingness to endure one's fate discouraged the use of education to change the world. For all the differences between its aspirations and its accomplishments, Christendom after Constantine did at least hold both these commitments together: Christian officials were obliged to seek justice for all God's children. Enlightenment liberals inherited and affirmed this aspect of the older tradition; and thus achieving greater justice was from the beginning one of the goals of state-supported secular education.

There are thus good historical reasons why their common concern with justice can serve as a congenial point of convergence between Catholic schools and a secular academic environment that is politically liberal and occasionally radical (Steinfels, 2000). In both traditions, education was supposed to produce a good result even though it could separate us "from one another, from our families, from our communities, sometimes . . . even from our very own selves" (Steinfels, 2000, p. 138). Indeed in the secular context, it was this very ability to dissolve old beliefs and allegiances that made education a crucial instrument in the drive to progress. Descartes revolutionized philosophy with his method of radical doubt, and ever since a self-compounding circle has dominated. Both the encounter with other, sometimes radically different, traditions and the growing willingness to suspend uncritical attachment to our own tradition have meant that action within and between societies must be coordinated in post-traditional ways. If that was not to mean total war—and of course it did mean that far too often—we had to learn to reason together more effectively. And that meant being even more willing to ferret out and suspend belief in suspect traditional patterns of thought, hoping to discover some common core of reason. On this model, education intentionally threw things "out of balance" (Steinfels, 2000, p. 138), for it achieved its purpose that way.

But if the secular tradition aimed to shake up students by means of education, that goal had to be even more central to a religious tradition which recognized not only the continuing actuality of injustice but also the alienation from self and others rooted in sin. In their attempt to leaven the whole culture, Catholic schools thus had a biblical mandate to separate students from their families, their communities, and even from themselves —or better, they were charged to undermine students' attachments to false selves in order to awaken them to the true selves who alone could build an eternal community. Recall Jesus' shockingly vivid metaphor for the renunciation of all that gets in the way: one cannot be a disciple of Jesus "without hating father, mother, wife, children, brothers, sisters, yes and your own life too" (Luke 14:25–27, New American Version). Earthly love may be very good, but it is only an image of and cannot be preferred to the divine. Celibacy, the many other forms of voluntary renunciation, and more recently the preferential option for the poor: all of these were biblically motivated ways of overturning longstanding and in some cases age-old traditions in the name of the City of God. Indeed the historic affirmation of "witnesses" to the faith—i.e., martyrs—suggests that the Church and her institutions have been at their most distinctive when they have questioned the usual ways of the world.

In both secular and Catholic contexts, then, education raised questions about the traditions which students had inherited through family, ethnic, national, and gender-identities. Both shared the view that this process of unsettling traditions could achieve some good and thus that it was not intrinsically bad. But this unsettling process was not intrinsically good, either. For despite the common aim of achieving justice, the results in both secular and religious practice were decidedly mixed. Education could be and has been, as Steinfels (2000) suggests, a catalyst for injustice. Indeed education can catalyze injustice in at least the following five ways:

(a) Education can separate us from ourselves and from one another in other trivial but potentially destructive ways. I'm sure I'm not the only one who returned from a year at college proud of my advancement to the status of "wise fool" (sophomore). And what of the many unintended costs of valuing education in our culture: e.g., the superior attitude of those who've succeeded toward those who have not—blaming the victim, in many cases, given the virtual planning of failure so graphically documented by Jonathan Kozol (1991); or the cost to the poorer or emotionally less sturdy children of ambitious families for whom failure means, figuratively and sometimes literally, death. Pride finds opportunities everywhere.

(b) Moreover education's destabilizing effect on old presuppositions and prejudices is morally ambiguous. Often education merely legitimates and institutionalizes old prejudices. Sometimes it dissolves old prejudices in the name of new, much more destructive ones, in the manner of Dickens's Messrs. Gradgrind and Choakumchild, the fearsome educators in *Hard Times* (1854). And even as education dissolves ignorance, it also dissolves bonds, forcing granddaughters to choose between the "sensible future" of their parents and siblings on one side of the fence, and "the other, unkempt side of the fence" with their grandparents, "where the past—the real past, not of history but of mythic, granite secrecy which is ignorance—refused to lie down and play dead" (Hampl, 1981, p. 48).

(c) Education's effect on the perception of justice in particular is problematic, since it often unintentionally sustains old or produces new injustices. Some effectively "educate" students to a form of moral and political blindness, using sophisticated arguments to justify the conclusion that the injustice around us is inevitable, unconquerable, or perhaps not even injustice. But unintended injustice has not been the sole preserve of educators committed to the status quo ante. How many lives have been lost in wars and revolutions fought in the name of justice since the first two successful ones fomented by *philosophies* two centuries ago? Even the political center cannot claim clean hands, since its incrimentalism in fact allows the continuation of injustice, offering, at best, justice delayed. That conservatives, centrists, and revolutionaries have typically been well-intentioned cannot completely excuse the injustice each has directly or indirectly caused.

(d) Fourth, and more systemically: our wide reliance on educational qualification for work theoretically levels the economic playing field, since individuals earn positions on the basis of merit demonstrated at school. But as Ivan Illich (1971) has pointed out so incisively, schools function as a "radical monopoly," and thus not only allow but effectively ensure unequal representation in the professions, in business, and in government. This becomes clear to common sense once one grasps the concept of a radical monopoly. According to Illich, a business becomes a monopoly when it alone furnishes a product that we all desire, as would be the case if General Motors made all cars. A *radical* monopoly occurs when society itself is restructured so that one way of meeting a common need becomes the only possible way. Los Angeles, for example, was restructured when, in mid-century, it let its formerly effective public transit system fall into disrepair (it had been sold—how about that?—to General Motors), and which then built freeways and low-density suburbs that both encouraged cars and discouraged any alternate forms of transportation.

In this century, schools and universities have gained a radical monopoly on professional certification, and thus they function as gatekeepers in the processes of initial job application and of promotion. And insofar as access to education is unevenly distributed, the very certification process which was to ensure equality of opportunity at the same time ensures inequality of results both within and between nations. Richer individuals can always forgo productive income longer than poorer, thus giving them a permanent advantage in seeking qualifications. The resulting process of educational "inflation" has become even more obvious in the twenty-eight years since Illich (1971) wrote: a GED is virtually required in order to haul garbage, and a masters degree such as an MSW or an MBA is now the entry-level qualification in many fields where formerly a BA sufficed. Illich does not question our legitimate interest in certification in the huge and anonymous post-industrial societies of the West; and I, at least, would find the UCLA diploma on my doctor's wall reassuring if she were soon to anaesthetize me and cut me open with a knife. But there are many contexts in which a less formal training through apprenticeship might constitute an equivalent or even a superior preparation for certification—and not least, in the fields we most closely associate with professionalism, such as medicine and the law. In the absence of other, less costly alternatives, schools play at best an ambiguous role in the struggle to equalize opportunity well enough that people can be chosen on the basis of merit.

(e) And finally, of course, there are those who intentionally use education to promote injustice. The old debate between Socrates and the sophists continues still, and many of the sophists' students (and—God help me—surely mine too) find highly remunerative employ for the skills they've learned at school in, e.g., ad agencies, political and market lobbying groups, and public relations firms. I don't think it's unduly cynical to suspect that at least some know they are using their skills in ways destructive of the common good.

In at least these five respects, then, education is emphatically *not* neutral from the point of view of justice. Given the hope of achieving some good and the obvious possibilities for evil, what was the historic rationale for education in the Christian context?

In his *Confessions*, Augustine baptized a Platonic argument. Plato was well aware that education, like rhetoric—education's metonym in Socrates' debate with Gorgias—could be used either to liberate or emiserate individuals and whole communities. Education is thus a good, but it is not the only or the highest good; it is—in the old way of speaking—subservient to a higher end. In a similar way, Augustine found biblical support for the study of classical authors through the metaphor of "Egyptian gold," recalling the night when the escaping Israelites took their masters' gold—in the form of household idols—to finance their flight out of Egypt. The suspicious form of the gold could be overlooked as long as it was used for higher ends; so also, Augustine argued, the fruits of pagan philosophy, literature, and art (Augustine, 1960, p. 170). Like the employment of our senses, our health, our intelligence, and our creativity, education could be enjoyed for its own sake only as long as its enjoyment was constrained by the necessity of achieving our highest end. Christians don't get to heaven by knowing the Bible or by having a sophisticated theology, but through the godly foolishness and humility to accept and respond to a gift of amazing grace; so also the desire to know everything human through the study of pagan literature and philosophy must serve the Christian's final aim of becoming fully human for God.

Education, in the Christian context, is thus ultimately a means to an end even higher than (though one that includes) justice. Steinfels draws attention to this point in metaphorical form when she suggests that Gerard Manley Hopkins, in saying that "The just man justices," has

> . . . something more personal and more immediate in mind, something that Hopkins reflected in so much of the rest of his poetry: a Creator everywhere and *all ways* present . . . "the world is charged with the grandeur of God."

> . . . his views would run against the idea of justice as a program or as a project. I think he is talking about justice as a way of life and as a way of being. (Steinfels, 2000, p. 140)

Augustine would agree: justice cannot be a program. One of the casualties of modern philosophy has been the old sense of "righteousness," understood as living in right relationships. The Christian view that justice must be subsumed in love does not allow one to ignore an education for justice. That view demands such an education, but sees it as contributing to the larger task of developing whole people, people who really *are* just because they are not *merely* just. But if an education for justice is a means to a higher end in a Christian context, it is a means to a higher end in a secular context as well.

The dependence of justice on higher ends in a secular context becomes most obvious when we riffle through the long list of apparently intractable debates that step up as pinch-hitter subjects on talk radio during slow news days. Capital punishment, abortion, affirmative action, environmental protection, parole and sentencing reform, the legalization of recreational drugs: there is a reason why all of these topics keep being recycled. They are essentially contested; but they are not merely controversial in the way of arguments about sports or fashion, since their resolution would say much about who we think we are or ought to be. And that's the problem: while all these controversies involve issues of justice, none can be resolved without taking into account much more than our views about justice. Their resolution depends on controversial claims about what is most real, most fulfilling, most fundamentally good.

Yet liberalism, the reigning Enlightenment political theory, is very quiet on these issues. Moreover its silence is no accident, for liberalism took its name from its fundamental commitment to individual freedom. As a political theory, liberalism thematizes the *boundaries* of public discourse and action. A liberal government (and I mean "liberal" in the generic sense, as opposed to feudal or socialist) must in principle refuse to favor a particular interpretation of the good life; we citizens are on our own here, as long as we respect the equal liberty of others. What does this mean in practice? Prayer in schools and Sunday shopping laws cannot be sustained even in a country with a less consistent commitment to liberalism such as Canada, let alone in the United States. But in the very act of maximizing individual liberty, liberal governments intentionally blind themselves to the deeper kind of freedom which had been the focus of classical Greek and Christian political theory: i.e., to freedom as human flourishing. Is it actually good for us, let alone for the unfortunate clerks, to be able to shop around the clock? A good liberal will not answer; she attempts to make do with a "thin" theory of the good, one which is as neutral as possible toward "thicker," more substantive and controversial claims about what makes life worth living.

Historically speaking, there were tremendous virtues in this approach. After centuries of religious and political wars which only succeeded in fertilizing the battlefields of Europe with blood, it must have been a relief to agree to disagree, and to practice the moral discipline of averting one's eyes from one's profoundest differences with others. Moreover even though they were as agnostic as possible with respect to questions of the good, liberal theories of justice were not vacuous. Two substantive principles gave bite to liberal commitments—freedom and equality—and these principles straightforwardly ruled out many kinds of injustice. Progress could be measured in terms of the affronts against freedom and equality identified and defeated.

But if the liberal commitments to freedom and equality could have clear and substantive implications, each of the two principles also generated ambiguities. What does our affirmation of the general principle of equality mean: equality of results or equality of opportunity? And if the latter, as most in the United States would say, which kinds of equality matter and what counts as equality? Opportunities to learn to ski or to sail are very unevenly distributed, but most of us do not find that disparity of access upsetting. Yet other, more obviously important, opportunities are also distributed un-equally. The way we fund public education generates huge inequalities between different, sometimes contiguous, school districts. Yet we require students everywhere to attend schools until they are at least sixteen. This means, as Kozol points out, that "the state, by requiring attendance but refusing to require equality, effectively requires inequality" (Kozol, 1991, p. 56)—and that in an area highly prejudicial to the equal opportunity of economically deprived students.

Finally, even where opportunities are evenly distributed by law, we must wonder whether that legal equality is really meaningful. There is, for instance, no legal barrier to my daughter's becoming President. But in an age when even President Bush's commission on affirmative action testified to the continuing existence of a glass ceiling, her odds are significantly lower than those of her male cousins. Are barriers formed by private prejudices sufficient to ground legal complaint? Here as elsewhere, our ultimate conclusions about what equality of opportunity should mean will depend on our views about what it means to be fully human; but as we have seen, the liberal tradition resists making public commitments on this question.

Moreover ambiguity of interpretation is not the only problem; in many cases, our two fundamental principles conflict with one another. To return to the last issue with an unlikely but relevant example: the best way to achieve strict equality of opportunity would be to follow Plato's lead in the *Republic*, instituting a state-sponsored upbringing for children who—in the best of all possible worlds—would not even know who their biological parents were. Yet most of us would find such an approach to family life unattractive, and we would strongly resist any attempt to impinge on our freedom to raise our children in the best way we saw fit. How should we resolve this apparent conflict between freedom and equality? Plato's suggestion would clearly be out of bounds if we could show that it was not merely pleasurable but necessary to form intimate and particular attachments. But is this true? Again, our answer will depend on what it means to be fully human, and liberalism as a political theory can give us no help on this issue.

Admittedly, liberalism does allow and even encourage us to have individual opinions about the good, and thus while the government may not be able to resolve certain questions of justice unilaterally, we may resolve them together when necessary through voting. But are the opinions which guide our voting rational? This is a pressing concern, because if suspect

individual opinions become popular, voting becomes merely the aggre-
gation of prejudices to the great detriment of the less powerful. And thus
the hope as old as universal suffrage: that we may keep citizens from going
too far astray through universal education.

But if, under the constraints of liberalism, no government can impose
its view of the good, state-sponsored education in a liberal country is not
much better placed to help shape individual views about the good and thus
about justice. For the restrictions liberal theory imposes on the government
also affect all educational institutions which accept government funds.
Teachers in public schools, in consequence, must observe fundamental
constraints when leading discussions about the common good. Indeed this
presupposition is so deeply embedded in our culture that I—a teacher of
political philosophy at a Catholic university—regularly hear the following:
not only that I should not influence my students' political views, but that I
should ideally keep my views out of the classroom entirely. Naturally, I do
not aspire to demagoguery, but I would argue that such a self-extinction
was misguided, irrational, and in any case, impossible.

Be that as it may, public education can still be tremendously helpful
even under its severe constraints. Teachers have a number of valuable tools
at their disposal in the project of shaking students awake and challenging
them to rethink their views:

(a) Good teachers collect as many facts as appear to be relevant to the
justice questions considered in their classrooms. The TV images of African-
American "welfare queens" and of poor people sucking the lifeblood out of
the United States economy, for instance, have been at least partially
undermined by research demonstrating that most welfare recipients are
white and that middle-class homeowners (and of course the very rich)
benefit far more from government handouts than poor people do (benefits
go to the better-off in the form of tax credits rather than in the direct form
of money or coupons; there is more money in their pockets, all the same).

(b) Educators work out connections between the facts and possible
goals through careful means-end reasoning. To take a crude example: even
United States budget hawks might decide to invest in the prenatal care of
poor mothers once they had discovered that this initial cost is many times
lower than the statistically likely long-term health-care and criminal-justice
costs of low-birthweight babies.

(c) Educators may connect facts and insist on consistency. United
States negotiators toned down their denials that American SO_2 emissions
were causing acid rain–related damage in Canada once they realized that
they'd be on the other side of the table when talking to Mexico about a
number of extremely dirty factories near the border there.

(d) And finally, educators can insist that students learn about and
seriously consider as many models of living and as many accounts of the

good as seem plausible; thus the proliferation of requirements to study other traditions and cultures in many liberal arts colleges.

But while these tools may rule out some interpretations of the good, they are insufficient either singly or in concert to determine which of the many remaining conceptions students should adopt. Indeed in some cases, they can distort the discussion in the attempt to help it along. Consider the nature of a typical "environmental review," which usually takes the crude form of a cost-benefit analysis. As useful as this may be in cases which involve measurable costs and benefits (where, for instance, the long-term benefit of eco-tourism may match or outweigh the benefit of exploiting the land for immediate profit), such an analysis also distorts the discussion where costs are either economically invisible or immeasurable. Who, for instance, could put a price on the many little birdies and beasties which the eco-tourists *don't* come to see, and yet which play a role in helping manage the homeostasis of the whole; or on the obscure plant which may yet be the source of the cure for cancer or the subject of a beautiful ode by a poet yet unborn?

What are the consequences of such an agnostic approach to education for a liberal political culture? I'm not sure; I think that the jury is still out on this, though I'd hazard that we can read important evidence out of the political and crime pages of the daily papers. Nor do I think that this suggestion simply reflects my religiously motivated prejudices. Toward the end of the first pan-European disaster of this century, the impeccably secular sociologist Max Weber (1919, trans. 1946) praised the liberal separation of facts and values even while acknowledging that this separation allowed demagogues to use ever-more destructive technologies in the service of their wars of gods and idols. Handicapped by its principled unwillingness to discuss the good, an education for justice as conceived by our secular liberal friends is in principle unable to determine the answers to many important questions of justice. My point is not that such an education is unnecessary or unimportant, but merely that it is insufficient to do all that is needed. The Catholic tradition, to its credit, has other resources to draw on, and thus its education for justice—subsumed as it must be under a characteristic account of the good—will inevitably be as distinctive as the tradition itself.

An example to illustrate the point: there are many places where a religiously motivated tradition must resist naturalism and its illegitimate child, materialism—not least in connection with justice. Steinfels (2000) notes that there are many different types of justice, and wonders whether a Catholic university must be focused on one or another type. I'm not at all tempted to reduce the Catholic focus on justice to a subset of justice questions; this would seem an offense against its commitment to treating people holistically. But Steinfels's distinction of types of justice does invite another observation. As befits their largely naturalistic approach, secular schools have tended to focus on questions of distributive justice, since they are somewhat more conducive to objective measurement. We can empirically determine whether poor children get enough calories to live, or whether the minimum wage in this country can provide an honest living. But these are not the only significant justice questions—and indeed there are distributive questions which cannot conveniently be measured or resolved this way. We can measure calories, but not the love and support that children need at least as much to thrive; and we can measure the wage differential that a university degree will likely provide, but not the sense of entitlement and competency to face down bureaucracies that knowledge, the ability to communicate, and the opportunity to meet powerful families can give. It's unlikely that we will ever be able to measure these goods in a plausible way. But in the light of a richer account of the good, we can at least acknowledge and discuss them.

Having finished my central argument, I will close by reviewing its structure. In one sense, reflection on justice cannot distinguish a Catholic education because it is common to the secular tradition as well. Yet many questions concerning justice can only be answered by reflecting on one's fundamental view of the good. This raises a severe problem at a secular school—at least insofar as it is committed to educating its students for justice—since there are severe institutional constraints on its ability to fulfill the requirement of reflection on the good. In a Catholic school, on the other hand, those working on questions of justice may and indeed must take advantage of the Church's broad and rich tradition of reflection on the good. Just because of its commitment to justice, again, it cannot avoid "the bothersome religious issues, especially a belief in a transcendent reality," and it must face the tensions between transcendent reality and the reigning academic ethos of naturalism (Steinfels, 2000). In short, an education for justice in a Catholic context must be distinctive—richer, I would suggest, but in any case, more particular—than that education could hope to be in a secular context. Shared reflection on what makes life worth living should be both more native and more productive for justice in this soil.

Though I will not pursue them, I cannot close without at least mentioning two issues which deserve further reflection. First, we cannot simply ransack the past for models of how to educate students for justice—or better, we must look at past models with the creativity to see how they can be suited to our present. This volume reminds us that the dynamic of Word becoming flesh in history—the core of the Christian revelation—prohibits us from uncritically adopting or maintaining the patterns that have given meaning and stability in the past. Steinfels (2000) invites and challenges us not to restore an old paradigm of Christian education but to construct a new one. This invitation and challenge is inescapable, for as Fr. Privett points out, tradition cannot be maintained by sheer repetition, and thus always requires debates about what constitutes our tradition (Privett, 2000). Why must this be so? The evidence involves the commonplace that someone who merely "repeats what is said . . . does not need to distort consciously, and yet he will change the meaning of what is said" (Gadamer, 1991, p. 467). Effective interpretation thus always requires saying "the same thing in a different way, and, precisely by virtue of saying it in a different way, to say the same thing" (Ebeling, quoted by Linge, 1976, p. xxvii). Fr. O'Malley (2000) highlights the special historical role of intellectuals in this process of maintaining the same message in new circumstances—a challenge that, as Fr. Engh (2000) notes, has had a history at Loyola Marymount University as at other places. And this challenge is particularly pressing at a time when secular researchers are drawing attention to the necessity of listening to "justice in a different voice" (Keane, 2000). Attention to the dynamics of history—to the refracting influence of new environments—must enliven, and will certainly complicate, any discussion of how to shape a distinctively Catholic institution.

Second, I have argued that an education for justice in a Catholic school not only may, but must, take advantage of the rich Catholic tradition of reflection on the good. But if this concern must characterize the institution in general, we might wonder whether it should characterize the work of all participating students and scholars. More concretely: Should all contribute to the project of articulating a Catholic vision of justice, or may this only be the concern of the subset of Catholics on campus? I have explored a metaphor for resolving this issue elsewhere and won't repeat those observations here; suffice to say, there must at least be a core of scholars concerned with this issue, there must be institutional support for these concerns, and it should at least be possible to ask all scholars (and perhaps even all students) on a Catholic campus what their research and reflection might have to say about this endeavor. To teach and to learn is in large measure to be part of a community of discussion, and each such community has boundaries which define what questions are more and less pertinent. Those of us who are not Catholic have, I believe, an obligation to understand the Catholic intellectual tradition into which we've stepped, and to have some sort of reasoned response to it. As Fr. Privett (2000) notes, the Church has had the humility since Vatican II to see itself not only as a teaching but also as a learning institution. She has invited us here to facilitate that project; and we non-Catholics owe, at very least, the courtesy of a reply.

References

Augustine, St. (1960). *The confessions of Saint Augustine* (J. K. Ryan.,Trans.). New York, NY: Doubleday Image.

Dickens, C. (1854). *Hard times: For these times.* London: Bradbury & Evans.

Engh, M.E., S.J. (2000). Just ones past and present at Loyola Marymount University. In M. K. McCullough (Ed.), *The just one justices: The role of justice at the heart of Catholic higher education* (pp. 21–36). Scranton, PA: University of Scranton Press.

Gadamer, H. G. (1991). *Truth and method* (2nd Rev. Ed.) (W. Glen-Doepel, Ed. J. Cumming, & G. Barden. Rev. J. Weinsheimer, & D. G. Marshall, Trans.). New York, NY: Crossroads.

Hampl, P. (1981). *A romantic education.* Boston, MA: Houghton Mifflin.

Illich, I. (1971). *Deschooling society.* New York, NY: Harper & Row.

Keane, E.M., R.S.H.M. (2000). Justice in a different voice. In M. K. McCullough (Ed.), *The just one justices: The role of justice at the heart of Catholic higher education* (pp. 89–95). Scranton, PA: University of Scranton Press.

Kozol, J. (1991). *Savage inequalities: Children in America's schools.* New York, NY: Crown.

Linge, D. E. (1976). Editor's Introduction. In H-G. Gadamer, *Philosophical hermeneutics.* Berkeley, CA: University of California.

O'Malley, T. P., S.J. (2000). At the heart of Catholic Christianity. In M. K. McCullough (Ed.), *The just one justices: The role of justice at the heart of Catholic higher education* (pp. 1–9). Scranton, PA: University of Scranton Press.

Plato (1987). *Gorgias* (D. J. Zeyl, Trans.). Indianapolis, IN: Hackett.

Privett, S., S.J. (2000). The Jesuit university and the struggle for justice. In M. K. McCullough (Ed.), *The just one justices: The role of justice at the heart of Catholic higher education* (pp. 49–58). Scranton, PA: University of Scranton Press.

Steinfels, M. O. (2000). The value of higher education as a catalyst for justice. In M. K. McCullough (Ed.), *The just one justices: The role of justice at the heart of Catholic higher education* (pp. 135–145). Scranton, PA: University of Scranton Press.

Weber, M. (1946). Science as a vocation. In *From Max Weber: Essays in sociology.* (H. H. Gerth & C. W. Mills, Trans.). Oxford: Oxford University.

INSTITUTIONALIZING SOCIAL JUSTICE: NOW WHAT?

Mary K. McCullough

The spirit of humility guides me in this final reflection and summation of the 1998 President's Institute at Loyola Marymount University: The Just One Justices. As a lay woman and mother of two Jesuit-educated sons, I have great respect for the Marymount tradition of care and concern for the total growth of each person, commitment to social justice, and the liberal arts education of women. I also embrace the Jesuit dialogic tradition and perspective of "commitment, discernment, self-criticism, and continual adaptation to changing needs" (McShane, 1999, p. 20). In keeping with the ecumenical nature of the Institute, Nancy Fox (1998) succinctly describes the essence of the Jesuit tradition from a Jewish perspective: "This style is intellectual, humanistic, generous, questioning yet affirming, God-based yet in many ways 'worldly' . . . It cares about justice . . . And its final goal is service—service of God and of others" (Fox, 1998, p. 49). The goal of social justice for all guides both traditions and thus the work of the President's Institute, and indeed, the entire University.

The Institute provided two key elements for entering into a dialogue on the promotion of social justice in higher education: a respite from the busy academic calendar, and an opportunity for faculty to engage in cross-curricular, collegial conversations about a topic at the heart of Catholic higher education. The merger of the Marymount and Jesuit traditions, the respect for the variety of faiths represented by the participants, and the focus on social justice served as challenging topics for faculty discussion and reflection. It is the hope of the participants, all contributing to this volume, that our reflection might inform discussion and practice in other Catholic institutions of higher education.

The Institute produced the following three benefits: (1) an opportunity for faculty members to meet colleagues from a variety of disciplines and faith traditions, (2) the luxury of time to discuss and reflect on issues related to justice, and (3) the call to explore ideas and future action steps to ensure the integration and implementation of justice throughout the University. At the end of the Institute, many of the participants did not want to stop with the weeklong exploration of justice. A focus group was formed to meet and discuss the following: issues of poverty and the sociopolitical needs of the campus community, the role and voice of women on campus and in higher education, gender as a category of social justice, and the communal life of the university. The main question for the focus group, which was led by Sister Ellen Marie Keane, R.S.H.M, and met an additional four times, was "How is social justice institutionalized at a Catholic university?" Specifically, the dialogue continued on the role of women in Catholic higher education. The group recommended concrete ways to eliminate mechanisms that lead to the marginalization of women at the university and ways to enhance the women's voice at all levels within the university community. My contribution to this volume includes a summary of the discussions and is organized around the following three questions: (1) What are the issues? (2) What do we need? (3) What critical questions must we raise to move to the next level of institutionalizing social justice?

What are the issues?

The Focus group explored several topics: faculty service, part-time faculty, campus activities, and curriculum issues. In the area of faculty service the discussion centered on connecting, in a meaningful way, the expectation of all faculty members embracing the mission of the University. The group suggested the University review the current system of evaluation of faculty and incorporate questions such as: How does our teaching, research, and/or service further the mission of the University? How does faculty service answer the call to social justice?

The issue of social justice for part-time faculty was raised. Does a Catholic university have the obligation to offer a benefits package to part-time faculty for their service to the university? The group felt strongly about exploring some level of benefits for part-time faculty. As a result of the group discussions, this issue was raised with two campus committees and the faculty senate. Offering a benefits package to part-time faculty is now being researched by the Academic Vice President and appropriate faculty committees.

The topic of campus community and symbolic activities on campus was explored. Should major celebrations reflect the ongoing mission of the university? What are these symbolic activities? Who is involved in ensuring social justice is integrated throughout the campus calendar of activities? Is there a need for a broader scope of activities to include more ecumenical activities? For example, the focus group participants suggested analyzing the purpose and restructuring the use of the convocation hour, a weekly common time on campus. The original intent was to extend the conversation by getting together to talk about, among other topics, the Catholic identity of the University, and to take the time to reflect, pause, and dialogue on what is important. Does this original intent match current practice?

In exploring curriculum issues the focus group discussed the content of the core curriculum through the following questions: What about exploring the institution of a language requirement as an issue of social justice? Is it time to evaluate the American Cultures program as it relates to international cultures? The American Cultures program has a multicultural focus, is part of the core curriculum for all students, and explores issues of culture from three different perspectives. What about including a service learning component as part of coursework?

What do we need?

After looking at the mechanisms already in place to advance social justice on campus, the Focus group brainstormed ideas and additional avenues for implementation. How do we come together as a socially just community? What is the relationship of the university to the local Catholic community? How do we connect with each other and the local community to provide support? Some of the ideas for future areas of growth include:

• Conduct interdisciplinary conversations on curriculum reform. Explore ways faculty and students can work together across disciplines to incorporate issues of justice and service in the curriculum. One idea is to add a service learning component to coursework. Another idea is to develop a Catholic Studies program, by building a network of conversations without re-entering the isolation of the ghetto.

• Publish a booklet highlighting the social justice endeavors shared by faculty and students. Each year the University publishes a handbook that could be expanded to include service activities of faculty, staff, and students.

• Produce a video reflecting the history and mission of the University. The Focus group acknowledged the importance of including a discussion of mission, identity, and service in promotion and recruiting materials and new faculty orientation.

• Establish a teaching center to carry on the values of social justice in the art of teaching. Fortunately, a Center for Teaching Excellence was opened in Fall 1998. The Center is coordinated by a member of the faculty, and concentrates on curriculum integration and professional development. The next step will be to ensure social justice is the continued focus and design for the ongoing work and outreach of the Center.

- Strive for commonality of discussion across campus. Involve all stakeholders in conversations around topics that matter: institutionalizing social justice. The end is not merely to conduct conversations, but to ignite action. But what would be explored? How does a university nurture intellectual commonality? How does a university explore and integrate reflective practice?

- Connect with the Center for Parish Life and other agencies in the local community. Conduct an outreach campaign to local parishes and other agencies in need of ongoing support.

- Continue the work of the President's Institute on Catholicity. As a part of future Institutes, include an element of outreach to a place where people need assistance and care. Ensure the Institute continues to incorporate its theoretical work with the practical application of service to those in need.

What are the critical questions?

As the focus group brainstormed ideas on elements and integration of social justice, we kept coming back to the central issue of purpose. What do we mean by social justice? How do we ensure it is embedded in the core, fiber, and everyday life of the University? To this end, the group raised the following questions for ongoing dialogue and action:

- How do we draw students into the conversation on justice? How do we link co-curricular programs with the curriculum? How do we engage students in reflection on their service activities?

- How do we promote interdisciplinary collegiality?

- How do we connect with other institutions both locally and nationally? How do we connect with the law school?

- How do we continue the conversation on justice with a wider constituency?

The conversation must continue and focus on why the university often neglects the role and voice of women and children. Sometimes there is a presumption made, particularly in settings of male-dominated leadership, that conversations include equals talking with equals. This is not always the case. Sexism might be worse than racism. According to Carol Gilligan (1982), "Women perceive and construe social reality differently from men and that these differences center around experiences of attachment and separation . . . because women's sense of integrity appears to be entwined with an ethic of care, so that to see themselves as women is to see themselves in a relationship of connection" (p. 171). "In addition, since race and sex are not the only advantaging systems at work, we need to similarly examine the daily experience of having age advantage, or ethnic advantage, or physical ability, or advantage related to nationality, religion, or sexual orientation" (McIntosh, 1995, p. 85).

Informed by the work of Annette Baier (1994), Catholic institutions of higher education face four challenges in realizing inclusive dialogue:

1. Acknowledging the challenge of individualism: Noninterference in the lives and needs of others leads to neglect and assumes no harm is done. Is this concept of noninterference active in moral theory? Sometimes institutional and intellectual settings assume an equality that does not exist. The assumption of equality and the practice of non-interference can lead to marginalization of whole groups of people. "Gilligan reminds us that noninterference can, especially for the relatively powerless, such as the very young, amount to neglect, and even between equals can be isolating and alienating" (Baier, 1994, p. 110).

2. Confronting the habit of inattention to issues of inequality. What about the role and voice of women and children? A basic respect of difference must form the fabric of the institution. Women bring to the table inclusive skills and a desire to share power. What is the institutional consciousness of the connected vs. the separated? What are the safeguards against the pattern of inequality? A pattern in dialogue emerges in which someone is excluded, then is included, and then becomes the excluder. The Jesuits promote connecting issues of faith and justice to issues of women: "explicit teaching of the essential quality of women and men in Jesuit ministries, especially in schools, colleges, and universities" (*Documents*, 1995, p. 38).

3. Is the scope of choice or the pattern of decision-making a question of oversight, a question of inclusion, or an incidence of non-recognition of all the players? Is not choosing to be engaged in the dialogue or not being invited to the dialogue a way of institutionalizing social injustice? In things that matter to the institution: Who is invited to sit at the decision-making table? Who ultimately makes the decisions? The outcome of the Jesuit's Thirty-Fourth General Congregation (*Documents*, 1995) is clear about the following practical ways the scope of choice can be widened: support of liberation movements, attention to violence against women, presence of women in Jesuit

ministries and institutions, involvement of women in decision making, cooperation with female colleagues, promotion of the education of women, and elimination of discrimination.

4.   Reintegrating the role of emotion. Is rationality alone a traditional means of not including the voice of women? Currently, intuition is being recognized as playing a role in science. How does emotion factor into the dialogue on social justice in higher education? "It is clear . . . the best moral theory has to be a cooperative product of women and men, has to harmonize justice and care" (Baier, 1994, p. 118).

Next Steps

The fruits of the Institute are being manifested in ongoing conversations, plans, and actions. The members of the focus group continue to explore the following topics, each seen as an issue of justice, in their individual and collective work: spirituality, leadership, teaching and learning, campus life, and careers. The following outlines the plans and action items developed, and recommendations made in each category. At this writing, some of the action items have been addressed and others are becoming part of the ongoing campus dialogue.

Spirituality

*   Continue the ongoing dialogue on issues of social justice. Continue and encourage the Jesuit dialogue on the role of women in the Church. Plan and conduct a call to "Conversation" on the Jesuit Decrees (*Documents*, 1995) on women. All members of the University community must be involved in helping the Jesuits live out their mission and goals as expressed in their documents. "Above all we want to commit the Society in a more formal and explicit way to regard this solidarity with women as integral to our mission" (p. 40).

*   Discuss the role of gender, specifically the role of women in the Church. Consider the Mass of the Holy Spirit, Baccalaureate, and other large community liturgical celebrations, and how they incorporate women in planning, ceremony, and celebration. In Fall 1998, members of the focus group served on the planning committee for the Mass of the Holy Spirit and some changes were made in the inclusion of women in the celebration. As the Jesuit Documents reflect, "respectful reconciliation can flow only from our God of love and justice, who reconciles all and promises a world in which 'there is neither Jew nor Greek, there is neither slave nor free, there is neither male nor female,

for you are all one in Christ Jesus' (Gal. 3:28)" (*Documents*, 1995, p. 40).

Leadership

- Raise the visibility of women in roles of leadership and decision making. Ask the question: Who holds "the power to decide whether to commit themselves to more equitable distributions of power"? (McIntosh, 1995, p. 84). Review statistics of campus groups (1998–99) to determine where women are included in the leadership of the University:

	men	women
Administration/Dean's Council	86%	14%
Board of Trustees	84%	16%
Board of Regents	86%	14%
Chairs	79%	21%
Faculty	69%	31%
Students	48%	52%

- Keep the Marymount tradition alive. Without the continuing consciousness of exploring the Marymount tradition, elements of institutional vitality could be lost. July 1998 marked the 25-year anniversary of the merger. In Spring 1999, a liturgical celebration and reception were held to celebrate and honor this tradition and the merger.

Teaching and Learning

- Ensure the Center for Teaching Excellence includes instructional practices from updated pedagogical methods to help all students learn, i.e., cooperative learning, and alternative assessment. The Center has been actively supporting faculty, beginning in Spring 1999, by offering professional development activities. Through ongoing dialogue and support, the Center could assist in transforming pedagogy on campus to include all stakeholders: gender, race, culture, and disability.

- Explore gender issues in the curriculum and in the classroom. Raise the consciousness of white and male privilege. Is sexism worse than racism? What about women in science and math? Sponsor institutes in science and math for female students at the high school and college level. Recommend that the Core Curriculum Committee consider Women's Studies as part of the core.

Campus Life

- Suggest the University committee on the Status of Women look at the application of justice in the life of the community.

- Ensure gender, race, ethnicity, and disability are included in the discussions of affirmative action on campus.

- Encourage the Enrollment Management Committee to review admissions brochures, videos, and policies with regard to issues of diversity and full inclusion.

- Build an environment that is liberating and empowering for all. Continue to include the role of women in planning major campus celebrations. Encourage women to find their own voice and explore interests in the arts, sciences, leadership, etc.

- Enlighten from the top-down and the bottom-up. The University must take the lead in celebrating women and the merger of two religious traditions. The student body, which is a majority female, must be empowered to take leadership roles and contribute to institutional-ization of social justice.

- Insist on the use of inclusive language throughout the university community. Ensure an environment that is liberating and empowering for all.

Careers

- Respect the role of parents by building a child care center. In Spring 1999, through the work of the faculty and staff senates, a joint committee was formed to go beyond the feasibility stage and investigate the implementation of a long-awaited and much-needed child care center. The development of this center is seen as a statement of social justice.

- Explore the creation of doctoral programs in areas that will empower women and men to gain leadership roles in their careers, for example, in areas of Educational Administration and Theology.

In light of the ideals promoted by the President's Institute and current Jesuit documents, the Institute focus group was energized by exploring ways the faculty can bring the dialogue of justice into everyday reality. The participants of the Institute are committed to serving in and reflecting on campus-wide activities, renewing liturgical events to ensure the inclusion of women, catering to symbolic examples of spirituality for all, and creating spiritual experiences to increase student involvement.

To the Jesuits, the Institute participants say, "We appreciate being invited into the implementation of your documents." To the University, the Institute participants challenge all stakeholders to embrace each person as a concrete manifestation of justice. To all institutions of Catholic higher education, the Institute participants challenge university communities to institutionalize social justice as the recognition of the life of the Spirit, the mission of the life of the mind, and the heart of a community rooted in respect and full inclusion. "A Jesuit university must be outstanding in its human, social, spiritual, and moral formation, as well as for its pastoral attention to its students and to the different groups of people who work in it or are related to it" (*Documents*, 1995, p. 48).

This commitment and call to action, social justice, and full inclusion bring the work of the Institute and the goal of Catholic higher education full circle: the just one justices. In reflecting on Gerard Manley Hopkins poem, "As Kingfishers Catch Fire," the title expresses the call to action described by the contributing authors in this volume. The fruits of the Institute are yet to be realized in action. As the Hopkins poem (in Phillips, 1995, p. 115) suggests, this is our life's work:

Keeps grace: that keeps all his goings graces; (Line 10)

Grace is the "action, activity on God's part by which, in creating or after creating, he carries the creature to or towards the end of its being" (Phillips, 1995, p. 210). In the words of my catechism days, we are created, in God's image, to love, honor, and serve God in this world. The act of self-sacrifice is the ultimate act of love, the work of salvation, which requires our need for grace from God. The work of God in harmony with humanity, requires a full union, which Hopkins describes as:

Acts in God's eye what in God's eye he [she] is—
      Christ (Lines 11–12)

Hopkins seeks the individuality of each as a work of God, "a reflexive work, with the purpose of glorifying the Creator" (Johnson, 1997, p. 177). Our task then, according to Christ, expressed by Hopkins, is simply to be a reflection of God in this world: social justice lived.

References

Baier, A. (1994). *Moral prejudices: Essays on ethics*. Cambridge, MA: Harvard University Press.

Documents of the thirty-fourth general congregation of the Society of Jesus (1995). St. Louis, MO: Institute of Jesuit Sources.

Fox, N. R. (1998, Fall). Letter. *Conversations on Jesuit Higher Education*, 14, 49.

Gilligan, C. (1982). *In a different voice: Psychological theory and women's development*. Cambridge, MA: Harvard University Press.

Johnson, M. (1997). *Gerard Manley Hopkins and Tractarian poetry*. Aldershot, England: Ashgate Publishing, Ltd.

McIntosh, P. (1995). White privilege and male privilege: A personal account of coming to see correspondences through work in women's studies. In M. Anderson & Collins (Eds.), *Race, class, gender* (2nd ed.). New York, NY: Wadsworth.

McShane, J.M., S.J. (1999, Spring). The heart of the matter: The core and the task of core revision. *Conversations on Jesuit Higher Education, 15*, 19–23.

Phillips, C. (Ed.). 1995. *Gerard Manley Hopkins*. Oxford, England: Oxford University Press.

CONTRIBUTORS

Linda Bannister, Ph.D., is Professor and Chair of the Loyola Marymount University English Department and specializes in Rhetoric, Stylistics, and Theory of Metaphor. She has written articles on cross-cultural and cross-gendered literature, metaphor, Joyce Carol Oates, and Virginia Woolf.

Lance H. Blakesley, Ph.D., is an Associate Professor of Political Science at Loyola Marymount University, where he teaches courses in urban politics and public policy analysis. His current research focuses upon public policies directed at the problems of concentrated inner-city poverty in the United States. He is presently writing a book which examines the urban agenda of the Clinton presidency.

Barbara J. Busse, M.A., is Associate Professor of Communication Studies at Loyola Marymount University. She began teaching at Marymount College at Loyola University of Los Angeles in 1969. During her tenure she has served as Associate Academic Vice President (1989–91), as Acting Dean of the College of Communication and Fine Arts (1991–92), as Chair of Theatre, Speech, and Dance and Speech Communication Coordinator. She has been named California Women in Higher Education Woman of the Year (1991) and Teacher of the Year (1993–94). Her areas of concentration include organizational communication, argumentation and debate, conflict management, communication consulting, and gender communication.

W. Scott K. Cameron, Ph.D., Associate Professor of Philosophy, Loyola Marymount University, received his bachelor's and master's degrees from Queen's University, Kingston, Ontario, Canada. He completed his Ph.D. at Fordham University. During his doctoral studies, he joined the Mennonite church, which has had a major influence on his current religious perspective. His research interests include political theory and hermeneutics.

Olga Celle de Bowman, Ph.D., Formerly an Assistant Professor of Sociology at Loyola Marymount University, has a bachelor of science degree from the Universidad Nacional Federico Villareal in Peru and a Ph.D. from the University of California, Santa Cruz.

John Coleman, S.J., Ph.D., is the Charles Casassa Professor in Social Values at Loyola Marymount University. He holds a Ph.D. in sociology from the University of California, Berkeley, and did advanced study in social ethics at the Divinity School, The University of Chicago. He is the author of several books, including *The Evolution of Dutch Catholicism* (1978), *An American Strategic Theology* (1983), and *One Hundred Years of Catholic Social Teaching* (1991). At the Thirty-Fourth General Congregation of the Jesuits, he was the principal redactor of the document on "Jesuits and University Life."

Steven Combs, Ph.D., Associate Professor of Communication Studies, Loyola Marymount University, specializes in rhetoric and public address, specifically rhetorical theory and criticism. His current research interests are classical Daoist rhetorical theory and the application of communication to legal practice. He is also a communication consultant to social service agencies.

Jan C. Costello, J.D., is a Professor of Law at Loyola Law School. She teaches and writes in the areas of Children and the Law, Mental Disability Law, and Family Law. She received her B.A., M.A., and J.D. from Yale University, and before joining the Loyola faculty practiced public interest law for eight years, representing children in the juvenile justice system and people with mental disabilities. She has worked with state and national associations concerned with legal rights of people with disabilities, and presently volunteers as a board member of two disability rights organizations.

Michael E. Engh, S.J., Ph.D., Associate Professor History, received his doctorate at the University of Wisconsin–Madison and has taught at Loyola Marymount University since January 1988. Specializing in the history of the American West, his publication and research interests have focused on Los Angeles, as well as on religion and society in the West. He co-founded and has continued as coordinator of the Los Angeles History Seminary at the Huntington Library. Through his historical methods class, he has directed extensive undergraduate student research into and interviews about the history of Loyola Marymount University. Fr. Engh is grateful to these students for their assistance over the years in compiling material on the school's history which he used in parts of his essay. At present he serves as Rector of the Jesuit Community at LMU.

Diane D. Glave, Ph.D., has been an Assistant Professor in the African-American Studies Department at Loyola Marymount University since Fall 1998. She graduated with an M.A. and Ph.D. in History, emphasizing African-American and environmental history at the University Center at Stony Brook. She has been awarded several fellowships, grants, and scholarships. Dr. Glave is revising two articles entitled, "The African American Cooperative Extension Service: A Folk Tradition in Conservation in the Early Twentieth Century" and "Azaleas and Yams: African American Women in Gardening in the Progressive Period." Her community work includes women's discipleship at Faithful Central Missionary Baptist Church in Inglewood and the Children's Nature Institute in Santa Monica.

Victoria L. Graf, Ph.D., is a Professor in the School of Education at Loyola Marymount University. Her area of expertise is the preparation of Special Education teachers who teach students with exceptional needs from diverse cultural and linguistic backgrounds. Her research interests include the connection between the preparation of teachers and the moral purpose of education and schooling. This is related to work she has completed regarding the beliefs and attitudes of teachers regarding exceptionality and cultural diversity. Her work also includes the incorporation of the principles of social justice into the preparation of teachers through the development of service learning projects.

Ellen Marie Keane, R.S.H.M., Ph.D., is Associate Professor of Philosophy in the Department of Philosophy and Religious Studies at Marymount College, Tarrytown, New York. Her areas of specialization include Ethics, Greek Philosophy, Women's Studies, and Justice Studies.

Barbara E. Marino, Ph.D., is currently serving as an Assistant Professor in the Department of Electrical Engineering and Computer Science at Loyola Marymount University. She graduated with a B.S.E.E. from Marquette University in 1989 and a Ph.D. in electrical engineering from the University of Notre Dame in 1996. Her research interests are in the areas of color image processing and the human visual system.

Timothy M. Matovina, Ph.D., is a faculty member in the Department of Theological Studies at Loyola Marymount University. His area of specialization is faith and culture, particularly Latino religion in the United States. He has participated extensively in community organizing efforts, the United Farm Workers, and other attempts to promote justice in contemporary life.

Herbert A. Medina, Ph.D., Associate Professor of Mathematics at Loyola Marymount University, was born in El Salvador and immigrated to the United States at the age of eight. He received his B.S. in Mathematics/Computer Science in 1985 from UCLA and his Ph.D. in Mathematics in 1992 from U.C. Berkeley. His mathematical research interests center on functional analysis, harmonic analysis, ergodic theory, and wavelets. His work on social justice issues includes co-directing the Summer Institute in Mathematics for Undergraduates (SIMU) at the University of Puerto Rico–Humacao, a program whose goal is to increase the number of Chicanos/Latinos and Native Americans earning graduate degrees in mathematics; involvement in making a university education possible for undocumented students; and his board membership in the Central American Resource Center (CARECEN), a community-based organization serving immigrants and their families in Los Angeles.

Mary K. McCullough, Ph.D., Associate Professor in the School of Education at Loyola Marymount University, coordinates the Educational Administration Masters and credential program which prepares public and private school administrators. She received her Ph.D. in Policy, Planning, and Administration from the University of Southern California. She is currently serving as the editor of the journal, *Educational Leadership and Adminis-tration: Teaching and Program Development.* Her research interests include leadership, the change process, and school reform.

Margaret O'Brien Steinfels is the editor of *Commonweal*, which is available on the World Wide Web: http://www.commonwealmagazine.org.

Thomas P. O'Malley, S.J., Litt.D., President of Loyola Marymount University, 1991 to 1999. A graduate of Boston College and Fordham University, Fr. O'Malley was ordained in Brussels in 1961 and was awarded a doctorate in early Christian Latin and Greek literature from the University of Nijmegen in 1967. He returned to Boston College, where he chaired the Departments of Classics and Theology and also was Dean of the College of Arts and Sciences from 1973 to 1980. He was President of John Carroll University from 1980 to 1988; a guest professor at the Catholic Institute of West Africa in Port Harcourt, Nigeria; and an assistant editor and theatre critic for *America* magazine. After a brief stint as Rector of the Jesuit Community at Fairfield University, he became President of Loyola Marymount University on July 1, 1991.

Stephen A. Privett, S.J., Ph.D., is Provost at Santa Clara University and oversees programs in academic affairs and student development.

INDEX